Translation of Chinese Classics:
Selected Readings

21世纪英语专业系列教材

英译中国古典名著选读

李文婷 主编

马平 副主编

刘婷婷 赵惠君 张从成 赵奂 编者

图书在版编目 (CIP) 数据

英译中国古典名著选读 / 李文婷主编 . —北京：北京大学出版社，2020.7
21 世纪英语专业系列教材
ISBN 978-7-301-31178-3

Ⅰ. ①英… Ⅱ. ①李… Ⅲ. ①英语 – 阅读教学 – 高等学校 – 教材 ②中国文学 – 古典文学 – 文学欣赏 Ⅳ. ① H319.4：I

中国版本图书馆 CIP 数据核字 (2020) 第 025235 号

书　　　名	英译中国古典名著选读 YINGYI ZHONGGUO GUDIAN MINGZHU XUANDU
著作责任者	李文婷　主编
责任编辑	李　娜
标准书号	ISBN 978-7-301-31178-3
出版发行	北京大学出版社
地　　　址	北京市海淀区成府路 205 号　100871
网　　　址	http://www.pup.cn　新浪微博：@ 北京大学出版社
电子信箱	lina@pup.cn
电　　　话	邮购部 010-62752015　发行部 010-62750672　编辑部 010-62754382
印　刷　者	河北滦县鑫华书刊印刷厂
经　销　者	新华书店
	787 毫米 ×1092 毫米　16 开本　15.75 印张　564 千字 2020 年 7 月第 1 版　2020 年 7 月第 1 次印刷
定　　　价	56.00 元

未经许可，不得以任何方式复制或抄袭本书之部分或全部内容。
版权所有，侵权必究
举报电话：010-62752024　电子信箱：fd@pup.pku.edu.cn
图书如有印装质量问题，请与出版部联系，电话：010-62756370

前　言

中国文化"走出去"是国家"十二五"规划对我国新时期文化发展战略提出的重要目标之一，"十二五"规划明确指出："要增强我国文化软实力，创新文化'走出去'模式，增强文化国际竞争力。"党的十八大报告也明确提出进一步加快中国文化"走出去"的步伐。在这次大会精神的指导之下，中国文化"走出去"已成为重要的国家文化战略。中国典籍外译工程进行得轰轰烈烈，为加强中国文化的对外宣传提供了大量的有用资料。英语专业的学生将要承担弘扬中国文化、促进对外宣传的重要任务，不仅应该熟悉中国的传统文化和经典名著，还应该具备用英文介绍和阐释这些经典名著的能力。

英语专业学生已经具备一定的英语语言功底和阅读能力，但在学习西方语言和文化的同时，往往忽略了本国的传统文化。因此，作为一门训练英语专业二年级学生听、说、读、写、译综合能力的精读课程，有必要将中国古典名著的经典英译本的精读纳入课堂内外的学习中，引导学生用英语阅读、赏析、背诵、翻译和评介古典名著，强化学生精通中国传统文化的"国民精神"，也有利于实现与英语专业高年级的中国文化"走出去"的人才培养课程的衔接。

本教材精选中国经典名著的原文及汉译本进行对照学习，按历时线索分章节呈现，选篇涵盖面广，包括《诗经》、唐诗、宋词、元曲、《水浒传》《三国演义》《西游记》《牡丹亭》《桃花扇》《聊斋志异》《红楼梦》《老残游记》。本教材所节选的译文，尽量保留了原本的内容和格式。例如：闵福德翻译《画皮》时，所有对话均使用单引号来表示引用，大卫·霍克斯翻译《红楼梦》时亦是如此，本书中完全保留了译本的单引号。对于译文中极少数的拼写错误，本书在更正的同时，还加上括号以提示区别，最大限度地为读者呈现译文的原貌。本教材将会帮助学生在信息碎片化的今天，提高对中国古典名著主要脉络的了解程度，极大提高学生评价和鉴赏汉英译文的能力。此外，在精读课本中编写鉴赏导读，引导学生进行自学和批判性思考，也是本教材的一大特色。

本教材编写的体例：Text A 选取市面上流传较广的英译本，提供单词表、注释和对照的中文原文。课前设有鉴赏导读、预习要求、预习思考题，课后设有练习题（词形变化、语法词汇、古词翻译、句子翻译、关键词造句、情境仿写等）；Text B 提供另一版本的英译本，提供单词表和注释，这样学生可以对比欣赏不同译本。教材最后附练习题的参考答案，以满足学生自学需求。

本教材共分十二个单元，分工如下：李文婷老师和马平老师负责全书的策划工作；赵惠君老师负责第一单元导读以及第三单元、第九单元、第十一单元的编写并参与了校对工作；刘婷婷老师负责第二单元、第四单元、第八单元、第十二单元的编写并参与了校对工作；

李文婷老师负责第一单元（导读部分除外）、第五单元、第六单元、第七单元、第十单元的编写并参与了校对工作；张从成老师负责全书终稿的校对工作；赵奂老师为选篇、制定体例等工作提供了宝贵的建议，在此对以上老师的辛勤付出深表谢忱。

本教材在编写过程中还得到了四川外国语大学英语学院院长张旭春教授的大力支持，英语学院张婷老师的积极协助，北京大学出版社的刘文静女士、李娜女士的悉心帮助，特此致谢！此外，教材的编写得到了四川外国语大学"特色教材"项目资助，在此一并表示感谢。最后，特别感谢我的家人对我一如既往的支持，没有他们的支持，这本小书也不可能得以付梓。

由于编者水平有限，书中错谬难免，恳请国内同行不吝赐教，也恳请读者批评指正，共同促进教材的完善和建设。

编　者

2020 年 2 月

Contents

Unit 1　The Poems Selected from *The She King* ························1
　Text A　James Legge's Version ····························· 3
　Text B　Wang Rongpei's Version ························· 23

Unit 2　The Selected Tang Poems ·····························32
　Text A　Witter Bynner's Version ························· 33
　Text B　Xu Yuanchong's Version ························ 42

Unit 3　The Selected Song Lyrics ····························46
　Text A　Xu Yuanchong's Version ························ 47
　Text B　Yang Hsien-yi & Gladys Yang's Version ········ 59

Unit 4　The Selected Yuan Qu Songs ························63
　Text A　Gu Zhengkun's Version ························· 65
　Text B　Zhou Fangzhu's Version ························ 77

Unit 5　Instructor Wang Secretly Makes His Escape; Shi Jin Gets His Defences into Shape (excerpt) ······························81
　Text A　John Dent-Young & Alex Dent-Young's Version ········ 82
　Text B　Sidney Shapiro's Version ······················ 94

Unit 6　Kongming Borrows Cao Cao's Arrows Through a Ruse; Huang Gai Is Flogged Following a Secret Plan (excerpt) ···············99
　Text A　Moss Roberts's Version ······················ 100
　Text B　C. H. Brewitt-Taylor's Version ················ 112

Unit 7　The Cadaver Demon Three Times Mocks Tripitaka Tang; The Holy Monk in Spite Banishes Handsome Monkey King (excerpt) ······119
　Text A　Anthony C. Yu's Version ····················· 121
　Text B　W.J.F. Jenner's Version ······················ 131

Unit 8   Pursuing the Dream ·· **136**
    Text A   Cyril Birch's Version ··· 138
    Text B   Wang Rongpei's Version ··· 155

Unit 9   The Rejected Suit ··· **164**
    Text A   Chen Shih-Hsiang, Harold Acton & Cyril Birch's Version ··············· 166
    Text B   Xu Yuanchong & Frank M. Xu's Version ·· 179

Unit 10   The Painted Skin ·· **186**
    Text A   Herbert A. Giles's Version ··· 188
    Text B   John Minford's Version ·· 197

Unit 11   Lin Ru-Hai Recommends a Private Tutor to His Brother-in-Law and Old Lady Jia Extends a Compassionate Welcome to the Motherless Child (excerpt) ··· **202**
    Text A   David Hawkes's Version ·· 204
    Text B   Yang Hsien-yi & Gladys Yang's Version ··· 213

Unit 12   At the Foot of Mount Li the Traces of an Ancient Emperor; By the Side of Lake Ming the Song of a Beautiful Girl (excerpt) ············· **217**
    Text A   Harold Shadick's Version ·· 219
    Text B   Yang Hsien-yi & Gladys Yang's Version ··· 229

Key to the Exercises ··· **233**

Unit 1

The Poems Selected from *The She King*

Reading Guide

The She King or *The Book of Poetry* is considered as the oldest existing collection of Chinese poetry. With 305 works in it, the book contains four main parts: Lessons from the States (ancient folk songs of the common people from different regions), Minor Odes of the Kingdom (works of aristocrats of high status), Greater Odes of the Kingdom (works of aristocrats of both high and low status) and Odes of the Temple and the Altar (works of ministers to eulogize the monarchs' achievements and virtues), ranging from the Western Zhou Dynasty (1046 BC—771 BC) to the middle of the Spring and Autumn period (700 BC). It mirrors the circumstances, the lives and the thoughts of people, aristocrats and civilians alike.

The poems selected from *The She King* were translated by James Legge, the great 19th century Scottish sinologist, missionary and scholar, known for his translation of classical Chinese texts into English, such as *Confucian Analects*, *The Great Learning*, *The Doctrine of the Mean*, *The I Ching: The Books of Changes* and *Book of Rites*. He made significant and invaluable contributions to the dissemination of Chinese classics. As is in the words of William Jennings, translator of *The Shi King, the Old "Poetry Classic" of the Chinese* (1891), "His work will doubtlessly remain always the standard one for students; and the erudition, the evidence of wide reading, and the patience and care displayed in it, make one indeed stand aghast."[①]

Before Reading

I. Preview Requirements: Please make a preparatory research on the background information, key words and phrases of this text.

1. Do research on the translator James Legge.

---

① This review is quoted from "Online Library of Liberty", and the website is http://oll.libertyfund.org/titles/school-the-shi-king-the-old-poetry-classic-of-the-chinese#lf1440_head_001.

2. Do research on how the poems in *The She King* were collected and compiled.
3. Do research on King Wen and his influence in the Chinese history.
4. Do research on other translators of *The She King* such as *Ezra Pound, Arthur Waley, William Jennings, Jone A. Turner, Yang Hsien-yi* and *Gladys Yang, Xu Yuanchong*, and *Su Manshu*.
5. Underline the new words in the text and make some study on them such as *tender, reverence, plaster, yoke, fetid, spinner,* and *libation*.
6. Learn the useful expressions in the text such as *give out, spring up, from age to age, deliver one's instructions, display one's virtue* and *repose confidence in*.

II. Preview Questions: Please answer some questions about the understanding of the main content of the text.

1. Why do people refer to *The She King* as *300 Poems*? What are the major topics of Lessons from the State, Minor Odes of the Kingdom, Greater Odes of the Kingdom, and Odes of the Temple and the Altar in *The She King*? Was *The She King* compiled for instructive purposes in the ancient China?
2. What is the main content of "Qi Yue"? What kinds of activities should the farmers do during a whole year? Did they live a happy life or a hard one? What could determine their living standards?
3. What is the author's purpose of repeating the first line "In the seventh month, the Fire Star passes the meridian" for three times in "Qi Yue"? What kind of rhetorical devices does the author use?
4. What is the theme of "Cai Wei"? What kind of life did people yearn for? Could it be possible for people to live a comfortable and stable life? Try to find out the obstacles that prevented people from going back home.
5. What is the tone set in "Wen Wang"? Is it solemn or casual? What were people's attitudes towards King Wen? Why did King Wen enjoy such a high prestige at that time?
6. What kind of image does the author try to project for King Wen in "Wen Wang"? Please try to find some descriptive details about King Wen.
7. Can you feel a joyful atmosphere in "Pan Shui"? What achievements did the marquis of Lu make? Why did the marquis of Lu go to his college with the semi-circular water? What was his college with the semi-circular water built for?
8. A Chinese literary critic Liu Xie once criticized the last paragraph of "Pan Shui" as rhetorical exaggeration in *Carving a Dragon at the Core of Literature* (《文心雕龙》). How do you view his comment?
9. What kind of influence did Confucius exert on the compilation of *The She King*? How did Confucianism influence the dissemination of *The She King*?

Unit 1
The Poems Selected from *The She King*

Text A

James Legge's Version

Qi Yue

In the seventh month, the Fire Star passes the meridian;
In the 9th month, clothes are given out.
In the days of (our) first month, the wind blows cold;
In the days of (our) second, the air is cold;—
Without the clothes and garments of hair,
How could we get to the end of the year?
In the days of (our) third month, they take their ploughs in hand;
In the days of (our) fourth, they take their way to the fields.
Along with my wife and children,
I carry food to them in those south-lying acres.
The surveyor of the fields comes, and is glad.

In the seventh month, the Fire Star passes the meridian;
In the ninth month, clothes are given out.
With the spring days the warmth begins,
And the oriole utters its song.
The young women take their deep baskets,
And go along the small paths,
Looking for the tender (leaves of the) mulberry trees.
As the spring days lengthen out,
They gather in crowds the white southernwood.
That young lady's heart is wounded with sadness,
For she will (soon) be going with one of our princess as his wife.

In the seventh month, the Fire Star passes the meridian;
In the eighth month are the sedges and reeds.
In the silkworm month they strip the mulberry branches of their leaves,
And take their axes and hatchets,
To lop off those that are distant and high;
Only stripping the young trees of their leaves.
In the seventh month, the shrike is heard;
In the eighth month, they begin their spinning; —

They make dark fabrics and yellow.
Our red manufacture is very brilliant,
It is for the lower robes of our young princes.

In the fourth month, the Small grass is in seed.
In the fifth, the cicada gives out its note.
In the eighth, they reap.
In the tenth, the leaves fall.
In the days of (our) first month, they go after badgers,
And take foxes and wild cats,
To make furs for our young princes.
In the days of (our) second month, they have a general hunt,
And proceed to keep up the exercises of war.
The boars of one year are for themselves;
Those of three years are for our prince.

In the fifth month, the locust moves its legs;
In the sixth month, the spinner sounds its wings.
In the seventh month, in the fields;
In the eighth month, under the eaves;
In the ninth month, about the doors;
In the tenth month, the cricket Enters under our beds.
Chinks are filled up, and rats are smoked out;
The windows that face (the north) are stopped up;
And the doors are plastered. "Ah! our wives and children,
Changing the year requires this:
Enter here and dwell. "

In the sixth month they eat the sparrow-plums and grapes;
In the seventh, they cook the Kui and pulse,
In the eighth, they knock down the dates;
In the tenth, they reap the rice;
And make the spirits for the spring,
For the benefit of the bushy eyebrows.
In the seventh month, they eat the melons;
In the eighth, they cut down the bottle-gourds;
In the ninth, they gather the hemp-seed;
They gather the sowthistle and make firewood of the Fetid tree;

To feed our husbandmen.

In the ninth month, they prepare the vegetable gardens for their stacks,
And in the tenth they convey the sheaves to them;
The millets, both the early sown and the late,
With other grain, the hemp, the pulse, and the wheat.
" O my husbandmen, Our harvest is all collected.
Let us go to the town, and be at work on our houses.
In the day time collect the grass,
And at night twist it into ropes;
Then get up quickly on our roofs; —
We shall have to recommence our sowing."

In the days of (our) second month, they hew out the ice with harmonious blows;
And in those of (our) third month, they convey it to the ice-houses,
(Which they open) in those of the fourth, early in the morning,
Having offered in sacrifice a lamb with scallions.
In the ninth month, it is cold, with frost;
In the tenth month, they sweep clean their stack-sites.
The two bottles of spirits are enjoyed,
And they say, "Let us kill our lambs and sheep,
And go to the hall of our prince,
There raise the cup of rhinoceros horn,
And wish him long life, — that he may live for ever. "

Cai Wei

Let us gather the thorn-ferns, let us gather the thorn-ferns;
The thorn-ferns are now springing up.
When shall we return?
When shall we return? It will be late in the (next) year.
Wife and husband will be separated,
Because of the Xian-yun.
We shall have no leisure to rest,
Because of the Xian-yun.

Let us gather the thorn-ferns, let us gather the thorn-ferns;

The thorn-ferns are now tender.

When shall we return? When shall we return?

Our hearts are sorrowful;

Our hearts are sad and sorrowful;

We shall hunger, we shall thirst.

While our service on guard is not finished,

We can send no one home to enquire about our families.

Let us gather the thorn-ferns, let us gather the thorn-ferns;

The thorn-ferns are now hard.

When shall we return? When shall we return?

The year will be in the tenth month.

But the king's business must not be slackly performed;

We shall have no leisure to rest.

Our sorrowing hearts are in great distress;

But we shall not return from our expedition.

What is that so gorgeous?

It is the flowers of the cherry tree.

What carriage is that?

It is the carriage of our general.

His war carriage is yoked;

The four steeds are strong.

Dare we remain inactive?

In one month we shall have three victories.

The four steeds are yoked,

The four steeds, eager and strong; —

The confidence of the general,

The protection of the men.

The four steeds move regularly, like wings; —

There are the bow with its ivory end, and the seal-skin quiver.

Shall we not daily warn one another?

The business of the Xian-yun is very urgent.

At first, when we set out,

The willows were fresh and green;

Now, when we shall be returning,
The snow will be falling in clouds.
Long and tedious will be our marching;
We shall hunger; we shall thirst.
Our hearts are wounded with grief,
And no one knows our sadness.

Wen Wang

King Wen is on high;
Oh! bright is he in heaven.
Although Zhou was an old country,
The (favouring) appointment lighted on it recently.
Illustrious was the House of Zhou,
And the appointment of God came at the proper season.
King Wen ascends and descends,
On the left and the right of God.

Full of earnest activity was King Wen,
And his fame is without end.
The gifts (of God) to Zhou,
Extend to the descendants of King Wen; —
To the descendants of King Wen,
In the direct line and the collateral branches for a hundred generations.
All the officers of Zhou,
Shall (also) be illustrious from age to age.

They shall be illustrious from age to age,
Zealously and reverently pursuing their plans.
Admirable are the many officers,
Born in this royal kingdom.
The royal kingdom is able to produce them, —
The supporters of (the House of) Zhou.
Numerous is the array of officers,
And by them King Wen enjoys his repose.

Profound was King Wen;
Oh! continuous and bright was his feeling of reverence.

Great is the appointment of Heaven!
There were the descendants of (the sovereigns) of Shang; —
The descendants of the sovereigns of Shang,
Were in number more than hundreds of thousands;
But when God gave the command,
They became subject to Zhou.

They became subject to Zhou.
The appointment of Heaven is not constant.
The officers of Yin, admirable and alert,
Assist at the libations in (our) capital; —
They assist at those libations,
Always wearing the hatchets on their lower garment and their peculiar cap.
O ye loyal ministers of the king,
Ever think of your ancestor!

Ever think of your ancestor,
Cultivating your virtue,
Always striving to accord with the will (of Heaven).
So shall you be seeking for much happiness.
Before Yin lost the multitudes,
(Its kings) were the assessors of God.
Look to Yin as a beacon;
The great appointment is not easily (preserved).

The appointment is not easily (preserved),
Do not cause your own extinction.
Display and make bright your righteousness and name,
And look at (the fate of) Yin in the light of Heaven.
The doings of High Heaven,
Have neither sound nor smell.
Take your pattern from King Wen,
And the myriad regions will repose confidence in you.

Pan Shui

Pleasant is the semi-circular water,
And we will gather the cress about it.
The marquis of Lu is coming to it,
And we see his dragon-figured banner.
His banner waves in the wind,
And the bells of his horses tinkle harmoniously.
Small and great,
All follow the prince in his progress to it.

Pleasant is the semi-circular water,
And we will gather the pondweed in it.
The marquis of Lu has come to it,
With his horses looking so grand.
His horses are grand.
His fame is brilliant.
Blandly he looks and smiles;
Without any impatience he delivers his instructions.

Pleasant is the semi-circular water,
And we will gather the mallows about it.
The marquis of Lu has come to it,
And in the college he is drinking.
He is drinking the good spirits;
And may there be given him the old age that is seldom enjoyed!
May he accord with the grand ways,
So subduing to himself all the people!

Very admirable is the marquis of Lu,
Reverently displaying his virtue,
And reverently watching over his deportment,
The pattern of the people.
With great qualities truly civil and martial,
Brilliantly he affects his meritorious ancestors.
In everything entirely filial,
He seeks the blessing for himself.

Very intelligent is the marquis of Lu,
Making his virtue illustrious.
He has made this college with its semicircle of water,
And the tribes of the Huai will submit in consequence.
His martial-looking, tiger leaders,
Will here present the left ears (of their foes).
His examiners, wise as Gao-tao,
Will here present their prisoners.

His numerous officers,
Men who have enlarged their virtuous minds,
With martial energy conducting their expedition,
Will drive far away those tribes of the east and south.
Vigorous and grand,
Without noise or display,
Without having appealed to the judges,
They will here present (the proofs of) their merit.

How they draw their bows adorned with bone!
How their arrows whizz forth!
Their war chariots are very large!
Their footmen and charioteers never weary!
They have subdued the tribes of the Huai,
And brought them to an unrebellious submission!
Only lay your plans securely,
And all the tribes of the Huai will be got!

They come flying on the wing, those owls,
And settle on the trees about the college;
They eat the fruit of our mulberry trees,
And salute us with fine notes.
So awakened shall be those tribes of the Huai;
They will come presenting their precious things,
Their large tortoises and their elephants' teeth,
And great contributions of the southern metals.

Unit 1
The Poems Selected from *The She King*

Notes on the Text

1. James Legge

James Legge (1815—1897), a Scottish sinologist, missionary, and scholar, was best known as an early and prolific translator of classical Chinese texts into English. He was the first Professor of Chinese at Oxford University (1876—1897). After studying at the Highbury Theological College in London, James Legge went to China as a missionary in 1839. Convinced of the need for missionaries to be able to comprehend the ideas and culture of Chinese people, in 1841, he began to translate many volumes of the Chinese classics, a monumental task that he completed a few years before his death. During his residence in Hong Kong, he translated Chinese classic literature into English with the help of Wang Tao and Hong Rengan. Among his translated Chinese classics are *The I Ching: The Books of Changes, Confucian Analects, The Great Learning, The Doctrine of the Mean*, and *The She King*.

2. the horn cups

The horn cups are a kind of wine vessel used in ancient times, especially popular in the Shang Dynasty and the early Western Zhou Dynasty. They were made of horns at first, and then copper, jade, wood, pottery, bronze, and so on.

3. King Wen

King Wen of Zhou (1152 BC—1056 BC) was King of Zhou during the later Shang Dynasty in ancient China. Although it was his son King Wu who conquered the Shang Dynasty following the Battle of Muye, King Wen was honored as the founder of the Zhou Dynasty. A large number of the hymns in *The She King* are praises to the legacy of King Wen.

4. the Tribes of Huai

The Tribes of Huai lived around the Huai River at that time, and was not ruled by the Zhou Dynasty, thus threatening the princes of the Zhou Dynasty. Many princes, including the marquis of Lu, had expeditions towards the Tribes of Huai.

Glossary

assessor /əˈsesə/   *n.* a person who judges how well sb. has done in an exam, a competition, etc.
e.g.: *College lecturers acted as external assessors of the exams results.*

beacon /ˈbiːk(ə)n/   *n.* a light that is placed somewhere to guide vehicles and warn them of danger
e.g.: *He was a beacon of hope for the younger generation.*

bushy /ˈbʊʃɪ/   *adj.* growing thickly
e.g.: *His eyebrows were thick and bushy.*

eaves /iːvz/   *n.* the lower edges of a roof that stick out over the walls
e.g.: *birds nesting under the eaves*

garment /ˈgɑːm(ə)nt/	*n.* a piece of clothing
	e.g.: *a strange shapeless garment that had once been a jacket*
gorgeous /ˈgɔːdʒəs/	*adj.* 1. very beautiful and attractive; giving pleasure and enjoyment
	e.g.: *You look gorgeous!*
	2. with very deep colours; impressive
	e.g.: *exotic birds with feathers of gorgeous colours*
illustrious /ɪˈlʌstrɪəs/	*adj.* very famous and much admired, especially because of what you have achieved
	e.g.: *The composer was one of many illustrious visitors to the town.*
plaster /ˈplɑːstə/	*v.* to cover sb./sth. with a wet or sticky substance
	e.g.: *She plastered herself in suntan lotion.*
quiver /ˈkwɪvə/	*v.* to shake slightly; to make a slight movement
	e.g.: *Her lip quivered and then she started to cry.*
	n. an emotion that has an effect on your body; a slight movement in part of your body
	e.g.: *He felt a quiver of excitement run through him.*
recommence /ˌriːkəˈmens/	*v.* to begin again; to start doing sth. again
	e.g.: *Work on the bridge will recommence next month.*
slack /slæk/	*n.* a king, queen, or other royal ruler of a country
	e.g.: *In March 1889, she became the first British sovereign to set foot on spanish soil.*
	adj. not putting enough care, attention or energy into sth. and so not doing it well enough
	e.g.: *He's been very slack in his work lately.*
sovereign /ˈsɒvrɪn/	*n.* a king, queen, or other royal ruler of a country
	e.g.: *In March 1889, she became the first British sovereign to set foot on Spanish soil.*
tinkle /ˈtɪŋk(ə)l/	*v.* to make a series of light high ringing sounds; to make sth. produce this sound
	e.g.: *A bell tinkled as the door opened.*
utter /ˈʌtər(r)/	*v.* to say sth. or to make a sound with your voice
	e.g.: *He uttered a snorting laugh.*

Unit 1
The Poems Selected from *The She King*

While Reading

I. Please fill in the blanks with the words in the parentheses with the appropriate part of speech.

1. The meeting between the two friends was as joyful as their parting had been _____. (sorrow)
2. _____ back-benchers are threatening to vote against the government. (rebel)
3. China has always been known as a land of property and _____. (right)
4. Nowadays, he is seen less as the sober pragmatist and more as the dangerously revolutionary _____. (zealously)
5. Even the native Americans, who were massacred almost to the point of _____, escaped the curse of race slavery. (extinct)
6. It is common knowledge among those familiar with the rabbinic tradition that Human was considered as a _____ of the Amalekites. (descend)
7. They are often characterized as benevolent and _____; when we do the same, we are angry and unreasonable. (admire)
8. In response, voters thought voting for Madison was inconsistent with their _____ for free booze. (thirsty)
9. She could choose her own partner in matrimony, as long as she gave no _____ to her passions and emotions. (utter)
10. Your lenders will then send their own _____ to value the property. (survey)

II. Please choose one word or phrase that best completes the sentence.

1. In questions where freedom is involved, it is not necessary to _____ the truth by the torture of those whose status is in dispute.
   A. seek for   B. seek   C. look for   D. search
2. Now, more consideration is paid to whether the government's actions _____ realistic principles.
   A. qualify   B. accord on   C. suit   D. accord with
3. _____ what you want, even though you may not believe that it is possible.
   A. Go into   B. Go in   C. Go after   D. Go with
4. The Australian research team _____ to see whether the intensity of these desires affects our ability to concentrate on other things.
   A. set about   B. set for   C. set out   D. set aside
5. The convention acknowledges that the exercises of this right may be _____ certain restrictions.
   A. subjected to   B. subject to   C. apt to   D. prone to

6. The baby's mother escaped from the fire _____ two other children.
   A. besides   B. along with   C. except   D. apart from

III. Translation

1. Please translate the following from English into Chinese.

1) The Fire Star passes the meridian.   2) to get to the end of the year
3) The spring days lengthen out.   4) to wish sb. long life
5) One's heart is sad and sorrowful.   6) The willows are fresh and green.
7) The snow is falling in clouds.   8) a hundred generations
9) Numerous is the array of officers.
10) You shall be seeking for much happiness.
11) with great qualities truly civil and martial

2. Please translate the following from Chinese into English.

1）举趾   2）春日载阳
3）载绩   4）公子
5）鸣蜩   6）陨萚
7）春酒   8）始播百谷
9）莫知我哀   10）旧邦
11）其马跻跻

3. Please translate each sentence with at least one key word or its derivative.

Key Words: proceed, dwell, convey, assist, display

1）他先简单介绍了一下计划，接着又进一步详细地解释。
2）他不顾一切地试图说明情况是多么紧急。
3）他们为这片森林及居住于此的印第安人的命运而担心。
4）我们正在寻找愿意协助该团体工作的人。
5）警方坚持认为迈克尔没有按照正确的程序申请签证。
6）这里有一些有价值的信息来源，可以帮助你做出最佳选择。
7）通常，只有在母亲面前，他的情感才会如此外露。
8）一旦你登上顶峰，就只会有一个愿望：往下走入最深的峡谷，和那里的人民一起生活。
9）管道将热水从锅炉输送到暖气片。
10）在政党改革中，他表现出了非凡的勇气。

Unit 1
The Poems Selected from *The She King*

After Reading

I. Please make a sentence with the words and expressions you have learnt from the text.

1. to yoke together:
2. to plaster:
3. to quiver:
4. to hew out:
5. to subdue to:

II. Paragraph Writing

1. Please write a paragraph of around 150 words about how an old farmer spent his first day of spring sowing.

2. Please write a paragraph of around 100 words with the following words and expressions you have learnt from the text. Make sure that the paragraph you have written is grammatically correct and coherent.

> slack; tinkle; for the benefit of; lop off; cut down

Original Edition in Chinese

七 月

七月流火，
九月授衣。
一之日觱发，
二之日栗烈。
无衣无褐，
何以卒岁？
三之日于耜，
四之日举趾。
同我妇子，

馌彼南亩。
田畯至喜。

七月流火，
九月授衣。
春日载阳，
有鸣仓庚。
女执懿筐，
遵彼微行，
爰求柔桑。
春日迟迟，
采蘩祁祁。
女心伤悲，
殆及公子同归。

七月流火，
八月萑苇。
蚕月条桑，
取彼斧斨。
以伐远扬，
猗彼女桑。
七月鸣鵙，
八月载绩。
载玄载黄，
我朱孔阳，
为公子裳。

四月秀葽，
五月鸣蜩。
八月其获，
十月陨萚。
一之日于貉，
取彼狐狸，
为公子裘。
二之日其同，
载缵武功。
言私其豵，
献豜于公。

五月斯螽动股,
六月莎鸡振羽。
七月在野,
八月在宇,
九月在户,
十月蟋蟀入我床下。
穹窒熏鼠,
塞向墐户。
嗟我妇子,
曰为改岁,
入此室处。

六月食郁及薁,
七月亨葵及菽。
八月剥枣,
十月获稻。
为此春酒,
以介眉寿。
七月食瓜,
八月断壶,
九月叔苴。
采荼薪樗,
食我农夫。

九月筑场圃,
十月纳禾稼。
黍稷重穋,
禾麻菽麦。
嗟我农夫,
我稼既同,
上入执宫功。
昼尔于茅,
宵尔索绹;
亟其乘屋,
其始播百谷。

二之日凿冰冲冲,
三之日纳于凌阴。

四之日其蚤,
献羔祭韭。
九月肃霜,
十月涤场。
朋酒斯飨,
曰杀羔羊。
跻彼公堂,
称彼兕觥,
万寿无疆!

采　薇

采薇采薇,
薇亦作止。
曰归曰归,
岁亦莫止。
靡室靡家,
玁狁之故。
不遑启居,
玁狁之故。

采薇采薇,
薇亦柔止。
曰归曰归,
心亦忧止。
忧心烈烈,
载饥载渴。
我戍未定,
靡使归聘。

采薇采薇,
薇亦刚止。
曰归曰归,
岁亦阳止。
王事靡盬,
不遑启处。
忧心孔疚,
我行不来。

彼尔维何?
维常之华。
彼路斯何?
君子之车。
戎车既驾,
四牡业业。
岂敢定居?
一月三捷。

驾彼四牡,
四牡骙骙。
君子所依,
小人所腓。
四牡翼翼,
象弭鱼服。
岂不日戒?
玁狁孔棘!

昔我往矣,
杨柳依依。
今我来思,
雨雪霏霏。
行道迟迟,
载渴载饥。
我心伤悲,
莫知我哀!

文 王

文王在上,
於昭于天。
周虽旧邦,
其命维新。
有周不显,
帝命不时。
文王陟降,
在帝左右。

亹亹文王，
令闻不已。
陈锡哉周，
侯文王孙子。
文王孙子，
本支百世，
凡周之士，
不显亦世。

世之不显，
厥犹翼翼。
思皇多士，
生此王国。
王国克生，
维周之桢；
济济多士，
文王以宁。

穆穆文王，
於缉熙敬止。
假哉天命，
有商孙子。
商之孙子，
其丽不亿。
上帝既命，
侯于周服。

侯服于周，
天命靡常。
殷士肤敏，
祼将于京。
厥作祼将，
常服黼冔。
王之荩臣，
无念尔祖。

无念尔祖，
聿修厥德。
永言配命，

自求多福。
殷之未丧师,
克配上帝。
宜鉴于殷,
骏命不易。

命之不易,
无遏尔躬。
宣昭义问,
有虞殷自天。
上天之载,
无声无臭。
仪刑文王,
万邦作孚。

泮　水

思乐泮水,
薄采其芹。
鲁侯戾止,
言观其旂。
其旂茷茷,
鸾声哕哕。
无小无大,
从公于迈。

思乐泮水,
薄采其藻。
鲁侯戾止,
其马蹻蹻。
其马蹻蹻,
其音昭昭。
载色载笑,
匪怒伊教。

思乐泮水,
薄采其茆。
鲁侯戾止,

在泮饮酒。
既饮旨酒,
永锡难老。
顺彼长道,
屈此群丑。

穆穆鲁侯,
敬明其德。
敬慎威仪,
维民之则。
允文允武,
昭假烈祖。
靡有不孝,
自求伊祜。

明明鲁侯,
克明其德。
既作泮宫,
淮夷攸服。
矫矫虎臣,
在泮献馘。
淑问如皋陶,
在泮献囚。

济济多士,
克广德心。
桓桓于征,
狄彼东南。
烝烝皇皇,
不吴不扬。
不告于讻,
在泮献功。

角弓其觩,
束矢其搜。
戎车孔博,
徒御无斁。
既克淮夷,

Unit 1
The Poems Selected from *The She King*

孔淑不逆。
式固尔犹,
淮夷卒获。

翩彼飞鸮,
集于泮林。
食我桑黮,
怀我好音。
憬彼淮夷,
来献其琛。
元龟象齿,
大赂南金。

Text B

Wang Rongpei's Version

Month Seven

In Month Seven the Fire Star is hardly spotted;
In Month Nine winter coats are allotted.
In Month Eleven the north wind blows cold;
In Month Twelve severe weather will hold.
Without a cloth coat coarse or fine,
How can we last through the winter time!
In Month One we repair the plough;
In Month Two we begin to mow.
Women and children leave the house
And carry food to the fields down south;
The farmers take the food to his mouth.

In Month Seven the Fire Star is hardly spotted;
In Month Nine winter coats are allotted.
When the weather turns warm in spring,
The orioles wake and start to sing.
Carrying deep baskets in their hands,
The maidens walk to the farmland
To gather mulberries by the strand.

As the spring sun goes its course,
They pick baskets of wormwood outdoors.
Yet they are worried when they are alone,
For fear the dandies will take them home.

In Month Seven the Fire Star is hardly detected;
In Month Eight we have reeds collected.
When we trim mulberries in Month Three,
We use both axes and hatchets
To cut the long boughs and branches,
And pick the leaves from soft branches.
In Month Seven the shrikes shriek overhead;
In Month Eight we twist the hempen thread
And dye it black, or yellow instead.
We may dye it red, which is so bright,
To make skirts for the young knight.

In Month Four the milkworts are in seeds;
In Month Five the cicadas chirp in the trees.
In Month Eight we gather in the corps;
In Month Ten leaves from the trees drop.
In Month Eleven we hunt the raccoon-dogs
And go on to skin the fox
To make fur coats and frocks.
In Month Twelve we have a grand chase,
To complete the hunt with good grace.
We keep the yearlings for our hoard;
We present the old boars to the lord.

In Month Five the grasshoppers hop about;
In Month Six the crickets start to skip out.
In Month Seven they live in the fields;
In Month Eight they stay under the eaves;
In Month Nine in the room they keep;
In Month Ten under the bed they sleep.
We smoke the mice and stop the holes;
We seal the doors and the windows.
Wretched are our children and spouses;

Unit 1
The Poems Selected from *The She King*

Not until the new year comes around
Can they move into those small houses.

In the Month Six we eat plums and wild grapes;
In Month Seven we cook mallows and beans.
In Month Eight we knock down the dates;
In Month Ten we take in the grains.
With the grains we make rice wine;
Drinking the wine grants us long life.
In Month Seven we eat the melons;
In Month Eight we cut the gourds;
In Month Nine we collect the hemps.
We pick wild herbs and cut firewood;
These things make our livelihood.

In Month Nine we prepare the threshing floor;
In Month Ten we put the crops in store.
There's rice, sorghum and glutinous millet,
Also sesame, bean, wheat and millet.
We farmers have much to deplore;
As soon as we put the crops in store,
We must build houses for the lord.
We gather thatch grass in the morning
And twist ropes in the evening.
When we are finished with houses,
We are busy again at the ploughs.

In Month Twelve we chop the ice with hammers;
In Month One we move it to the cellars.
In Month Two we use it in sacrifice,
To preserve the lamb and the chive.
In Month Nine it is cold with frost;
In Month Ten we clean the threshing floor.
With two pitchers of wine in our hands,
We then begin to kill the lambs.
Together we go to the lord's hall,
And raise the horn cups above us all,
Wishing a long life to our lord.

Picking Vetches

We pick the vetches, the vetches;
Springing up are the vetches.
When, oh when can we go back?
The year is the end of its track.
I have no house, I have no home;
To fight the Huns I leave my home.
I have no peace, I have no rest;
To fight the Huns I give up rest.

We pick the vetches, the vetches;
Fresh and tender are the vetches.
When, oh when can we go back?
My heart is very, very sad.
My sad heart will burst
With hunger and thirst.
I'm stationed here, I'm stationed there;
The tidings from my home are rare.

We pick the vetches, the vetches;
Withered and tough are the vetches.
When, oh when can we go back?
It's now Month Ten of the almanac!
The king's warfares never end;
I have no leisure time to spend.
I am sad, I am distressed;
No sympathy has been expressed.

What flowers are in full bloom?
Kerria flowers are in full bloom.
What carriage is magnificent?
The lord's chariot is magnificent.
His war-chariot is on the way;
Four steeds gallop and neigh.
We never settle down once,
With three battles in a month.

The four steeds are on the way;
How they prance and neigh!
The lord rides with pretension;
The footmen seek protection.
With prances the four steeds go;
Seal-skin quiver goes with ivory bow.
We are guarding the frontier;
The Huns run rampant far and near.

When I set out so long ago,
Fresh and green was the willow.
When now homeward I go,
There is a heavy snow.
The homeward march is slow;
My hunger and thirst grow.
My heart is filled with sorrow;
Who on earth will ever know!

Lord Wen

Lord Wen inhabits now on high,
And lords it over us from the sky.
Although the State of Zhou is old,
It starts a history now twice old.
The State of Zhou is shining bright;
Lord Wen enjoys divine right.
Between heaven and earth he rides;
By God of Heaven he abides.

The diligent Lord Wen
Enjoys a fame that'll never end.
His bounties spread in Zhou;
From son to son they go.
They pass from son to son;
For generations they will run.
For those who serve the House of Zhou,
Their glories always last and grow.

With glories that last and grow,
They give their counsels from below.
As courtiers of the topmost rate,
They are born in this great state.
Bred and brought up on this land,
They serve well at the king's command.
With all those courtiers there allied,
Lord Wen can in full peace reside.

August is Wen the mighty lord,
Revered at home, revered abroad.
When Heaven issues its decree,
Shang's offspring cannot but agree.
Is it not true that heirs of Shang
Do form a populous large clan?
Yet the God's will they obey,
Subject to Zhou in every way.

Subject to Zhou in every way,
They know that fortunes never stay.
As men of fame and high renown,
They make libations in the capital town.
They make libations in success,
In their former caps and dress.
Oh, loyal courtiers of the king,
To your ancestors always cling!

To keep your ancestors in mind,
You'll never leave your faith behind.
Always follow Heaven's will
And you will always have your fill.
Before Yin-Shang had lost control,
Divine and royal was its role.
Yin has undergone decline and fall;
Heaven's will disposes all.

Since Heaven's will disposes all,
Be alert against your own downfall.

Carry on the good fame of Lord Wen,
And learn from lessons of the Yin.
Heaven's will can never tell;
It makes no sound and gives no smell.
Take your pattern from Lord Wen
And you will lord it over then.

Merry Waves

Merry are the waves in the pond of Pan,
Where we gather cresses as we can.
Now arrives respected Marquis Lu,
His dragon-banners coming into view.
His banners flutter in the wind;
Bells tinkle on steeds well-disciplined.
Officials high in rank or low,
Behind the prince they go.

Merry are the waves in the pond of Pan,
Where we gather pondweed as we can.
Now arrives respected Marquis Lu,
His team of steeds a splendid view.
On his coach and four he comes to town,
The prince of high renown.
So kind is he, with a smile on his face;
With patience, he instructs his race.

Merry are the waves in the pond of Pan,
Where we gather mallows as we can.
Now arrives respected Marquis Lu,
His banquet there a superb view.
He drinks the excellent wine,
That will ensure a long lifetime.
He follows those time-honoured ways
In subduing all the race.

Reverent is Marquis Lu,
Renowned for noble virtue.

His manners stimulate our awe,
A model fit for one and all.
He has excelled in peace and wars,
A true successor to the cause.
Faithful to the ancestors in every way,
He seeks their blessing every day.

Intelligence is Marquis Lu,
Illustrious for his noble virtue.
He builds the royal school of Pan,
And quells the barbarous Huai clan.
His valiant marshals offer here
The enemy chieftain's ears.
He questions skillfully as Gaoyao
The captives here and now.

His numerous marshals and knights
Are gifted with virtue and insights.
On the march, their valour never ceased;
They qulled the foe in the south and east.
Full of vigour, full of grace,
They do not boast out of place.
They do not argue, they do not plead;
Here in Pan they announce their deed.

The horn-tipped bows hang slack;
The sheaves of arrows pile in a stack.
The mighty chariots are retired;
Footmen and riders are not tired.
When the Huai tribes are subdued,
They are no longer fierce and rude.
As Marquis Lu's plans are carried out,
The tribes of Huai are put to rout.

The owls flutter on the wing,
And in the woods of Pan they cling.
They eat the mulberry fruits
And pay back with pleasant hoots.

So do the tribes of Huai,
Who bring their gifts thereby:
Ivory and tortoise-shell,
And gold from where they dwell.

Notes on the Text

1. About the text

The present text is taken from *The Book of Poetry* translated by Wang Rongpei, published by Hunan People's Publishing House in 2008.

2. chariot

A chariot is an ancient horse-drawn two-wheeled vehicle used in war, race and processions. It was usually used by armies as transportation vehicles or mobile archery platforms for hunting or racing.

Unit 2

The Selected Tang Poems

Reading Guide

This text is excerpted from *The Jade Mountain: A Chinese Anthology* translated by Witter Bynner, who was an American poet, writer and scholar. In Chinese literature, the Tang Dynasty (618—907) is considered as the golden age of Chinese poetry. The original Chinese version of *300 Tang Poems* is an anthology of poems from the Tang Dynasty compiled by Sun Zhu in the Qing Dynasty. Sun made his own selection of Tang poems based on their popularity and effectiveness in cultivating character. Because it represented equally well each of the classical poetic forms and the best works by the most prominent Tang poets, Sun's collection became a "best seller" soon after its publication and is still a classic today, its popularity undiminished.

This text selects six poems written by three great Tang poets, Li Bai, Du Fu and Wang Wei. These poems are about various topics including eulogy of love, frustration in officialdom, idyllic life and ladies' life, and so on. The translation is idiomatic, apprehensible, and in rhyming whenever possible.

Before Reading

I. *Preview Requirements: Please make a preparatory research on the background information, key words and phrases of this text.*
   1. Do research on the translator Witter Bynner.
   2. Do research on Tang poems. Get to know five-character quatrain, seven-character quatrain, five-character metrical verse and seven-character metrical verse.
   3. Do research on poetry translation. Pay attention to the forms, rhymes and artistic conception of Tang poems in the translation.
   4. Find and study the new words in the text such as *trot, tag, tumble, companion, woe, whimper* and *flush*.

Unit 2
The Selected Tang Poems

5. Learn the useful expressions in the text such as *turn to, sweep away, drop down,* and *roll on.*

II. Preview Questions: Please answer some questions about the understanding of the main content of the text.

1. What is the theme of "A Song of Changgan"? In what order is the song developed, by time or space? How many phases of the woman's life are described, and what are they?
2. In "A Song of Changgan", how does the description of the scene in the garden in autumn help to show the woman's sorrow for missing her husband?
3. What is "Drinking Alone with the Moon" mainly about? What are the things described in the scene? Do you find the scene a little dull? What feelings does the scene bring to you?
4. "Drinking Alone with the Moon" describes three phases of the poet's mood. What are the three phases? How does the description help to set the tone for different phases of the poet's emotion?
5. What is the theme of "A Long Climb"? What kind of thoughts and feelings does the poem try to express?
6. What are the things described in the first four lines of "A Long Climb"? What tone does the description set? How does the description of the scene help to express the poet's feelings?
7. What is the theme of "A View of Taishan"? In what order is the poet's view described, from the bottom to the top, or something else?
8. How does the poet show the magnificence of Taishan? How is the description of Taishan related to the emotion the poet wants to express?
9. What is the theme of "An Autumn Evening in the Mountains"? What is the poet's purpose of describing the empty mountain, the moonlight, the brook and so on? How does the description of the scene help to set the tone of the poem?
10. What is the theme of "One-Hearted"? What does the red berry symbolize in the poem?
11. Please read a chapter of the epic *Odyssey*, and try to contrast Tang poems with *Odyssey*. Consider their themes, meters and rhymes.

Text A

Witter Bynner's Version

A Song of Changgan

Li Bai

My hair had hardly covered my forehead.
I was picking flowers, paying by my door,

When you, my lover, on a bamboo horse,
Came trotting in circles and throwing green plums.
We lived near together on a lane in Ch'ang-kan,
Both of us young and happy-hearted.
...At fourteen I became your wife,
So bashful that I dared not smile,
And I lowered my head toward a dark corner
And would not turn to your thousand calls;
But at fifteen I straightened my brows and laughed,
Learning that no dust could ever seal our love,
That even unto death I would await you by my post
And would never lose heart in the tower of silent watching.
...Then when I was sixteen, you left on a long journey
Through the Gorges of Ch'u-t'ang, of rock and whirling water.
And then came the Fifth-month, more than I could bear,
And I tried to hear the monkeys in your lofty far-off sky.
Your footprints by our door, where I had watched you go,
Were hidden, every one of them, under green moss,
Hidden under moss too deep to sweep away.
And the first autumn wind added fallen leaves.
And now, in the Eighth-month, yellowing butterflies
Hover, two by two, in our west-garden grasses
And, because of all this, my heart is breaking
And I fear for my bright cheeks, lest they fade.
...Oh, at last, when you return through the three Pa districts,
Send me a message home ahead!
And I will come and meet you and will never mind the distance,
All the way to Chang-feng Sha.

Drinking Alone with the Moon

Li Bai

From a pot of wine among the flowers
I drank alone. There was no one with me –
Till, raising my cup, I asked the bright moon
To bring me my shadow and make us three.
Alas, the moon was unable to drink

And my shadow tagged me vacantly;
But still for a while I had these friends
To cheer me through the end of spring...
I sang. The moon encouraged me.
I danced. My shadow tumbled after.
As long as I knew, we were boon companions.
And then I was drunk, and we lost one another.
...Shall goodwill ever be secure?
I watch the long road of the River of Stars.

A Long Climb

Du Fu

In a sharp gale from the wide sky apes are whimpering,
Birds are flying homeward over the clear lake and white sand,
Leaves are dropping down like the spray of a waterfall,
While I watch the long river always rolling on.
I have come three thousand miles away. Sad now with autumn
And with my hundred years of woe, I climb the height alone.
Ill fortune has laid a bitter frost on my temples,
Heart-ache and weariness are a thick dust in my wine.

A View of Taishan

Du Fu

What shall I say of the Great Peak? –
The ancient dukedoms are everywhere green,
Inspired and stirred by the breath of creation,
With the Twin Forces balancing day and night.
...I bare my breast toward opening clouds,
I strain my sight after birds flying home.
When shall I reach the top and hold
All mountains in a single glance?

An Autumn Evening in the Mountains

Wang Wei

After rain the empty mountain
Stands autumnal in the evening,
Moonlight in its groves of pine,
Stones of crystal in its brooks.
Bamboos whisper of washer-girls bound home,
Lotus-leaves yield before a fisher-boat –
And what does it matter that springtime has gone,
While you are here, O Prince of Friends?

One-Hearted

Wang Wei

When those red berries come in springtime,
Flushing on your southland branches,
Take home an armful, for my sake,
As a symbol of our love.

Notes on the Text

1. Witter Bynner

Witter Bynner (1881—1968), an American poet, writer and scholar, was born in Brooklyn, New York. He attended Harvard University, where he was invited by Wallace Stevens to join the *Harvard Advocate*. After his graduation from the university, he edited *McClure's* in New York for four years. His collections of poetry include *An Ode to Harvard* (1907), *The Beloved Stranger* (1919), *Pins for Wings* (1921), *Indian Earth* (1929), and *New Poems* (1960). The style of Bynner's early poetry is comparable to that of A. E. Housman. His later poetry reflects his familiarity with Japanese and Chinese poetry, becoming less traditionally structured in forms. Bynner translated *The Jade Mountain: A Chinese Anthology* from the texts of Kian Kang-Hu. He also translated a version of the *Tao Te Ching—The Way of Life According to Laotse* (1949).

2. three Pa

the name of an area in the eastern part of Sichuan Province, namely Ba county, the Eastern Ba, and the Western Ba.

3. Changgan

Changgan is a gathering place for boatpeople in the south of Nanjing city. "A Song of Changgan," a topic of Yue Fu Poetry, is a ballad in the downstream of the Yangtze River, mainly describing the life of the boat women.

4. Chang-feng Sha

a place along the Yangtze River in Anqing City of Anhui Province, which is 700 miles from Nanjing City.

5. Taishan

Taishan, usually known as Mount Tai, is a mountain of historical and cultural significance located in the north of Tai'an City, Shandong Province. The tallest peak is the Jade Emperor Peak. Mount Tai is known as the eastern mountain of the Five Great Mountains of China. It is associated with sunrise, birth, and renewal, and is often regarded as the foremost of the five. Mount Tai has been a place of worship for at least 3,000 years and served as one of the most important ceremonial centers of China.

Glossary

bashful /ˈbæʃfl/   *adj.* shy and easily embarrassed
e.g.: *He seemed bashful and awkward.*

boon /buːn/   *n.* something that is very helpful and makes life easier for you
e.g.: *The new software will prove a boon to Internet users.*

dukedom /ˈdjuːkdəm/   *n.* the rank or position of a duke
e.g.: *The marquis will succeed to the dukedom at his father's death.*

gale /geɪl/   *n.* an extremely strong wind
e.g.: *The gale blew down hundreds of trees.*

lofty /ˈlɒfti/   *adj.* (of buildings, mountains, etc.) very high and impressive
e.g.: *lofty ceilings/ rooms/ towers*

moss /mɒs/   *n.* a small flowerless green plant that spreads over damp surfaces, rocks, trees, etc.
e.g.: *The moss was soft and furry to the touch.*

tag /tæg/   *v.* to fasten a label onto sth./sb.
e.g.: *Each animal was tagged with a number for identification.*

trot /trɒt/   *v.* to move forward at a speed that is faster than a walk and slower than a canter
e.g.: *She trotted her pony around the field.*

tumble /ˈtʌmbl/   *v.* to fall downwards, often hitting the ground several times, but usually without serious injury; to make sb./sth. fall in this way
e.g.: *He slipped and tumbled down the stairs.*

vacant /ˈveɪkənt/	*adj.* empty; not being used
	e.g.: *The seat next to him was vacant.*
whirl /wɜːl/	*v.* to move, or make sb./sth. move, around quickly in a circle or in a particular direction
	e.g.: *She whirled around to face him.*
whimper /ˈwɪmpə(r)/	*v.* to make low, weak crying noises; to speak in this way
	e.g.: *The child was lost and began to whimper.*

While Reading

I. Please fill in the blanks with the words in the parentheses with the appropriate part of speech.

1. The President could continue to _____ Democrats as being soft on crime. (bashful)
2. We employed a lawyer to _____ our legal tangle. (straight)
3. His _____ spirit has greatly attracted and activated others. (loft)
4. Her unexpected maternity leave will create a temporary _____ . (vacant)
5. The _____ that young boys receive builds a greater self-confidence. (encourage)
6. He found very little congenial _____ in this casual Western city. (companion)
7. The _____ forces had to intervene to prevent the situation from worsening. (secure)
8. _____, the storm only did minimal damage to the farmer's crops. (fortune)
9. India's myths and songs are the _____ for her books. (inspire)
10. _____ people are usually very determined and thrive on overcoming obstacles. (creation)

II. Please choose one word or phrase that best completes the sentence.

1. They value your perspective on matters and _____ you for advice.
   A. turn to   B. turn on
   C. turn over   D. turn up
2. Newspaper editorials spoke of the need to _____ corruption.
   A. get over   B. sweep away
   C. put away   D. clear up
3. He had to cancel some engagements _____ tiredness.
   A. account for   B. thanks to
   C. because of   D. regardless of
4. Fruits soon _____ when they get ripe.
   A. tear apart   B. come off
   C. fall through   D. drop down

5. As my exams are coming next month, I'll take advantage of the weekend to _____ on some reading.
   A. pick up   B. make up
   C. clear up   D. catch up
6. You just work day in and day out so the world can _____ and other people can live.
   A. roll on   B. roll around
   C. roll away   D. roll back

III. Translation

1. Please translate the following from English into Chinese.

1) to pick flowers   2) green plums
3) to lower the head   4) to straighten one's brows
5) a pot of wine   6) to drink alone
7) to raise the cup   8) washer-girls
9) an empty mountain   10) a fisher-boat

2. Please translate the following from Chinese into English.

1）两小无嫌猜   2）千唤不一回
3）举杯邀明月   4）对影成三人
5）无边落木萧萧下   6）不尽长江滚滚来
7）明月松间照   8）清泉石上流
9）愿君多采撷   10）此物最相思

3. Please translate each sentence with at least one key word or its derivative.

Key Words: trot, tag, tumble, whimper, stain

1）向导在前面带路，我们紧跟在他后面。
2）在英国，爵士音乐不再仅限于精英人士欣赏，它正吸引着越来越多的听众。
3）今天东京股市的股价继续暴跌。
4）我们不想哭泣着离开，我们知道必须要小心谨慎，但不能谨慎过度。
5）一块深红色的污渍正在他的衬衫上渗开。
6）那姑娘突然小步跑了起来，拐过街角不见了。
7）这个国家不愿意再被称为第三世界国家。
8）双方摔跤运动员都使出了全身气力想把对手摔倒。
9）我咬紧牙关，一声不出。
10）你可以用这种特制的液体来染这块木料，使它看起来赏心悦目。

After Reading

I. *Please make a sentence with the words and expressions you have learnt from the text.*

1. to await:
2. to seal one's love:
3. to whirl:
4. to fade:
5. to stir:
6. to flush:

II. *Paragraph Writing*

1. Please write a paragraph of around 150 words to describe the dismay of the wife being miles away from her husband.

2. Please write a paragraph of around 100 words with the following words and expressions you have learnt from the text. Make sure that the paragraph you have written is grammatically correct and coherent.

> shadow; inspire; moss; woe; weariness

Original Edition in Chinese

长干行

李 白

妾发初覆额，折花门前剧。
郎骑竹马来，绕床弄青梅。
同居长干里，两小无嫌猜。
十四为君妇，羞颜未尝开。
低头向暗壁，千唤不一回。
十五始展眉，愿同尘与灰。
常存抱柱信，岂上望夫台！

十六君远行,瞿塘滟滪堆。
五月不可触,猿声天上哀。
门前迟行迹,一一生绿苔。
苔深不能扫,落叶秋风早。
八月蝴蝶黄,双飞西园草。
感此伤妾心,坐愁红颜老。
早晚下三巴,预将书报家。
相迎不道远,直至长风沙。

月下独酌
李 白

花间一壶酒,独酌无相亲。
举杯邀明月,对影成三人。
月既不解饮,影徒随我身。
暂伴月将影,行乐须及春。
我歌月徘徊,我舞影零乱。
醒时同交欢,醉后各分散。
永结无情游,相期邈云汉。

登 高
杜 甫

风急天高猿啸哀,渚清沙白鸟飞回。
无边落木萧萧下,不尽长江滚滚来。
万里悲秋常作客,百年多病独登台。
艰难苦恨繁霜鬓,潦倒新停浊酒杯。

望 岳
杜 甫

岱宗夫如何,齐鲁青未了。
造化钟神秀,阴阳割昏晓。
荡胸生层云,决眦入归鸟。
会当凌绝顶,一览众山小。

山居秋暝
王　维

空山新雨后，天气晚来秋。
明月松间照，清泉石上流。
竹喧归浣女，莲动下渔舟。
随意春芳歇，王孙自可留。

相　思
王　维

红豆生南国，春来发几枝。
愿君多采撷，此物最相思。

Text B

Xu Yuanchong's Version

Ballad of a Trader's Wife

Li Bai

My forehead barely covered by my hair,
Outdoors I pluck'd and played with flower fair.
On hobby horse you came upon the scene;
Around the well we played with mumes still green.
We lived, close neighbors on Riverside Lane,
Carefree and innocent, we children twain.
At fourteen years when I became your bride,
I'd often turn my bashful face aside.
Hanging my head, I'd look on the dark wall;
I would not answer your call upon call.
I was fifteen when I composed my brows;
To mix my dust with yours were my dear vows.
Rather than break faith, you declared you'd die.
Who knew I'd live alone in tower high?
I was sixteen when you went far away,

Passing Three Gorges studded with rocks grey,
Where ships were wrecked when spring flood ran high,
Where gibbons' wails seemed coming from the sky.
Green moss now overgrows before our door;
Your footprints, hidden, can be seen no more.
Moss can't be swept away, so thick it grows,
And leaves fall early when the west wind blows.
In yellow autumn butterflies would pass
Two by two in west garden o'er the grass.
This sight would break my heart and I'm afraid,
Sitting alone, my rosy cheeks would fade.
O when are you to leave the western land?
Do not forget to tell me beforehand!
I'll walk to meet you and not call it far
E' en to go to Long Wind Sands where you are.

Drinking Alone Under the Moon

Li Bai

Among the flowers, from a pot of wine
I drink without a companion of mine.
I raise my cup to invite the Moon who blends
Her light with my Shadow and we're three friends.
The Moon does not know how to drink her share;
In vain my Shadow follows me here and there.
Together with them for the time I stay,
And make merry before spring's spent away.
I sing and the Moon lingers to hear my song;
My Shadow's a mess while I dance along.
Sober, we three remain cheerful and gay;
Drunken, we part and each may go his way.
Our friendship will outshine all earthly love;
Next time we'll meet beyond the stars above.

On the Height

Du Fu

The wind so swift, the sky so wide, apes wail and cry;
Water so clear and beach so white, birds wheel and fly.
The boundless forest sheds its leaves shower by shower;
The endless river rolls its waves hour after hour.
A thousand miles from home, I'm grieved at autumn's plight;
Ill now and then for years, alone I'm on this height.
Living in times so hard, at frosted hair I pine;
Cast down by poverty, I have to give up wine.

Gazing on Mount Tai

Du Fu

O peak of peaks, how high it stands!
One boundless green o'erspreads two States.
A marvel done by Nature's hands,
O'er light and shade it dominates.
Clouds rise therefrom and lave my breast;
My eyes are strained to see birds fleet.
Try to ascend the mountain's crest:
It dwarfs all peaks under our feet.

Autumn Evening in the Mountains

Wang Wei

After fresh rain in mountains bare
Autumn permeates evening air.
Among pine-trees bright moonbeams peer;
O'er crystal stones flows water clear.
Bamboos whisper of washer-maids;
Lotus stirs when fishing boat wades.

Unit 2
The Selected Tang Poems

Though fragrant spring may pass away,
Still here's the place for you to stay.

Love Seeds

Wang Wei

Red berries grow in southern land.
How many load in spring the trees?
Gather them till full is your hand;
They would revive fond memories.

Notes on the Text

About the text

The text is excerpted from *300 Tang Poems* translated by Xu Yuanchong, published by Higher Education Press in 2000.

Unit 3

The Selected Song Lyrics

Reading Guide

Song Lyrics, a poetic form in classical Chinese poetry, represent a significant landmark of literature in the Song Dynasty. With fixed-rhythm, fixed-tone and variable line-length, Song lyrics have set musical song tunes. Each lyric is labeled "to the tune of (tune name)" and fits the meter and rhyme of the tune. Basically, Song Lyrics fall into two styles of writing: "heroic abandon" voicing heroic and patriotic sentiments, and "delicate restraint" depicting tender feelings. As most eminent exponents, Su Shi and Xin Qiji are seen as the epitome of the former; Li Qingzhao the latter.

The selected Song Lyrics of Su Shi, Xin Qiji and Li Qingzhao are translated by professor Xu Yuanchong, a distinguished Chinese translator known for his artistic translation of Chinese ancient poems into English and French. Professor Xu introduced the three-beauties-principle to translation theory, which indicates that a good translation should be as beautiful as the original in sense, sound and form. "He (Xu Yuanchong) advocates that the versions of poems should combine visual and aural beauties together, and they should reproduce the fusion of pictorial composition and musical arrangement."[①] Prof. Xu's translation of *The Selected Song Lyrics* in the text is to be appreciated from the angle of sense, sound and form.

Before Reading

I. Preview Requirements: Please make a preparatory research on the background information, key words and phrases of this text.
 1. Do research on the translator Xu Yuanchong.
 2. Do research on the writing styles of "heroic abandon" and "delicate restraint".

---

① Gao, Lei. "On English Translation of Classical Chinese Poetry: A Perspective from Skopos Theory". *Journal of Language Teaching and Research*, Vol.1, No.1 (January 2010), 84–89.

Unit 3
The Selected Song Lyrics

3. Do research on the lives of Su Shi, Xin Qiji and Li Qingzhao.
4. Find and study the new words in the text such as *abate, bumper, crystalline, drizzle, gallant, gauze* and *grizzle*.
5. Learn the useful expressions in the text such as *shed light on, take a dim view of,* and *acquaint sb. with sth.*

II. Preview Questions: Please answer some questions about the understanding of the main content of the text.

1. How do you state the theme of "Tune: Prelude to Water Melody"? Is the lyric sentimental? Or does it express optimism?
2. Note the image of moon in the second stanza of "Tune: Prelude to Water Melody". How is this image related to the theme?
3. What is the tone of "Tune: The Charm of a Maiden Singer"? Why does Su Shi use a historical narrative frame here?
4. What images in "Tune: The Moon over the West River" strike you as fresh and effective? Why? What do the details of magpies, cicadas, frogs, stars and raindrops do to emphasize the effect of the lyric?
5. In "Tune: Song of Ugly Slave", how do the repetitions in lines 2 and 3 and lines 6 and 7 contribute to the tone of the lyric?
6. How do you describe the tone of "Tune: Slow, Slow Song"? Do lines 1, 2 and 3 in the first stanza add to the dramatic power of the lyric? How are they related to the main theme?
7. What is Li Qingzhao's attitude toward spring in "Tune: Spring in Peach-Blossom Land"? Specify the details that make for her attitude.

Text A

Xu Yuanchong's Version

Tune: Prelude to Water Melody
Sent to Ziyou on Mid-autumn Festival

Su Shi

On the mid-autumn festival, I drank happily till dawn and wrote this in my cups while thinking of Ziyou.

When did the bright moon first appear?
Wine-cup in hand, I ask the blue sky.

I do not know what time of year
It would be tonight in the palace on high.
Riding the wind, there I would fly,
But I'm afraid the crystalline palace would be
Too high and too cold for me.
I rise and dance, with my shadow I play.
On high as on earth, would it be as gay?

The moon goes round the mansions red
With gauze windows to shed
Her light upon the sleepless bed.
Against man she should not have any spite.
Why then when people part is she oft full and bright?
Men have sorrow and joy, they part and meet again;
The moon may be bright or dim, she may wax or wane.
There has been nothing perfect since olden days.
So let us wish that man live as long as he can!
Though miles apart, we'll share the beauty she displays.

Tune: The Charm of a Maiden Singer
The Red Cliff

Su Shi

The great river eastward flows;
With its waves are gone all those
Gallant heroes of bygone years.
West of the ancient fortress appears
Red Cliff where General Zhou won his early fame
When the Three Kingdoms were in flame.
Rocks tower in the air and waves beat on the shore.
Rolling up a thousand heaps of snow.
To match the land so fair, how many heroes of yore
Had made great show!

I fancy General Zhou at the height
Of his success, with a plume fan in hand,

In a silk hood, so brave and bright,
Laughing and jesting with his bride so fair,
While enemy ships were destroyed as planned
Like castles in the air.
Should their souls revisit this land,
Sentimental, his bride would laugh to say:
Younger than they, I have my hair turned grey.
Life is but like a dream.
O Moon, I drink to you who have seen them on the stream.

Tune: The Moon over the West River
Home-Going at Night from the Yellow Sand Bridge

Xin Qiji

Startled by magpies leaving the branch in moonlight,
I hear cicadas shrill in the breeze at midnight.
The ricefields' sweet smell promises a bumper year;
Listen, how frogs' croaks please the ear!

Beyond the clouds seven or eight stars twinkle;
Before the hills two or three raindrops sprinkle.
There is an inn beside the village temple. Look!
The winding path leads to the hut beside the brook.

Tune: Song of Ugly Slave
Written on the Wall on My Way to Boshan

Xin Qiji

While young, I knew no grief I could not bear;
I'd like to go upstair.
I'd like to to upstair,
To write new verses with a false despair.

I know what grief is now that I am old;
I would not have it told.

I would not have it told,
But only say I'm glad that autumn's cold.

Tune: Slow, Slow Song

Li Qingzhao

I look for what I miss;
I know not what it is.
I feel so sad, so drear,
So lonely, without cheer.
How hard is it
To keep me fit
In this lingering cold!
Hardly warmed up
By cup on cup
Of wine so dry,
On, how could I
Endure at dusk the drift
Of wind so swift?
It breaks my heart, alas!
To see the wild geese pass,
For they are my acquaintances of old.

The ground is covered with yellow flowers,
Faded and fallen in showers.
Who will pick them up now?
Sitting alone at the window, how
Could I but quicken
The pace of darkness that won't thicken?
On broad plane leaves a fine rain drizzles
As twilight grizzles.
Oh, what can I do with a grief
Beyond belief!

Tune: Spring in Peach-Blossom Land

Li Qingzhao

Sweet flowers fall to dust when winds abate.
Tired, I won't comb my hair for it is late.
Things are the same, but he's no more and all is o'er.
Before I speak, how can my tears not pour!

'Tis said at Twin Creek spring is not yet gone.
In a light boat I long to float thereon.
But I'm afraid the grief-o'erladen boat
Upon Twin Creek can't keep afloat.

Notes on the Text

Ziyou
Ziyou is the courtesy name of Su Shi's younger brother, Su Zhe. Su Shi, Su Zhe and their father Su Xun were among "The Eight Great Men of Letters of the Tang and Song Dynasties". At this time Su Zhe was in Jinan City, Shandong Province, while Su Shi in Mi Prefecture.

Glossary

acquaintance /əˈkweɪntəns/	*n.* a person one knows slightly, but who is not a close friend e.g.: *Most people are content with having more acquaintances and very few friends.*
abate /əˈbeɪt/	*v.* (of sth. unpleasant or severe) become less intense or widespread e.g.: *Yet in the year that they had known each other his feelings had grown more intense rather than abated.*
bumper /ˈbʌmpə/	*adj.* exceptionally large, fine, or successful e.g.: *And another bumper crop is on the way thanks to abundant rain.*
crystalline /ˈkrɪstəlaɪn/	*adj.* having the structure and form of a crystal; composed of crystals e.g.: *Glass itself does not have a crystalline structure as minerals do.*

drizzle /ˈdrɪz(ə)l/   *v.* rain in very fine drops
e.g.: *It had been drizzling all day.*

gallant /ˈgæl(ə)nt/   *adj.* (of a person or their behavior) brave; heroic
e.g.: *She had made gallant efforts to pull herself together.*

gauze /gɔːz/   *n.* a transparent haze or film
e.g.: *They saw the grasslands through a gauze of golden dust.*

grizzle /ˈgrɪz(ə)l/   *v.* sulk or grumble
e.g.: *Then again, there's not much point in grizzling about it.*

jest /dʒest/   *v.* to say things that are not serious or true especially in order to make sb. laugh
e.g.: *Would I jest about such a thing?*

plume /pluːm/   *n.* a long, soft feather or arrangement of feathers used by a bird for display or worn by a person for ornament
e.g.: *Ornamental bird plumes, by weight, were more valuable than gold.*

prelude /ˈpreljuːd/   *n.* the introductory part of a poem or other literary work
e.g.: *The lines form a prelude to his long narrative poem.*

shrill /ʃrɪl/   *adj.* (of a voice or sound) high-pitched and piercing
e.g.: *A piercing and shrill sound could be heard in the distance.*

thereon /ðerˈɒn/   *adv.* on or following from the thing just mentioned
e.g.: *Parents, students and teachers should be free to determine what is learnt and employers and society should be free to pass judgment thereon.*

wax /wæks/   *v.* (of the moon) to show a large bright area that gradually increases until the moon is full
e.g.: *The moon was waxing, and I was sure it would be full the next night.*

wane /weɪn/   *v.* (of the moon) to appear slightly smaller each day after being round and full
e.g.: *I know Sarah would come in the same way I knew the moon would grow and wane in cycles.*

yore /jɔː/   *n.* of long ago or former times (used in nostalgic or mock-nostalgic recollection)
of yore e.g.: *While they make for funny dinner conversation now, in days of yore these words were taken very seriously.*

Unit 3
The Selected Song Lyrics

While Reading

I. Please fill in the blanks with the words in the parentheses with the appropriate part of speech.

1. _____ salons are polluting the water as they _____ people's appearance. (beauty)
2. Tragic literature dignifies _____ and disaster. (sorrowful)
3. Many top athletes are _____ who drive themselves to excel. (perfect)
4. Knowing the risks is important and will likely keep you _____ regardless of the water conditions. (float)
5. The fog _____ as the sun tries to peek through the cloud of mist below. (thick)
6. Marguerite hoped it would be the _____ to a book she wanted to write, and asked if I could get it published somewhere. (preludial)
7. It offers some _____ lessons in how we look at ourselves as well as how we perceive the stage of reality around us. (startle)
8. Peter was not a _____ person—in public he wasn't—but he had an honesty in his songwriting that just touches you. (sentiment)
9. The stone is about twelve feet in _____ and four in breadth with the hole near the top. (high)
10. But in the Chinese as well as Western ideology, isn't it the _____ personality in an individual that counts? (hero)

II. Please choose one word or phrase that best completes the sentence.

1. He added that the council _____ people using disabled parking spaces, which is why the fine was so high.
   A. took a dim view on
   B. took a dim point of
   C. adopted a dim view on
   D. took a dim view of
2. The problem is that there are not enough resources to _____.
   A. go round
   B. go about
   C. come around
   D. come about
3. Living together as a prelude _____ marriage is now considered acceptable in many countries.
   A. to
   B. on
   C. toward
   D. over
4. Police said they wanted to speak to a man seen in the area who might be able to _____ what happened.
   A. shed a light on
   B. shed light to
   C. shed light on
   D. shed a light to
5. Over time, levels of criminal behavior have _____.
   A. wax and wane
   B. waxes and wanes
   C. waxed and waned
   D. waxes and waned

6. We joined the party, and we all ate sliced fresh tomatoes drizzled with olive oil and _____ with chunky sea salt.

   A. splashed   B. sprayed
   C. scattered   D. sprinkled

III. Translation

1. Please translate the following from English into Chinese.

1) Oh, what can I do with a grief beyond belief!
2) Things are the same, but he's no more and all is o'er.
3) While young, I knew no grief I could not bear.
4) to write new verses with a false despair
5) Men have sorrow and joy, they part and meet again.
6) The moon may be bright or dim, she may wax or wane.
7) When did the bright moon first appear?
8) Wine-cup in hand, I ask the blue sky.
9) There has been nothing perfect since olden days.
10) I rise and dance, with my shadow I play.

2. Please translate the following from Chinese into English.

1）欲说还休   2）旧时相识
3）爱上层楼   4）人生如梦
5）乱石穿空   6）惊涛拍岸
7）七八个星天外   8）两三点雨山前
9）但愿人长久   10）千里共婵娟

3. Please translate each sentence with at least one key word or its derivative.

Key Words: shed, dim, part, gay, acquaintance

1）要他戒除那些奢侈的习惯可真不容易。
2）在英国，至少在我所熟知的放慢生活节奏的中产阶级人士（downshifters）中，追求简化生活的原因各有不同。
3）她虽然年事已高，但记忆并未模糊。
4）在未来几年里，研究人员也很有可能会阐明语言对知觉的更细微领域的影响。
5）家庭是我爷爷生活的重心，全家团聚是他最幸福的时刻。
6）直到最近，商界仍倾向于对气候正在变化的说法持怀疑态度。
7）苏格拉底告诉我们，当一个年轻人成长时，他有充分的机会去熟悉所在社会的生活方式。

8）街上旗帜鲜艳、彩灯缤纷，显出一派欢乐景象。

9）我不喜欢那暗淡的光线，第二天便自己掏钱装了个瓦数高点的灯泡。

10）正确发音极其重要，因此要重复练习新结识的朋友的名字，以确保自己发音正确。

After Reading

I. Please make a sentence with the words and expressions you have learnt from the text.

1. to abate:
2. to drizzle:
3. to grizzle:
4. to shrill:
5. to win one's fame:

II. Paragraph Writing

1. Please write a paragraph of around 150 words describing the characteristics of the writing styles of Su Shi, Xin Qiji and Li Qingzhao.

2. Please write a paragraph of around 100 words with the following words and expressions you have learnt from the text. Make sure that the paragraph you have written is grammatically correct and coherent

> bumper; gauze; gallant; grief; wane

Original Edition in Chinese

水调歌头
苏 轼
丙辰中秋，欢饮达旦，大醉，作此篇，兼怀子由。

明月几时有，
把酒问青天。

不知天上宫阙，
今夕是何年。
我欲乘风归去，
惟恐琼楼玉宇，
高处不胜寒。
起舞弄清影，
何似在人间。

转朱阁，
低绮户，
照无眠。
不应有恨，
何事长向别时圆。
人有悲欢离合，
月有阴晴圆缺，
此事古难全。
但愿人长久，
千里共婵娟。

念奴娇
赤壁怀古
苏　轼

大江东去，
浪淘尽、千古风流人物。
故垒西边，
人道是、三国周郎赤壁。
乱石穿空，
惊涛拍岸，
卷起千堆雪。
江山如画，
一时多少豪杰。

遥想公瑾当年，
小乔初嫁了，
雄姿英发。
羽扇纶巾，
谈笑间、强虏灰飞烟灭。

故国神游,
多情应笑我,
早生华发。
人生如梦,
一樽还酹江月。

西江月
夜行黄沙道中
辛弃疾

明月别枝惊鹊,
清风半夜鸣蝉。
稻花香里说丰年,
听取蛙声一片。

七八个星天外,
两三点雨山前。
旧时茅店社林边,
路转溪桥忽见。

丑奴儿
书博山道中壁
辛弃疾

少年不识愁滋味,
爱上层楼。
爱上层楼,
为赋新词强说愁。

而今识尽愁滋味,
欲说还休。
欲说还休,
却道"天凉好个秋"!

声声慢
李清照

寻寻觅觅。

冷冷清清，
凄凄惨惨戚戚。
乍暖还寒时候，
最难将息。
三杯两盏淡酒，
怎敌他、晚来风急。
雁过也，
正伤心，
却是旧时相识。

满地黄花堆积，
憔悴损，
如今有谁堪摘。
守着窗儿，
独自怎生得黑。
梧桐更兼细雨，
到黄昏、点点滴滴。
这次第，
怎一个、愁字了得。

武陵春
李清照

风住尘香花已尽，
日晚倦梳头。
物是人非事事休。
欲语泪先流。

闻说双溪春尚好，
也拟泛轻舟。
只恐双溪舴艋舟，
载不动、许多愁。

Unit 3
The Selected Song Lyrics

Text B

Yang Hsien-yi & Gladys Yang's Version

Shui Diao Ge Tou

Su Shi

On the Mid-autumn Festival of the year Bingchen I drank happily till dawn and wrote this in my cups while thinking of Ziyou.

Bright moon, when was your birth?
Winecup in hand, I ask the deep blue sky;
Not knowing what year it is tonight
In those celestial palaces on high.
I long to fly back on the wind,
Yet dread those crystal towers, those courts of jade,
Freezing to death among those icy heights!
Instead I rise to dance with my pale shadow;
Better off, after all, in the world of men.

Rounding the red pavilion,
Stooping to look through gauze windows,
She shines on the sleepless.
The moon should know no sadness;
Why, then, is she always full when dear ones are parted?
For men the grief of parting, joy of reunion,
Just as the moon wanes and waxes, is bright or dim;
Always some flaw—and so it has been since of old,
My one wish for you, then, is long life
And a share in this loveliness far, far away!

Nian Nu Jiao
Memories of the Past at Red Cliff

Su Shi

East flows the mighty river,

Sweeping away the heroes of time past;
This ancient rampart on this western shore
Is Zhou Yu's Red Cliff of three Kingdom's fame;
Here jagged boulders pound the clouds,
Huge waves tear banks apart,
And foam piles up a thousand drifts of snow;
A scene fair as a painting,
Countless the brave men here in time gone by!

I dream of Marshal Zhou Yu in his day
With his new bride, the Lord Qiao's younger daughter,
Dashing and debonair,
Silk-capped, with feather fan,
He laughed and jested
While the dread enemy fleet was burned to ashes!
In fancy through those scenes of old I range.
My heart overflowing, surely a figure of fun.
A man gray before his time.
Ah, this life is a dream,
Let me drink to the moon on the river!

Xi Jiang Yue
Traveling at Night to Huangsha Ridge

Xin Qiji

The bright moon startles the crow on the slanting bough,
At midnight the breeze is cool, cicadas shrill;
The fragrance of the paddy foretells a good year
And frogs croak far and wide.

Seven or eight stars at the horizon,
Two or three drops of rain before the hill;
An old thatched inn borders the wood with the local shrine,
And where the road bends a small bridge is suddenly seen.

Chou Nu Er
Written on My Way to Boshan

Xin Qiji

As a lad I never knew the taste of sorrow,
But loved to climb towers,
Loved to climb towers,
And drag sorrow into each new song I sang.

Now I know well the taste of sorrow,
It is on the tip of my tongue,
On the tip of my tongue,
But instead I say, "What a fine, cool autumn day!"

Sheng Sheng Man

Li Qingzhao

Seeking, seeking,
Chilly and quiet,
Desolate, painful and miserable.
Even when it's warmer there is still a chill,
It is most difficult to keep well.
Three or two cups of light wine,
How can they ward off the strong morning wind?
Wild geese fly past, while I'm broken-hearted;
But I recognize they are my old friends.

Fallen chrysanthemums piled up on the ground,
So withered,
Who would pluck them?
Leaning on the window,
How can I pass the time till night alone?
The drizzle falls on the *wutong* trees,
Rain-drops drip down at dusk.

At a time like this,
What immense sorrow I must bear!

Wu Ling Chun

Li Qingzhao

The wind's stopped, the earth fragrant, but petals have fallen,
Rising late, I'm too weary to dress my hair.
Though these remain, everything's meaningless since I lost my loved ones.
Before I can speak, tears flow down my cheeks.

I've heard spring is still beautiful at Double Brook,
I wish to go boating in a light canoe, too.
But I fear the little boat at Double Brook
Could not support all my sorrows.

Notes on the Text

1. **About the text**

    The present text is taken from *Tang Poems Song Prose* translated by Yang Hsien-yi and Gladys Yang, published by Foreign Languages Press in 2004.

2. **Yang Hsien-yi and Gladys Yang**

    Yang Hsien-yi was a Chinese literary translator, and his wife Gladys Yang (also known as Dai Naidie) a British translator of Chinese literature. They met and got married at Oxford. After their marriage, the Beijing-based couple became prominent translators of Chinese literature into English during the latter half of the 20th century at the Foreign Languages Press. Their translating works include *A Dream of the Red Mansions*, *The Songs of the South: Chu Ci, The Book of Songs, The Travels of Lao Can* and some of Lu Xun's stories.

Unit 4

The Selected Yuan Qu Songs

Reading Guide

This text is excerpted from *150 Masterpieces in Yuan Qu Poetry* translated and edited by Gu Zhengkun. Yuan Qu comprises Yuan Zaju and Yuan Sanqu. This book is the first relatively complete English translation of Yuan Sanqu in China, published by Peking University Press in 2004. The selected songs are not only superior in sound, form and meaning, but also especially suited to the aesthetic taste and reading habit of western readers. The lyrics are characterized by plain and clear description. The translation is faithful to the original version and stays in the rule of rhyme.

This text selects ten songs by Ma Zhiyuan, Guan Hanqing and Bai Pu, three great Yuan Qu writers. Some are about the joy of spring and the melancholy of autumn; others are about the sorrow of travellers miles away from home and of lovers miles away from each other; still others are about the leisure of care-free life and pleasure of love. Prof. Gu highly emphasizes the proper use of rhyme in the translation, which is, according to him, the soul of Yuan Sanqu. Yuan Sanqu, deviating from the poetry paradigm of Tang and Song Poetry, is more spontaneous. But compared with the vernacular poem, which is too colloquial, it still retains the feature of poetry, which emphasizes rhyme. Therefore, Yuan Sanqu marks a great success in the experiment of poetry revolution.

Before Reading

I. Preview Requirements: Please make a preparatory research on the background information, key words and phrases of this text.

1. Do research on the translator Gu Zhengkun.
2. Do research on Yuan Qu, Yuan Zaju, Yuan Sanqu, short lyrics and the cycle of songs in traditional opera, and pay special attention to the origin and content of the Yuan Sanqu.

3. Do research on Cipai and Qupai. Find out the characteristics of the six types of Qupai of the songs in this text.
4. Find and study the new words in the text such as *gaunt, neigh, roam, croak, scour, secular,* and *girth*.
5. Learn the useful expressions in the text such as *add to, in vain, beyond compare, lock up, desire for, dream of, pine away, prevent from, sift through, cover up,* and *at ease*.

II. Preview Questions: Please answer some questions about the understanding of the main content of the text.

1. What is the theme of "Thoughts on Autumn: To the Tune of *Sky Scouring Sand* "? What is the preponderant mood of the poem? How is the mood created? What's the purpose of the part "A small bridge, the murmuring water and a thatched cottage nearby", which creates an atmosphere different from the dominating mood of the poem?

2. In "The Night Rain on the Xiaoxiang River: To the Tune of *Life-giving Sun*", what atmosphere does the expression "dim lamplight" create at the beginning of the poem? What does "At dawn in the lonely fishing boat I roam" imply about the narrator? Of the part "At dawn in the lonely fishing boat I roam" and the part "Like a traveler's passion-ridden tear in vain", which one is a direct expression of the narrator's feelings? What do "Thoughts on Autumn:To the Tune of *Sky Scouring Sand*" and "The Night Rain on the Xiaoxiang River: To the Tune of *Life-giving Sun*" have in common?

3. What is "Fine Clouds over the Mountain: To the Tune of *Life-giving Sun*" mainly about? What are the four scenes described in the first three lines? What's the order of describing the four scenes? How is "Fine Clouds over the Mountain: To the Tune of *Life-giving Sun*" different from "Thoughts on Autumn: To the Tune of *Sky Scouring Sand* "?

4. What are "Leisure (3): To the Tune of *Four Pieces of Jade*" and "Leisure (4): To the Tune of *Four Pieces of Jade*" mainly about? What similarities and differences do "Leisure (3) : To the Tune of *Four Pieces of Jade*" and "Leisure (4): To the Tune of *Four Pieces of Jade*" have?

5. In "Leisure (4): To the Tune of *Four Pieces of Jade*", the narrator refers to himself as "the fool", is he being modest?

6. What is "Untitled (1): To the Tune of *Green Jade Flute*" mainly about? What atmosphere does the first four lines create for the poem? What's the purpose of the description of the narrator's loins?

7. In "Untitled (5): To the Tune of *Green Jade Flute*", what can we know about the author's attitude toward autumn from the part "How wonderful is this autumn scene as a poetic theme" ? What are the autumn scenes described in the first four lines? What are the things and scenes described in the fifth and sixth line? What emotion do they help to express? How would you compare the autumn in "Untitled (5): To the Tune of *Green Jade Flute*" and that in "Thoughts on Autumn: To the Tune of *Sky Scouring Sand* "?

8. What does "Ode on Love (3): To the Tune of *Young Spring*" criticize? How would you describe the character of the girl, the narrator in the poem?
9. What features of the flute can you tell from the first four lines of "Blowing: To the Tune of *Stopping One's Steed to Listen*"? What rhetoric devices do the last two lines apply respectively to describe the uniqueness of the flute?
10. In "Spring: To the Tune of *Sky Scouring Sand* ", what's the order of depicting the scenes in spring in the first three lines? What attitude toward spring does the author express in the poem? How is "the wooden bridge, the flowing water, pin with flowers that fly" in "Spring: To the Tune of *Sky Scouring Sand* " different from "a small bridge, the murmuring water and a thatched cottage nearby" in "Thoughts on Autumn: To the Tune of *Sky Scouring Sand* "?

Text A

Gu Zhengkun's Version

Thoughts on Autumn
To the Tune of *Sky Scouring Sand*

Ma Zhiyuan

A withered vine, an old tree gaunt and a raven croaking on high;
A small bridge, the murmuring water and a thatched cottage nearby;
An ancient path, the west wind and a bony horse is heard to neigh;
Lo! The sun sets today;
At the earth-end a heart-broken traveller plods his weary way.

The Night Rain on the Xiaoxiang River
To the Tune of *Life-giving Sun*

Ma Zhiyuan

The lamplight is dim;
Broken is the stranger's dream
By drops of heart rending rain
Like a traveler's passion-ridden tear in vain,
At dawn in the lonely fishing boat I roam,
Thousands of miles away from my home.

Fine Clouds over the Mountain
To the Tune of *Life-giving Sun*

Ma Zhiyuan

Beyond the village of flower,
West of the thatched shops,
Evening glow in the sky is washed by a recent shower.
Around, the setting sun licks hill tops,
Like a brocade screen added to more green props.

Leisure (3)
To the Tune of *Four Pieces of Jade*

Guan Hanqing

Repressing my wish for fame,
Locking up my desire for game,
Out of this secular world I drop now,
To break those fond dreams I vow.
No longer in that vanity fair,
I worm into a cosy and peaceful nest with care.
Oh, this life of leisure is happy beyond compare.

Leisure (4)
To the Tune of *Four Pieces of Jade*

Guan Hanqing

Tao the poet once plows the southern drills,
Xie the scholar once dwells among the eastern hills.
Too many to narrate the things of worldly kind,
Calmly I try to measure them in my mind.
O.K. Let's believe he is the saint,
And I am the fool, so our life
Is prevented from a competitive strife.

Unit 4
The Selected Yuan Qu Songs

Untitled (1)
To the Tune of *Green Jade Flute*

Guan Hanqing

I fear to see the departure of spring,
Willow catkins flying from the boughs that swing.
Silently I close the door of my fragrant bower,
Outside the curtain songs of morning orioles come in shower.
How annoyed I am, hearing nothing from you at the end of earth.
Last night I dreamt of you under my quilt with green girth.
Loose now is my clothes below,
Because my loins thinner grow.
Love as deeply as I may,
I pine away with each passing day.

Untitled (5)
To the Tune of *Green Jade Flute*

Guan Hanqing

How wonderful is this autumn scene as a poetic theme!
Red leaves fill up mountain stream.
Good is the path winding through many a pine,
Around the eastern hedge chrysanthemums gloriously entwine.
I hold the goblet full of newly-made wine afore,
With the official servant encouraging me to have more.
But what on earth from all this can I discern?
Better return, return,
From Tao Yuanming, the drunkard and recluse, I will learn.

Ode on Love (3)
To the Tune of *Young Spring*

Bai Pu

Laughing, with red (sleeve), I cover up the silvery candle light,
Not to let you, my talented-man, read at night.
Please embrace me and kiss me as you choose,
For the official entrance exam you doggedly fight,
But even if you have succeeded, what's the use?

Blowing
To the Tune of *Stopping One's Steed to Listen*

Bai Pu

Splitting the rock and piercing the cloud,
The flute of jade whines so meditatively aloud.
An expanse of desert lies under the frosty skies,
In the wind a partridge beats and spies,
The twilight clouds blanket the Phoenix Tower
Like evening snow-flakes the music-charmed plum flower petals shower.
Quiet now.
The last blowing sends down the moon over the river-dominating tower.

Spring
To the Tune of *Sky Scouring Sand*

Bai Pu

The temperate sun, the verdant hills and the vernal breeze;
Towers, balustrades and curtained windows;
There in the yard are swings and willows at their ease;
Orioles chirping and swallows dancing in the sky,
The wooden bridge, the flowing water, pink with flowers that fly.

Unit 4
The Selected Yuan Qu Songs

Notes on the Text

1. vanity fair

the social life of those officials chasing after fame and wealth, or the world in general, considered as symbolizing worldly frivolity

2. Tao

Tao, or Tao Yuanming, also known as Tao Chien, was a Chinese poet who lived during the Eastern Jin (317—420) and Liu Song (420—479) Dynasties. He is considered to be one of the greatest poets of the Six Dynasties. Tao Yuanming spent most of his life in reclusion, living in a small cottage in the countryside, reading, drinking wine, receiving occasional guests, and writing poems in which he often reflected on the pleasures and difficulties of life in the countryside, as well as his decision to withdraw from civil service. His simple, direct, and unmannered style was at odds with the norms of literary writing in his time.

3. Xie

Xie, or Xie An, was a statesman in the Eastern Jin Dynasty. When he was at his early years, he was famous for his idle talks, and he led a reclusive life in Mountain Dong, Huiji County, touring mountains and rivers with Wang Xizhi and Xu Xun, and educating the children of the Xie family. After his family members who worked as officials passed away, he took up the responsibility for the Xie family and started to work as officials.

4. Chinese Imperial Examination (Official Entnance Exam)

Chinese Imperial Examination was a civil service examination system in imperial China to select candidates for the state bureaucracy. Although imperial examinations appeared as early as the Han Dynasty, the system became widely utilized as the major path to civil service only in the mid-Tang Dynasty, and remained so until its abolition in 1905.

5. Phoenix Tower

The site of Phoenix Tower, which was built during the Six Dynasties, is now in the southwest corner of Nanjing City. The Phoenix Tower got its name because phoenixes were gathering when it was built.

Glossary

croak /krəʊk/	*v.* to speak or say sth. with a rough low voice
	e.g.: *I had a sore throat and could only croak.*
discern /dɪˈsɜːn/	*v.* to know, recognize or understand sth., especially sth. that is not obvious
	e.g.: *It is possible to discern a number of different techniques in her work.*
dwell /dwel/	*v.* (*formal*, or *literary*) to live somewhere

	e.g.: *For ten years she dwelled among the nomads of North America.*
doggedly /ˈdɒɡɪdlɪ/	*adv.* showing determination; not giving up easily
	e.g.: *He was still doggedly pursuing his studies.*
entwine /ɪnˈtwaɪn/	*v.* to twist or wind sth. around sth. else
	e.g.: *They strolled through the park, with arms entwined.*
girth /ɡɜːθ/	*n.* a narrow piece of leather or cloth that is fastened around the middle of a horse to keep the seat or a load in place
	e.g.: *Loosen the girth a little.*
gaunt /ɡɔːnt/	*adj.* very thin, usually because of illness, not having enough food, or worry
	e.g.: *I cannot read what I have written with this gaunt hand.*
glow /ɡləʊ/	*n.* a gold or red colour
	e.g.: *The rising sun casts a golden glow over the fields.*
meditatively /ˈmedɪtətɪvlɪ/	*adv.* thinking very deeply; involving deep thought
	e.g.: *The old man looked meditatively at the dart board.*
neigh /neɪ/	*v.* when a horse neighs it makes a long high sound
	e.g.: *But only on north mountains Tatar horses neigh.*
ode /əʊd/	*n.* a poem that speaks to a person or thing or celebrates a special event
	e.g.: *The chorus was singing The Ode to Joy.*
pine /paɪn/	*v.* to become very sad because sb. has died or gone away
	e.g.: *She pined for months after he'd gone.*
plod /plɒd/	*v.* to walk slowly with heavy steps, especially because you are tired
	e.g.: *Our horses plodded down the muddy track.*
recluse /rɪˈkluːs/	*n.* a person who lives alone and likes to avoid other people
	e.g.: *The old recluse secluded himself from the outside world.*
roam /rəʊm/	*v.* to walk or travel around an area without any definite aim or direction
	e.g.: *The sheep are allowed to roam freely on this land.*
scour /ˈskaʊə(r)/	*v.* to clean sth. by rubbing its surface hard with rough material
	e.g.: *I had to scour out the pans.*
secular /ˈsekjələ(r)/	*adj.* not connected with spiritual or religious matters
	e.g.: *Ours is a secular society.*
strife /straɪf/	*n.* angry or violent disagreement between two people or groups of people
	e.g.: *The country was torn apart by strife.*

temperate /ˈtempərət/	*adj.* having a mild temperature without extremes of heat or cold e.g.: *Great Britain has a temperate climate.*
twilight /ˈtwaɪlaɪt/	*n.* the faint light or the period of time at the end of the day after the sun has gone down e.g.: *We went for a walk along the beach at twilight.*
verdant /ˈvɜːdnt/	*adj.* (*literary*) (of grass, plants, fields, etc.) fresh and green e.g.: *The garden is covered with verdant grass.*
vernal /ˈvɜːnl/	*adj.* (*formal*, or *literary*) connected with the season of spring e.g.: *He described the vernal migration of birds in detail.*
whine /waɪn/	*v.* 1. to complain in an annoying, crying voice e.g.: *"I want to go home," whined Toby.* 2. to make a long high unpleasant sound because you are in pain or unhappy e.g.: *The dog whined and scratched at the door.*

While Reading

I. Please fill in the blanks with the words in the parentheses with the appropriate part of speech.

1. Houston, where I have been working as a consultant, hardly qualifies as one of the most physically attractive or _____ cities. (temperature)
2. The pace of the book is _____, with enjoyable literary and historical asides. (leisure)
3. The richness of his novel comes from his _____ of it. (narrate)
4. Through superior production techniques they were able to gain the _____ edge. (compete)
5. This hotel is very popular, so please phone in your order three or more days prior to your _____ . (depart)
6. Even the most accomplished writers show their work-in-progress to _____ readers. (discern)
7. The win revived _____ memories of his championship-winning days. (glory)
8. She had been living a _____ life in Los Angeles since her marriage broke up. (recluse)
9. Take time to _____, it is the source of strength. (meditative)
10. The boy was brought up by his mother, who was a _____ influence in his life. (dominate)

II. Please choose one word or phrase that best completes the sentence.

1. We searched _____ for the missing child, and then we called the police for help.
   A. in fear
   B. in need
   C. in vain
   D. in danger

2. You can _____ a person physically, but you cannot imprison his heart.
   A. cover up   B. give up
   C. lock up   D. fill up
3. Not having lived the Holy Life, not having obtained wealth in their youth, men _____ like old herons in a lake without fish.
   A. pine away   B. wear away
   C. give away   D. put away
4. Just on the other side of the lake are natural waterways that _____ freshwater marsh.
   A. break through   B. see through
   C. walk through   D. wind through
5. The boy didn't feel completely _____ in the strange surroundings.
   A. at random   B. at ease
   C. at work   D. at hand
6. Put on rain boots when washing floor, to _____ slipping down.
   A. withdraw from   B. prevent from
   C. recover from   D. depart from

III. Translation

1. Please translate the following from English into Chinese.

1) a withered vine
2) Broken is the stranger's dream.
3) evening glow in the sky
4) to repress my wish for fame
5) vanity fair
6) beyond compare
7) willow catkins
8) official servant
9) official entrance exam
10) flute of jade

2. Please translate the following from Chinese into English.

1）小桥流水
2）几行清泪
3）渔灯暗
4）飞红
5）草店
6）安乐窝
7）红尘
8）世态人情
9）天涯
10）东篱
11）红袖
12）裂石穿云

3. Please translate each sentence with at least one key word or its derivative.

Key Words: plod, repress, whine, chirp, roam

1）你是否在办公室里埋头苦干了一整天呢？
2）我们努力抑制失望的情绪，然后负责任地完成肩负的使命。
3）那警官在抱怨最近工作有多辛苦。

Unit 4
The Selected Yuan Qu Songs

4）麻雀每天清晨在窗外喊喊喳喳地叫。

5）随着他"砰"的一声在我的签证上盖了戳，我就可以自由地在欧洲大部分地区漫游了。

6）在经历个人计算领域 20 多年的缓慢发展之后，大量新平台浮出了水面。

7）对话与协议应当取代暴力与镇压。

8）不要任由您的孩子抱怨或哭泣，因为这样做只会强化他的行为。

9）朦胧中你只能听见消防员带的定位设备吱吱地响，只能看到红色和黄色的灯在一闪一闪。

10）您可以向您的电讯服务供应商申请漫游服务。

After Reading

I. Please make a sentence with the words and expressions you have learnt from the text.

1. to neigh:
2. to croak:
3. to dwell:
4. to entwine:
5. to wind through:
6. to blanket:

II. Paragraph Writing

1. Please write a paragraph of around 150 words to describe the dismay of the travellers being miles away from home.

2. Please write a paragraph of around 100 words about the leisure of life with the following words and expressions you have learnt from the text. Make sure that the paragraph you have written is grammatically correct and coherent.

> secular; vanity fair; worm into; strife; beyond compare

Original Edition in Chinese

天净沙·秋思
马致远

枯藤老树昏鸦,
小桥流水人家,
古道西风瘦马。
夕阳西下,
断肠人在天涯。

寿阳曲·潇湘雨夜
马致远

渔灯暗,
客梦回。
一声声滴人心碎。
孤舟五更家万里,
是离人几行清泪。

寿阳曲·山市晴岚
马致远

花村外,
草店西,
晚霞明雨收天霁。
四围山一竿残照里,
锦屏风又添铺翠。

四块玉·闲适(三)
关汉卿

意马收,
心猿锁,
跳出红尘恶风波。
槐阴午梦谁惊破?
离了利名场,

钻入安乐窝，
闲快活！

四块玉·闲适（四）
关汉卿

南亩耕，
东山卧，
世态人情经历多。
闲将往事思量过。
贤的是他，
愚的是我，
争甚么！

碧玉箫·无题（一）
关汉卿

怕见春归，
枝上柳绵飞。
静掩香闺，
帘外晓莺啼。
恨天涯锦字稀，
梦才郎翠被知。
宽尽衣，
一搦腰肢细；
痴，
暗暗的添憔悴。

碧玉箫·无题（五）
关汉卿

秋景堪题，
红叶满山溪。
松径偏宜，
黄菊绕东篱。
正清樽斟泼醅，
有白衣劝酒杯。

官品极，
到底成何济？
归，
学取他渊明醉。

阳春曲·题情（三）
白　朴

笑将红袖遮银烛，
不放才郎夜看书。
相偎相抱取欢娱，
止不过迭应举，
及第待何如。

驻马听·吹
白　朴

裂石穿云，
玉管宜横清更洁。
霜天沙漠，
鹧鸪风里欲偏斜。
凤凰台上暮云遮，
梅花惊作黄昏雪。
人静也，
一声吹落江楼月。

天净沙·春
白　朴

春山暖日和风，
阑干楼阁帘栊，
杨柳秋千院中。
啼莺舞燕，
小桥流水飞红。

Unit 4
The Selected Yuan Qu Songs

Text B

Zhou Fangzhu's Version

Autumn Thought
To the Tune of Sky-clear Sand

Ma Zhiyuan

Withered vine, old tree, a raven at dusk crows,
Tiny bridge, thatched cottages, the stream flows,
Ancient road, bleak wind, a bony steed slows.
The setting sun in the west glows,
The sorrow of the heart-broken traveller grows.

Night Rain on the Xiaoxiang River
To the Tune of Life-donating Sun

Ma Zhiyuan

Light from the fishing boat is dim,
The passenger is out of dream,
Heart-broken at the pattering of raindrops.
On the lone boat I'm too far away from my home,
Running down the cheeks are my teardrops.

Mountain Mist over a Country Fair
To the Tune of Life-donating Sun

Ma Zhiyuan

Outside the cottages of flower,
To the west of the thatched shops,
Evening glow spreads in clear sky after the shower.
Bathed in the setting sunshine are the mountain tops,
Like verdancy added to the brocade curtain drops.

Leisure
To the Tune of Four Pieces of Jade

Guan Hanqing

Get my desires to bind,
In the right frame of mind.
Free from vanity world, the source of nightmare,
Life is but a fond dream nobody can tear.
Out of vanity fair,
Get into the cosy nest,
In a leisurely mood free from care.

Leisure
To the Tune of Four Pieces of Jade

Guan Hanqing

In the south fields I'm farming,
A secluded life I'm leading.
Having gone through all ways of the world.
I stay calm and weigh them in a right mood,
Worldly-wise they are,
Foolish I'm so far,
With whom can I spar?

To the Tune of Green Jade Flute

Guan Hanqing

Afraid of seeing spring declining,
With willow catkins dancing and flying.
Closing quietly the door of my fragrant boudoir,
But twitters of morning orioles are heard from afar.
Resenting my darling for his grudging letters to me,
Meeting him in the dream my quilt knows only.
Worn to shadow,

My waist is of willow.
Crazy,
I'm getting wan and sallow.

To the Tune of Green Jade Flute

Guan Hanqing

Autumn scenery well worth a poetic theme,
Red leaves are all over the mountain stream.
Hidden under pine trees is a path winding,
Around the east fence chrysanthemums are blooming.
It's high time to get good and drunk,
With page-boy urging me to swig around.
Worming into the top rank,
What's the effect in the end?
Secluding and drinking,
Follow the example of Yuanming.

Ode to Love
To the Tune of Spring

Bai Pu

With red sleeve and smile I shadow the candle light,
Stopping my darling talent from reading at night.
Snuggle up to me and caress me as you like.
For the imperial examination you're forced to fight,
Even if you succeed, what will be in sight.

Fluting
To the Tune of Stopping the Steed to Listen

Bai Pu

The flute sounds clear and pierces cloud,

Splitting the rock as it's melodiously loud.
Vast desert under the frosty sky,
Francolins are carried away and forget to fly.
Dusk clouds shadow the Phoenix Tower,
Startled, plum petals like flakes begin to shower.
At dead of night,
With the melody of flute fading is the moonlight.

Spring
To the Tune of Sky-clear Sand

Bai Pu

Green hills, warm sun and breeze blows,
Pavilions, banisters and curtained windows,
Swings in the courtyard and weeping willows.
Orioles are singing, swallows dancing,
Tiny bridge, petals flying and stream flows.

Notes on the Text

1. About the text

The present text is taken from *An English Translation of 200 Yuan Qu Poems* translated by Zhou Fangzhu, published by Anhui University Press in 2009.

2. Zhou Fangzhu

Zhou Fangzhu has been engaged in the research and teaching of translation theory and practice. He graduated from the English Department of Anhui University and once taught Chinese culture in the United States. His published works include *Pluralism of Translation Studies* and *Principles of Translation from English to Chinese*. He has also published over 40 papers in national core journals such as *Chinese Translators Journal*, *Chinese Science & Technology Translators Journal* and *Foreign Language Education*.

Unit 5

Instructor Wang Secretly Makes His Escape; Shi Jin Gets His Defences into Shape (excerpt)

Reading Guide

This text is an excerpt from the 2nd episode "Instructor Wang Secretly Makes His Escape; Shi Jin Gets His Defences into Shape" of *The Marshes of Mount Liang* translated and edited by John Dent-Yang and Alex Dent-Young. Like other earlier Chinese novels, *The Marshes of Mount Liang* underwent a long and complex evolution. Involving different traditions, including historical narrative, professional storytelling, and stage drama, as well as having to go through the phases of initial creation, expansion, revision, and editing, the full development and expansion of the novel was consummated with the appearance of the 120-chapter version during the early seventeenth century. It has become one of the most popular and acclaimed Chinese classic novels, reaching beyond its country of birth.

The translators Dent-Youngs have rendered *The Marshes of Mount Liang* in its most complete form, and made an effort to retain most of the numerous verses in various poetic forms that interpolate the narrative. Retaining the verses enables the Western readers to savor the unique flavor of the novel and appreciate Chinese vernacular fiction. Meanwhile, this version is highly readable, and it maintains the lively and humorous narrative style and rhythm of the Chinese original.[①]

Before Reading

I. Preview Requirements: Please make a preparatory research on the background information, key words and phrases of this text.

  1. Do research on the translators John Dent-Young and Alex Dent-Young.

[①] Wu, H. Laura. "Reviewed Work: The Broken Seals: Part One of *The Marshes of Mount Liang* by John Dent-Young, Alex Dent-Young." *China Review International,* Vol. 4, No. 1(SPRING 1997), 116–118.

2. Get to know the origin and the popularity of football in the Song Dynasty.
3. Read some materials related to the Clear Jade School of Taoism, especially the founder Emperor Hui Zong. Is there any relation between Emperor Hui Zong's religious beliefs and his way of ruling the country?
4. Find and study the new words in the text such as *banishment, beleaguered, profusely, usher, escort, signify, pander, squander, haunt,* and *heir*.
5. Learn the useful expressions in the text such as *be an adept at, lodge with, make one's way to, see no alternative but, make one's name, in obedience to, be obliged to do,* and *in deference to*.

II. Preview Questions: Please answer some questions about the understanding of the main content of the text.

1. What kind of influence did Gao-the-Ball's family background exert on him?
2. The author gives detailed descriptions to some customs and ornaments. Please find them out and think about what the author tries to convey.
3. John Dent-Young and Alex Dent-Young translate Gao Qiu's name by switching from Gao-the-Ball to Gao-le-bel. Can you account for this change?
4. How many people mainly contributed to Gao-the-Ball's success? Please elaborate on their characteristics.
5. What is the turning point in Gao-the-Ball's career? What are the major factors for ordinary people to succeed under Emperor Hui Zong's rule?
6. Can you imagine what Gao-the-Ball would be like when he finally became an official? Would it be a blessing or a curse? Give your opinions and reasons.
7. Do you know some people of similar experiences like Gao-the-Ball in Chinese history? Please tell their stories.
8. There are some differences between the image of Gao-the-Ball in *The Marshes of Mount Liang* and that in the historical records. Try to know more about Gao-the-Ball from history books, and think about the reasons why Gao-the-Ball is molded as such in this novel.

Text A

John Dent-Young & Alex Dent-Young's Version

Instructor Wang Secretly Makes His Escape; Shi Jin Gets His Defences into Shape (excerpt)

……

Now there was in those days in the Xuanwu district of the Eastern Capital, Bianliang, or

Unit 5
Instructor Wang Secretly Makes His Escape; Shi Jin Gets His Defences into Shape (excerpt)

Kaifeng as it is now called, a certain profligate son of a ruined family named Gao. He was the second son, and since his youth he had neglected family affairs and devoted himself entirely to the manipulation of sword or staff, and to football, at which he was very skilled. The people of the capital therefore referred to him not in the customary way as Second Brother Gao, but as Gao Qiu or Gao-the-Ball. Later, when he began to get on in the world, he transformed this nickname into Gao-le-Bel. He could play various instruments, wind and string, danced well, and had a good voice. He was an adept at martial arts, with spear or staff, and wrestling. He had some idea of rhyming and calligraphy, and could turn out a song or an ode. But of generosity, virtue, the rites, wisdom, trustworthiness, reliability, loyalty, or excellence he knew absolutely nothing. He spent his days within and without the walls of the capital, pandering to the rich and famous. He had abetted the son of a wealthy man, Mr. Wang, in squandering a fortune: the two of them used to haunt the pleasure gardens, where they were forever in and out of those Houses of the Wind, the Flowers, the Snow or the Moonlight. After this the father took out a writ against Gao, and the district court sentenced him to twenty lashes and banishment, forbidding any inhabitant of the capital to give him food or shelter. Thus beleaguered, Gao-the-Ball betook himself to Linhuaizhou, west of the River Huai, where he found refuge with the owner of a gaming parlour, one Gentleman Liu, or Liu Shiquan, to give him his proper name. The latter had devoted his life to harbouring and supporting riff-raff, and it was his pleasure to shelter miscreants from the four corners of the empire. Gao-the-Ball came to rest in Gentleman Liu's abode and lived there three years.

Later, Emperor Zhe Zong, having gone to offer sacrifices in the southern suburbs and procured propitious winds and timely rains, graciously proclaimed an amnesty throughout the empire. Accordingly in Linhuaizhou Gao-the-Ball received a remission of his sentence and began to plan his return to the capital. Liu Shiquan happened to have a relation in the capital, a certain Dong, who had a medicinal herbs shop under the Golden-Beam Bridge. Liu wrote him a letter which he gave to Gao, together with supplies and money for travel expenses, so that the latter on his return to the capital could lodge with the herbalist.

Gao-the-Ball bade farewell to Liu Shiquan, shouldered his bags, and departed from Linhuaizhou. He made his way to the Eastern Capital, where he went straight to the herbalist's shop under the Golden-Beam Bridge and presented his letter. After observing Gao-the-Ball and reading the letter from Liu Shiquan, Dong said to himself: " How can I take this Gao into my home? If he were an honest man it might be all right to let him have the run of the house. The children could learn something from him. But he's an idler and a vagabond, and simply not to be trusted. What's more, he's a convicted criminal. Such as he don't change their ways. If I let him live with us it will disturb the children and set a bad example to them. On the other hand, if I don't receive him it will be an offence to Liu Shiquan." So for the time being he saw no alternative but to feign a warm welcome. He took Gao in and invited him to dine and drink each day. After ten days or so, Dong worked out a tactic. He bought a new set of clothes and he wrote a letter. These two things he offered to Gao, saying: "My humble establishment fails to do you justice; I fear you will be held back. I in turn, therefore, would like to recommend you, to the young academician, Mr. Su. Sooner or later you are sure to make your name. How does this proposal strike you?"

Gao-the-Ball thanked him profusely. Dong detailed someone to deliver the letter and show Gao the way to the academician's. The doorman announced him. The moment the academician saw Gao and read the letter he recognized him for the dissolute good-for-nothing he was, and said to himself: " How can I take this one into my house? The best solution is to do him a favour, and recommend him to Wang Jinqing, the Emperor's son-in-law, as a personal aide. People have a name for Wang, they call him 'Marshal Wang, the Princeling', and this is just the type of person he likes." He wrote a reply to Dong, the herbalist, and invited Gao to stay the night. The next day he composed a deferential letter and dispatched it with a servant, who was to take Gao to the Princeling's house.

This Princeling Wang was in fact the husband Emperor Zhe Zong's younger sister and was the son-in-law of the later Emperor Shen Zong. He liked men of the world: such were the people to whom he gave employment. When academician Su's messenger brought him the letter and presented Gao, Princeling Wang was greatly taken with him, and immediately penned a reply to the academician, informing him that he would take Gao into his household as a personal aide. Gao's fortunes had turned, for from now on he came and went in Marshal Wang's house like one of the family. And, as the old saying goes, "Separate lives make separate thoughts; close living makes for close relations."

One day—it was his birthday—the Princeling ordered his household to prepare a banquet, at which the guest of honour was to be his brother-in-law, Prince Duan. This Prince Duan was the eleventh son of the late Emperor Shen Zong, younger brother to the Emperor Zhe Zong. He had been appointed superintendent of the Eastern Stables, and had the title of Ninth Royal Prince. This was a man of some intelligence and he cut a dashing figure. Of the various pastimes of the rich, the idle, and the dissolute there was none he did not know, none he was not skilled in, and none he did not love. Master of the lute, chess, calligraphy and painting, it goes without saying that he was good at kicking a ball and throwing bowls as at playing the flute, strumming a guitar, singing or dancing.

The feast that was prepared at Marshal Wang's house that day was furnished with the choicest fare from sea or land. It was an occasion when:

> *Incense burns in precious vessels, flowers are arranged in golden vases; brilliant musicians compete to produce the most striking harmonies, and everywhere the masterpieces of famous craftsmen are on show. There are crystal decanters overflowing with ambrosia, amber cups brimming with transparent distillations; there are tortoiseshell plates piled with luscious peaches and rare fruits, glass bowls heaped*

Unit 5
Instructor Wang Secretly Makes His Escape; Shi Jin Gets His Defences into Shape (excerpt)

with bear's paws and camel's hooves; there is meat of delicate fish parted in silver strands, and perfumed tea brewed from the herb's choicest tips. The dancing girl in the red skirt matches her steps to the ivory clappers and the trilling flute; the blue-sleeved singer pours out her rich notes in harmony with the orchestra and the pipes. Two rows of beauties are drawn up before the steps, and the orchestra sits close below the dais.

When Prince Duan arrived for the banquet, Marshal Wang ushered him to the place of honour, and himself sat down opposite. After a good many cups, and after two complete menus had been served, Prince Duan got up to wash his hands. Happening to enter the library to rest for a while, he noticed on the table a pair of paperweights made of mutton-fat jade and carved in the forms of lions. They were of especially fine workmanship, and the detail was exquisite. Prince Duan picked the lions up and after holding them in his hands and gazing at them a long while, exclaimed, "Magnificent!" Marshal Wang, seeing Prince Duan so taken with them, said: "There is also a jade brush-holder, in the shape of a dragon, from the hand of the same craftsman. I don't have it here at the moment, but I will get it tomorrow and send the complete set to you."

Prince Duan was delighted. "That is truly generous," he said. "I am most grateful. I imagine the brush-holder must be even more beautiful."

"Tomorrow I will send for it and have it delivered to your palace," Wang said, "and then you can judge."

Prince Duan thanked him again, and the two of them returned to the banquet, where they feasted on till dusk. They were quite drunk when the party broke up and Prince Duan returned to his palace.

The next morning Wang sent for the jade dragon brush-holder, and together with the two jade lion paperweights had it put in a little gold box, which was wrapped in yellow silk. He also wrote a respectful letter, and told Gao-le-Bel—as he now called himself—to deliver it.

In obedience to Marshal Wang's wishes, Gao-le-Bel took up the precious jade knick-knacks, slipped the letter into his breastpocket, and took himself off to Prince Duan's palace. Here the doorman announced him to the chamberlain, who in a little while appeared and asked: "Whose household are you from?"

Gao-le-Bel bowed and said: "I am from Marshal Wang's household. I am sent especially to present these jade ornaments to the Prince."

"His Highness is in the main central court," the Chamberlain said, "playing ball with some of the young palace attendants. You'd better go there and see him yourself."

"Be so good as to conduct me," Gao-le-Bel said. The Chamberlain escorted him to the gates of the court where Gao saw the Prince, wearing a turban of soft gauze in the Tang style, and a long purple tunic embroidered with dragons, fastened at the waist by a double silk belt, signifying military and civil rank; the tunic was hitched up and tucked into the belt in front. On his feet he wore gold slippers embroidered with a flying phoenix. Several young palace attendants were kicking the ball with him.

Not wishing to interrupt, Gao-le-Bel remained standing behind some servants awaiting his opportunity. It must have been Gao-le-Bel's destiny to make his fortune, for luck was with him that day: the ball sailed through the air, while Prince Duan tried in vain to reach it, and came down among the group of servants, where it rolled right to Gao's feet. Gao saw the ball coming, and plucking up his courage, gave it the special kick known as "a duck and drake" or a "double bend", which delivered it straight back to the Prince.

Prince Duan was enormously impressed. "Who are you, then?" he asked.

Gao-le-Bel took a step forward and knelt. "Your Highness, I am in the service of Marshal Wang," he said. "I come, on my master's instructions, to bring you two jade ornaments, which he begs you accept. There is also a letter, which I venture humbly to present to you."

The Prince smiled and said: "How gracious of my brother-in-law."

Gao-le-Bel took out the letter and presented it. Prince Duan opened the box, and looked at the jade objects, then gave them to a servant to take away. He paid no further attention to the knick-knacks or where they went, but said to Gao: "So you can play the football! What's your name?"

Gao bowed again and said: "My name is Gao-le-Bel. I play just a little."

"Good!" said the Prince. "You can come and play with us now."

"But Your Highness, I am no one," Gao protested, prostrating himself. "How can I play with Your Highness?"

"This is the Clouds Company, a club for players," the Prince said. "We call ourselves 'Kickers United'. What possible harm can there be in your playing with us?"

"How could I presume?" Gao said, prostrating himself again.

He refused five or six times, but the Prince was adamant, so Gao had no alternative but to knock his head on the ground in acknowledgement of the honour, remove his leggings and enter the field. To begin with he simply performed a few kicks, which the Prince applauded. Finally, in deference to the Prince, he was obliged to display the full range of his skill and talent. He played so brilliantly that the ball seemed literally glued to his body, and Prince Duan was so pleased with him he would not hear of Gao's returning home, but insisted he stay the night.

The next day the Prince organized a banquet for Marshal Wang and invited him to the palace. Marshal Wang, by the way, had been full of suspicions, when Gao did not return the night before, but now his doorman appeared and announced: "The Ninth Royal Prince's servant has arrived with a message for Your Grace: he wants to invite you to a banquet at his palace." After receiving the messenger and reading the invitation, Marshal Wang immediately mounted his horse and rode over to the palace. Arriving there he dismounted and entered. Prince Duan expressed great pleasure at his coming, and thanked him for the jade objects. During dinner, Prince Duan said: "That Gao-le-Bel is truly an extraordinary ball player, what would you say if I asked you to let me keep him in my service?"

Unit 5
Instructor Wang Secretly Makes His Escape; Shi Jin Gets His Defences into Shape (excerpt)

"If you find this person useful to you, then by all means let him stay here in the palace to serve you," the Marshal replied.

Prince Duan was delighted and expressed his gratitude in a toast. After that the two friends chatted for a while, and when the dinner party broke up that evening, Marshal Wang returned to his residence. We say no more of him.

As for Prince Duan, having taken Gao-le-Bel into his service he kept him in the palace, where he was lodged and fed. Gao, for his part, after being so fortunate as to be noticed by Prince Duan, followed his master all the time, never departing from his footsteps.

Less than two months later, Emperor Zhe Zong departed this world. There was no direct heir, and the civil and military authorities, after holding a council, declared Prince Duan emperor. He reigned as Emperor Hui Zong, and was also a Taoist grand master—founder of the Clear Jade School and master of the Way of Subtle Mystery. His reign was unremarkable. One day, however, he said to Gao-le-Bel: "It is our desire to advance you. But for a promotion to be possible, you really need some frontier service behind you. First we will have you listed at the War Ministry. Then you will be transferred to our personal guard."

Less than six months later the Emperor promoted Gao-le-Bel to the ranks of Grand Marshal of the Palace. It was like this:

Clouds Company pays degree no heed;
"Kickers United" knows not higher and lower;
Gao booted himself upwards with an agile kick,
And landed in the corridors of power.

Notes on the Text

1. **the Eastern Capital: Kaifeng**

   Formerly named Bianliang, Kaifeng is one of the major seven ancient capitals in China. According to some research, there were human activities around Kaifeng area as early as the capital of a number of dynasties such as the Later Liang Dynasty, the Later Jin Dynasty, the Han Dynasty and the Later Zhou Dynasty. In 960 AD, the Northern Song Dynasty was founded and made Kaifeng its capital, then known as "Dongdu"(the Eastern Capital). During the Northern Song Dynasty, with a population of 1.5 million, Kaifeng was not only the economic, political and cultural hub of China, but also the greatest international metropolis, and hence the title "thoroughfare of the world".

2. **Clouds Company**

   Clouds Company, which means football players can kick the ball into the clouds, was a football club organized among the people in the Northern Song Dynasty. At that time, Gao-the-Ball was regarded as one of the most famous football players in Clouds Company.

Glossary

abode /əˈbəʊd/   *n.* the place where somebody lives
e.g.: *You are most welcome to my humble abode.*

adamant /ˈædəmənt/   *adj.* determined not to change your mind or to be persuaded about sth.
e.g.: *The government remained adamant that there was no more money available.*

amnesty /ˈæmnəsti/   *n.* 1. an official statement that allows people who have been put in prison for crimes against the state to go free
e.g.: *The president granted a general amnesty for all political prisoners.*
2. a period of time during which people can admit to a crime or give up weapons without being punished
e.g.: *2000 knives have been handed in during the month-long amnesty.*

beleaguered /bɪˈliːgəd/   *adj.* 1. experiencing a lot of criticism and difficulties
e.g.: *The beleaguered party leader was forced to resign.*
2. surrounded by an enemy
e.g.: *supplies for the beleaguered city*

calligraphy /kəˈlɪgrəfi/   *n.* beautiful handwriting that you do with a special pen or brush; the art of producing this
e.g.: *a poem written in neat italic calligraphy*

deference /ˈdefərəns/   *n.* behavior that shows that you respect sb./sth.
e.g.: *The women wore veils in deference to the customs of the country.*

embroider /ɪmˈbrɔɪdə(r)/   *v.* to decorate cloth with a pattern of stitches usually using coloured thread
embroider A on B. e.g.: *She embroidered flowers on the cushion covers.*

humbly /ˈhʌmbli/   *adv.* in a way that shows you do not think you are as important as other people
e.g.: *I would humbly suggest that there is something wrong here.*

knick-knack /ˈnɪk ˌnæk/   *n.* a small decorative object in a house
e.g.: *There were no photographs, no knick-knacks: just a simple table and chairs.*

pluck /plʌk/   *v.* to pull out hairs with your fingers or with tweezers

Unit 5
Instructor Wang Secretly Makes His Escape; Shi Jin Gets His Defences into Shape (excerpt)

	e.g.: *She plucked out a grey hair.*
	pluck up (the) courage (to do sth.): to make yourself do sth. even though you are afraid to do it.
	e.g.: *I finally plucked up the courage to ask her for a date.*
remission /rɪˈmɪʃn/	*n.* 1. a period during which a serious illness improves for a time and the patient seems to get better
	e.g.: *The patient has been in remission for the past six months.*
	2. a reduction in the amount of time sb. spends in prison, especially because they have behaved well
	e.g.: *She has been granted a remission of sentence.*
strum /strʌm/	*v.* to play a guitar or similar instrument by moving your fingers up and down across the strings
	strum (on) sth. e.g.: *As she sang she strummed on a guitar.*
wrestle /ˈresl/	*v.* 1. to fight sb. by holding them and trying to throw or force them to the ground, sometimes as a sport
	e.g.: *She tried to wrestle with her attacker.*
	2. to struggle to deal with sth. that is difficult
	e.g.: *She has been wrestling to raise the money all year.*

While Reading

I. Please fill in the blanks with the words in the parentheses with the appropriate part of speech.

1. The prices in that restaurant are absolutely _____, and very few people can afford to have a dinner there. (ruin)
2. The children in our family are always _____ to their elders because they are taught to be obedient. (respect)
3. They make a lot of money by clever _____ of the Stock Market, and they are able to control and _____ events. (manipulate)
4. I don't think I would say he is free of cancer. I would say that he is in what we call a solid partial _____ which means that the majority of the cancer cells have disappeared. (remiss)
5. He gave the struggle his attention, as a(n) _____ might observe the feat of a juggler, without interest in the outcome. (idle)
6. She presumed on her father's _____ by borrowing money from him and not repaying it. (generous)
7. If something is probable, you mean that you can trust it; and so probability means _____. (trustworthy)

8. Cafés and coffee houses are an Austrian tradition, and it is _____ to take an afternoon break for a strong cup of coffee. (custom)

9. Any disclosure to an attorney, CPA, or financial planner would also result in _____. (banish)

10. The government was trying to stop the increasing flow of _____ entering the country because the economy was further burdened by a flood of _____. (refuge)

II. *Please choose one word or phrase that best completes the sentence.*

1. New entrants in Europe's national markets are also proving to be _____ marketing and promotion.
   A. an adept at   B. apt to
   C. good for   D. subject to

2. There was an interim before her successor actually came because she had to _____ her notice.
   A. work at   B. work for
   C. work out   D. work against

3. Do not fill bottles to the _____ with liquid products, because they can expand under the effect of heat.
   A. brim   B. edge
   C. verge   D. rim

4. Although the family's remaining valuables are now lodging _____ the bank, he has installed an electronic 999 dialing system.
   A. at   B. to
   C. without   D. with

5. The government might _____ put its money where its mouth is to prove its commitment.
   A. anticipate to   B. be obliged to
   C. consider to   D. be hesitant to

6. But as we all know, of all these _____ fuel vehicles, the most practical are electric vehicles.
   A. alterable   B. alterative
   C. alternate   D. alter

III. Translation

1. Please translate the following from English into Chinese.

1) to express one's gratitude in a toast
2) to neglect family affairs
3) to offer sacrifices
4) supplies and money for travel expenses
5) to bid farewell to somebody
6) to do somebody a favor
7) to prepare a banquet
8) to make one's fortune

Unit 5
Instructor Wang Secretly Makes His Escape; Shi Jin Gets His Defences into Shape (excerpt)

9) Luck was with him that day.

10) Separate lives make separate thoughts; close living makes for close relations.

11) never to depart from one's footsteps   12) to be held back

2. Please translate the following from Chinese into English.

1）鼓起勇气   2）想出计策
3）亲随   4）吹弹歌舞
5）喜爱   6）伺机
7）投奔   8）风调雨顺
9）大赦天下   10）挥霍财富
11）告状   12）上马

3. Please translate each sentence with at least one key word or its derivative.

Key Words: haunt, harbor, squander, convict, procure

1）几乎没有一个人能天天如此虚度光阴。
2）他将不断回想起威尔公园的那一幕。
3）那名逃跑的罪犯要服刑五年才能获得赦免。
4）任何人如果辜负了她的信任，她都会心怀怨恨的。
5）不过至少在给全国各地的学校安装电影屏幕这件事上，爱迪生并没有浪费大笔公共资金。
6）第二次世界大战结束时人们仍然很难获得食品、燃料和其他日用必需品。
7）川西的王朗自然保护区是大熊猫出没的地方。
8）我现在掌握了给这个年轻人定罪的所有必要证据。
9）我们已经与世界上的41个国家开展了合作，来改善政府采购的透明度、竞争性和效率。
10）至于爱我们但我们不爱的人，我们可能是不关心的，或者至少不会怀有这样一种深切的全面关心。

After Reading

I. Please make a sentence with the words and expressions you have learnt from the text.

1. to be obliged to do:
2. to feign:
3. to await:
4. to signify:
5. to venture:

II. Paragraph Writing

1. Please write a paragraph of around 150 words about the description of Gao-the-Ball's appearance, personality and hobbies in the story.

2. Please write a paragraph of around 100 words with the following words and expressions you have learnt from the text. Make sure that the paragraph you have written is grammatically correct and coherent.

> glue; deliver; perform; kick; be skilled at

Original Edition in Chinese

王教头私走延安府　九纹龙大闹史家村（节选）

……

且说东京开封府汴梁宣武军，一个浮浪破落户子弟，姓高，排行第二，自小不成家业，只好刺枪使棒，最是踢得好脚气毬，京师人口顺，不叫高二，却都叫他做高毬。后来发迹，便将气毬那字去了毛傍，添作立人，便改作姓高名俅。这人吹弹歌舞，刺枪使棒，相扑顽耍，颇能诗书词赋；若论仁义礼智，信行忠良，却是不会。只在东京城里城外帮闲。因帮了一个生铁王员外儿子使钱，每日三瓦两舍，风花雪月，被他父亲开封府里告了一纸文状，府尹把高俅断了四十脊杖，迭配出界发放。东京城里人民，不许容他在家宿食。高俅无计奈何，只得来淮西临淮州投奔一个开赌坊的闲汉柳大郎，名唤柳世权。他平生专好惜客养闲人，招纳四方干隔涝汉子。高俅投托得柳大郎家，一住三年。后来哲宗天子因拜南郊，感得风调雨顺，放宽恩大赦天下，那高俅在临淮州，因得了赦宥罪犯，思量要回东京。这柳世权却和东京城里金梁桥下开生药铺的董将士是亲戚，写了一封书札，收拾些人事盘缠，赍发高俅回东京，投奔董将士家过活。

当时高俅辞了柳大郎，背上包裹，离了临淮州，迤逦回到东京，竟来金梁桥下董生药家，下了这封信。董将士一见高俅，看了柳世权来书，自肚里寻思道："这高俅，我家如何安着得他！若是个志诚老实的人，可以容他在家出入，也教孩儿们学些好。他却是个帮闲的破落户，没信行的人，亦且当初有过犯来，被开封府断配出境的人，倘或留住在家中，倒惹得孩儿们不学好了。待不收留他，又撇不过柳大郎面皮。"当时只得权且欢天喜地，相

Unit 5
Instructor Wang Secretly Makes His Escape; Shi Jin Gets His Defences into Shape (excerpt)

留在家宿歇,每日酒食管待。住了十数日,董将士思量出一个缘由,将出一套衣服,写了一封书简,对高俅说道:"小人家下萤火之光,照人不亮,恐后误了足下。我转荐足下与小苏学士处,久后也得个出身,足下意内如何?"高俅大喜,谢了董将士。董将士使个人将着书简,引领高俅竟到学士府内。门吏转报小苏学士,出来见了高俅,看罢来书,知道高俅原是帮闲浮浪的人,心下想道:"我这里如何安着得他!不如做个人情,荐他去驸马王晋卿府里,做个亲随。人都唤他做'小王都太尉',便喜欢这样的人。"当时回了董将士书札,留高俅在府里住了一夜。次日,写了一封书呈,使个干人,送高俅去那小王都太尉处。

这太尉乃是哲宗皇帝妹夫,神宗皇帝的驸马。他喜爱风流人物,正用这样的人。一见小苏学士差人驰书送这高俅来,拜见了,便喜。随即写回书,收留高俅在府内做个亲随。自此高俅遭际在王都尉府中,出入如同家人一般。自古道:日远日疏,日亲日近。忽一日,小王都太尉庆诞生辰,分付府中安排筵宴,专请小舅端王。这端王乃是神宗天子第十一子,哲宗皇帝御弟,现掌东驾,排号九大王,是个聪明俊俏人物。这浮浪子弟门风、帮闲之事,无一般不晓,无一般不会,更无一般不爱。更兼琴棋书画,儒释道教,无所不通。踢毬打弹,品竹调丝,吹弹歌舞,自不必说。当日王都尉府中准备筵宴,水陆俱备。但见:

  香焚宝鼎,花插金瓶。仙音院竞奏新声,教坊司频逞妙艺。水晶壶内,尽都是紫府琼浆;琥珀杯中,满泛着瑶池玉液。玳瑁盘堆仙桃异果,玻璃碗供熊掌驼蹄。鳞鳞脍切银丝,细细茶烹玉蕊。红裙舞女,尽随着象板鸾箫;翠袖歌姬,簇捧定龙笙凤管。两行珠翠立阶前,一派笙歌临座上。

且说这端王来王都尉府中赴宴。都尉设席,请端王居中坐定,太尉对席相陪。酒进数杯,食供两套,那端王起身净手。偶来书院里少歇,猛见书案上一对儿羊脂玉碾成的镇纸狮子,极是做得好,细巧玲珑。端王拿起狮子,不落手看了一回,道:"好!"王都尉见端王心爱,便说道:"再有一个玉龙笔架,也是这个匠人一手做的,却不在手头。明日取来,一并相送。"端王大喜道:"深谢厚意。想那笔架必是更妙。"王都尉道:"明日取出来,送至宫中便见。"端王又谢了。两个依旧入席饮宴,至暮尽醉方散。端王相别回宫去了。

次日,小王都太尉取出玉龙笔架和两个镇纸玉狮子,着一个小金盒子盛了,用黄罗包袱包了,写了一封书呈,却使高俅送去。高俅领了王都尉钧旨,将着两般玉玩器,怀中揣了书呈,径投端王宫中来。把门官吏转报与院公。没多时,院公出来问:"你是那个府里来的人?"高俅施礼罢,答道:"小人是王驸马府中,特送玉玩器来进大王。"院公道:"殿下在庭心里和小黄门踢气毬,你自过去。"高俅道:"相烦引进。"院公引到庭前,高俅看时,见端王头戴软纱唐巾,身穿紫绣龙袍,腰系文武双穗绦,把绣龙袍前襟拽扎起,揣在绦儿边。足穿一双嵌金线飞凤靴,三五个小黄门,相伴着蹴气毬。高俅不敢过去冲撞,立在从人背后伺候。也是高俅合当发迹,时运到来,那个气毬腾地起来,端王接个不着,向人丛里直滚到高俅身边。那高俅见气毬来,也是一时的胆量,使个鸳鸯拐,踢还端王。端王见了大喜,便问道:"你是甚人?"高俅向前跪下道:"小的是王都尉亲随,受东人使令,赍送两般玉玩器来进献大王,有书呈在此拜上。"端王听罢,笑道:"姐夫直如此挂心。"高俅取出书呈进上。端王开盒子看了玩器,都递与堂候官收了去。那端王且不理玉玩器下落，却先问高俅道："你原来会踢气毬。你唤做甚么？"高俅叉手跪复道："小的叫做高俅，胡踢得几脚。"端王道："好！你便下场来踢一回耍。"高俅拜道："小的是何等样人，敢与恩王下脚。"端王道："这是'齐云社'名为'天下圆'，但踢何伤。"高俅再拜道："怎敢。"三回五次告辞，端王定要他踢。高俅只得叩头谢罪，解膝下场。才踢几脚，端王喝采。高俅只得把平生本事都使出来，奉承端王。那身分模样，这气毬一似鳔胶粘在身上的。端王大喜，那里肯放高俅回府去，就留在宫中过了一夜。次日，排个筵会，专请王都尉宫中赴宴。

却说王都尉当日晚不见高俅回来，正疑思间，只见次日门子报道："九大王差人来传令旨，请太尉到宫中赴宴。"王都尉出来见了干人，看了令旨，随即上马来到九大王府前，下马入宫来，见了端王。端王大喜，称谢两般玉玩器。入席饮宴间，端王说道："这高俅踢得两脚好气毬，孤欲索此人做亲随，如何？"王都尉答道："殿下既用此人，就留在宫中伏侍殿下。"端王欢喜，执杯相谢。二人又闲话一回，至晚席散，王都尉自回驸马府去，不在话下。

且说端王自从索得高俅做伴之后，就留在宫中宿食。高俅自此遭际端王，每日跟随，寸步不离。却在宫中未及两个月，哲宗皇帝晏驾，无有太子。文武百官商议，册立端王为天子，立帝号曰徽宗，便是玉清教主微妙道君皇帝。登基之后，一向无事，忽一日，与高俅道："朕欲要抬举你，但有边功，方可升迁。先教枢密院与你入名，只是做随驾迁转的人。"后来没半年之间，直抬举高俅做到殿帅府太尉职事。

Text B

Sidney Shapiro's Version

Arms Instructor Wang Goes Secretly to Yanan Prefecture Nine Dragons Shi Jin Wreaks Havoc in Shi Family Village (excerpt)

During the reign of Emperor Zhe Zong, who ruled a long time after Ren Zong, in Bianliang the Eastern Capital, in Kaifeng Prefecture previously called Xuanwu District, there lived a young scamp named Gao. A second son, he was quite useless. He cared only for jousting with spear and staff, and was an excellent football player. People in the capital were fond of making quips. They dubbed him Gao Qiu, or "Gao the Ball." Later, when he prospered, he changed "Qiu" to another character with the same sound but with a less inelegant meaning.

In addition to his skill with weapons, Gao Qiu could play musical instruments and sing and dance. He also learned a bit about poetry and versifying. But when it came to virtue and proper behavior, he didn't know a thing. He spent his time gadding about the city and its environs. Thanks to him, the son of Master Wang, an iron-shop owner, dissipated a considerable sum of money in theaters, gambling dens and brothels.

Unit 5
Instructor Wang Secretly Makes His Escape; Shi Jin Gets His Defences into Shape (excerpt)

For this reason the father made a written complaint against Gao to Kaifeng Prefecture. The prefect gave Gao twenty strokes, banished him from the city, and forbade the people of the Eastern Capital from either feeding him or giving him shelter. Gao Qiu's solution was to proffer his services to one Liu Shiquan, known as Liu the Eldest, who ran a gambling house in Linhuai Prefecture, west of the Huaihe River. Liu surrounded himself with idlers and riffraff from all over.

Gao Qiu remained with Liu for three years. Then Emperor Zhe Zong prayed to Heaven south of the city, and this caused the winds and rains to become very propitious. The emperor was moved to benevolence, and he declared a general amnesty. Gao Qiu was able to return to the capital. Liu the Eldest wrote a letter of introduction to Dong Jiangshi, a relative of his who ran a medicinal herb shop near the Bridge of Golden Girders, gave Gao some travelling money, and told him Dong would take care of him.

Gao said goodbye, shouldered his pack and returned to the city, where he delivered the letter to Dong. The druggist took one look at Gao, then read the letter.

"How can I put this man up in my home?" he mused. "It would be different if he were straight and honest. The children could learn from him. But he's just a loafer, an untrustworthy fellow who's been exiled for breaking the law, and not the kind likely to reform. If I keep him here he's liable to teach the children bad ways. Yet if I don't, I'll be offending Liu the Eldest."

He had no choice but to receive Gao into his home with pretended delight. Dong feasted him every day for ten days, then he got an idea. He presented Gao with a suit of clothes and handed him a letter of introduction.

"The light of my household is too feeble," he said. "It would only be holding you back to keep you here. I'm turning you over to Su Junior, the Court Scholar. With him you'll be able to make a start. How does that sound?"

Gao thanked him gratefully. Dong had a servant take the letter and escort Gao to the Court Scholar's residence. There, a gateman reported Gao's arrival. The scholar came out and greeted him. He saw from the letter of introduction that Gao was a scamp.

"I can't take this man in," thought the Scholar. "As a favor to Dong I'll send him to Wang Jinqing, the Young Prince Consort, to serve as a retainer. The Young Prince likes that sort of fellow."

He wrote Dong a reply and let Gao stay the night. The next day he wrote another letter and dispatched it with a steward who took Gao Qiu to the residence of the Young Prince.

Wang had married a younger sister of Emperor Zhe Zong before he took the throne and while Emperor Shen Zong still reigned. The Young Prince was partial to adventurous men, and he staffed his retinue with them. He liked Gao the moment he saw him with the Scholar's letter-bearing servant. He wrote an immediate reply, accepting him as a retainer. From then on Gao remained with the prince, coming and going like one of the family.

As the old saying has it: "Distant friends grow ever distant, friends at hand grow closer still." To celebrate his birthday, the Young Prince ordered that a feast be laid, and invited Prince

Duan, his wife's younger brother. Duan had been the eleventh child of Emperor Shen Zong and was a brother of the reigning emperor Zhe Zong. In charge of the imperial equipage, the Ninth Royal Prince, as he was called, was an intelligent, handsome young man, and a skilled dilettante in all forms of amusement. His accomplishments included the lute, chess, calligraphy, painting and football. He was also a good musician, singer and dancer.

That day, Wang the Young Prince spread a banquet of the finest delicacies of land and sea. He seated Duan the Ninth Royal Prince in the central chair or honor and sat down opposite. After several cups of wine and two courses, Prince Duan went out to relieve himself. He stopped by in the library on his return, where the Young Prince joined him. Duan was attracted by a pair of paper-weight lions carved of mutton-fat jade. They were extremely well made, in exquisite detail.

Prince Duan picked them up and couldn't set them down. "Beautiful," he murmured.

"The same artisan also made a jade rack carved like a dragon for writing brushes," said the Young Prince. "I don't have it handy, but I'll find it tomorrow and send it to you together with these paper-weights."

"That's awfully kind of you. I'm sure the dragon is carved even more finely than the lions."

"I'll send it to the palace tomorrow. You'll be able to see for yourself."

Prince Duan thanked him and they went back to the banquet table where they dined until dusk. Both were drunk when they parted. Prince Duan bade the prince consort farewell and returned to his palace.

The next day the Young Prince found the writing-brush rack carved like a dragon. He placed it in a small gold box together with the pair of jade paper-weight lions, wrapped the box in golden silk, wrote a covering letter, and told Gao to deliver the gifts. Gao proceeded directly to Prince Duan's palace. The gate-keeper reported his arrival to the steward, who came out.

"From which official residence are you?"

Gao Qiu bowed. "Prince Consort Wang has directed me to deliver these jade objects to the Royal Prince."

"His Highness is in the middle court playing football with some young eunuchs. You may go in."

"Could I trouble you to show me the way?"

The steward led Gao to the gate of the inner court. Four or five young eunuchs were kicking a ball with Prince Duan. He was wearing a soft Tang style silk hat and a purple robe embroidered with an imperial dragon. The robe was tucked up in front under the prince's official waist sash. Flying phoenixes embroidered in gold thread decorated his boots.

Gao dared not interrupt. He stood behind some servants and waited. Fortune favored him. The ball sailed past Prince Duan, who couldn't stop it, and rolled through the crowd to Gao Qiu. In a momentary seizure of boldness, he kicked it back to the prince with a "mandarin duck and drake twist."

Duan was delighted. "Who are you?" he asked.

Unit 5
Instructor Wang Secretly Makes His Escape; Shi Jin Gets His Defences into Shape (excerpt)

Gao fell on his knees, "A retainer of Prince Consort Wang. At my master's orders I bring Your Highness two jade gifts. I have a letter that goes with them."

The royal prince smiled. "Brother-in-law is always considerate."

Gao Qiu produced the letter. Prince Duan opened the box and looked at the jade pieces, then turned them over to his major-domo.

"So you know how to kick a ball," he said to Gao. "What's your name?"

Gao crossed his arms before his chest respectfully and dropped again to his knees. "Your servant is called Gao Qiu. I've spent a little time with a ball on the field."

"Good," said the prince. "Come and join the game."

"A man of my rank! I wouldn't dare play with your Highness."

"Why not? This is the Clouds-High League, known as the All-Round Circle. It's open to anyone."

Gao Qiu continued to refuse. But when the royal prince insisted, he kowtowed, begged forgiveness for his presumption, and trotted onto the field. He made a few passes with the ball and the prince shouted approval. Gao Qiu was inspired to show everything he had. His movements, his style, were a pleasure to behold. He stayed so close to the ball it seemed glued to his feet.

Prince Duan was enchanted. He wouldn't let Gao leave, and kept him overnight in the palace. The next day he ordered a feast and sent an invitation to the Young Prince.

When Gao failed to return the night before, the Young Prince began to wonder whether he could be trusted. Now, his gate-keeper announced: "A messenger from the Ninth Royal Prince is here with an invitation for Your Excellency to attend a banquet in the palace." The Young Prince went out and received the messenger and read the invitation. Then he got on his horse and rode to the palace. Dismounting, he proceeded directly to Prince Duan.

The Ninth Royal Prince thanked him for the two jade gifts. Together, they entered the dining-room.

"That Gao Qiu of yours plays a good game of football," said Prince Duan. "I'd like to have him as a retainer. How about it?"

"If he's of any use to Your Highness, let him serve in the Palace, by all means."

Prince Duan raised his wine cup and thanked the Young Prince. The two chatted and dined until evening. Then the Young Prince returned to his residence. Of him we'll say no more.

Let us talk rather of Gao Qiu. After he went into the service of Prince Duan he lived and dined in the palace and accompanied the prince every day, never taking so much as a step from his side. Before two months had elapsed, Emperor Zhe Zong died without leaving an heir. All the high civil and military officials conferred and made Prince Duan the emperor. He was known as Emperor Hui Zong and bore the title of High Priest of Jade Purity and Taoist Sovereign of Provident Truth.

Hui Zong assumed the throne and all went well. One day he said to Gao Qiu: "I'd like to raise you in rank, but you'll have to perform some meritorious deed on the border first. I'll have the Council of Military Affairs put you down as available for imperial appointment." Less than half a year later, he was able to make Gao Qiu a marshal commanding the Imperial Guards.

Notes on the Text

1. About the text

The present text is taken from *Outlaws of the Marsh* translated by Sidney Shapiro, published by Foreign Languages Press in 2012.

2. Sidney Shapiro

Sidney Shapiro (December 23, 1915—October 18, 2014) was an American-born Chinese translator and author who lived in China from 1947 to 2014. He lived in Beijing for over a half century and was a member of the Chinese People's Political Consultative Council. Through his literary translations he remained at the forefront of helping people overseas learn about China's past and present. His literary translations, which range from the classical to the modern, include the Ming Dynasty masterpiece *Outlaws of the Marsh* and the well-known 20th century outcries against bigotry and backwardness such as Ba Jin's *The Family* and Mao Dun's *Spring Silkworms*.

Unit 6

Kongming Borrows Cao Cao's Arrows Through a Ruse; Huang Gai Is Flogged Following a Secret Plan (excerpt)

Reading Guide

This text is an excerpt from the 46th episode "Kongming Borrows Cao Cao's Arrows Through a Ruse; Huang Gai Is Flogged Following a Secret Plan" of *Three Kingdoms* translated by Moss Roberts. *Three Kingdoms* was published by Foreign Languages Press in 1994 with three volumes and 1690 pages in total. Moss Roberts, professor of Chinese at New York University, also published an abridged translation of *Three Kingdoms* (Pantheon, 1976) and is the translator of *Chinese Fairy Tales and Fantasies* (Pantheon, 1979).

Professor Roberts managed to achieve a rare feat in producing a translation that is not only a fine example of meticulous scholarly translation, but also a highly entertaining novel which should be a delight to readers with or without any prior knowledge of Chinese literature. The translation itself is generally very accurate, and maintains fidelity to the original text without falling into the trap of pedantic literalism. In his previous abridged translation Roberts generally put dialogue in dramatic form, but in this complete translation he abandoned the dramatic style for a more natural, fluid style of writing which perfectly captures the feeling of the original Chinese text.① All in all, *Three Kingdoms* translated by Moss Roberts has been regarded as the best version by most scholars, translators, and sinologists.

---

① West, Andrew C.. "Review Work: Three Kingdoms: A Historical Novel by Luo Guanzhong". *Chinese Literature: Essays, Articles, Reviews*, Vol.17 (1995), 157–159.

Before Reading

I. Preview Requirements: Please make a preparatory research on the background information, key words and phrases of this text.

1. Do research on the translator Moss Roberts.
2. Do research on the fateful moment at the end of the Han Dynasty (206 BC—220 AD).
3. Do research on Kongming and Zhou Yu, especially their influence in the Han Dynasty.
4. Find and study the new words in the text such as *felicitation, temporize, divulge, snap, seclude, precede, agony, verse, stratagem,* and *epitome*.
5. Learn the useful expressions in the text such as *be taken up with, take in, favor with, strive to, set out, appeal to,* and *refrain from*.

II. Preview Questions: Please answer some questions about the understanding of the main content of the text.

1. What is the most dramatic moment of the story? Please try to describe it in your own words.
2. Was Zhuge Liang in a real predicament? Please supply some evidence and examples.
3. How do you view Lu Su in the text? Please comment on his behavior.
4. What elements contribute to Zhuge Liang's success? List them as many as possible.
5. As a Chinese saying goes, "If you know the enemy and know yourself, you can fight a hundred battles with no danger of defeat." Do you attribute Zhuge Liang's success of borrowing arrows to his prediction of the enemy's reaction? Why? Please give examples and evidence.
6. Please read *King Arthur and His Knights*, and try to find out something in common between the story and *Three Kingdoms*. Consider romantic myths of a misty never-never land of long ago.

Text A

Moss Roberts's Version

Kongming Borrows Cao Cao's Arrows Through a Ruse; Huang Gai Is Flogged Following a Secret Plan (excerpt)

ZHOU Yu sent Lu Su to find out if Kongming had detected the subterfuge. Kongming welcomed Lu Su aboard his little boat, and the two men sat face-to-face. "Every day I am taken up with military concerns and miss your advice," Lu Su began. "Rather, I am the tardy one, having yet to convey my felicitations to the chief commander," answered Kongming. "What

Unit 6
Kongming Borrows Cao Cao's Arrows Through a Ruse; Huang Gai Is Flogged Following a Secret Plan (excerpt)

felicitations?" asked Lu Su. "Why," replied Kongming, "for that very matter about which he sent you here to see if I knew." The color left Lu Su's face. "But how did you know, master?" he asked. Kongming went on: "The trick was good enough to take in Jiang Gan. Cao Cao, though hoodwinked for the present will realize what happened quickly enough—he just won't admit the mistake. But with those naval commanders dead, the Southland has no major worry, so congratulations are certainly in order. I hear that Cao Cao has replaced them with Mao Jie and Yu Jin. One way or another, those two will do in their navy!"

Lu Su, unable to respond sensibly, temporized as best he could before he rose to leave. "I trust you will say nothing about this in front of Zhou Yu," Kongming urged Lu Su, "lest he again be moved to do me harm." Lu Su agreed but finally divulged the truth when he saw the field marshal. Astounded, Zhou Yu said, "The man must die. I am determined." "If you kill him," Lu Su argued, "Cao Cao will have the last laugh." "I will have justification," answered Zhou Yu. "And he will not feel wronged." "How will you do it?" asked Lu Su. "No more questions now. You'll see soon enough," Zhou Yu replied.

The next day Zhou Yu gathered his generals together and summoned Kongming, who came eagerly. At the assembly Zhou Yu asked him, "When we engage Cao Cao in battle on the river routes, what should be the weapon of choice?" "On the Great River, bow and arrow," Kongming replied. "My view precisely, sir," Zhou Yu said. "But we happen to be short of arrows. Dare I trouble you, sir, to undertake the production of one hundred thousand arrows to use against the enemy? Please favor us with your cooperation in this official matter." "Whatever task the chief commander assigns, I shall strive to complete," replied Kongming. "But may I ask by what time you will require them?" "Can you finish in ten days?" asked Zhou Yu. "Cao's army is due at any moment," said Kongming. "If we must wait ten days, it will spoil everything." "How many days do you estimate you need, sir?" said Zhou Yu. "With all respect, I will deliver the arrows in three days," Kongming answered. "There is no room for levity in the army," Zhou Yu snapped. "Dare I trifle with the chief commander?" countered Kongming. "I beg to submit my pledge under martial law: if I fail to finish in three days' time, I will gladly suffer the maximum punishment."

Elated, Zhou Yu had his administrative officer publicly accept the document. He then offered Kongming wine, saying, "You will be well rewarded when your mission is accomplished." "It's too late to begin today," said Kongming. "Production begins tomorrow. On the third day send five hundred men to the river for the arrows." After a few more cups, he left. Lu Su said to Zhou Yu, "This man has to be deceiving us." "He is delivering himself into our hands!" replied Zhou Yu. "We did not force him. Now that he has publicly undertaken this task in writing, he couldn't escape if he sprouted wings. Just have the artisans delay delivery of whatever he needs. He will miss the appointed time; and when we fix his punishment, what defense will he be able to make? Now go to him again and bring me back news."

Lu Su went to see Kongming. "Didn't I tell you not to say anything?" Kongming began. "He is determined to kill me. I never dreamed you would expose me. And now today he actually pulled this trick on me! How am I supposed to produce one hundred thousand arrows in three days? You have to save me!" "You brought this on yourself," said Lu Su. "How can I save you?" "You must lend me twenty vessels," Kongming went on, "with a crew of thirty on each. Lined up on either side of each vessel I want a thousand bundles of straw wrapped in black cloth. I have good use for them. I'm sure we can have the arrows on the third day. But if you tell Zhou Yu this time, my plan will fail." Lu Su agreed, though he had no idea what Kongming was up to, and reported back to Zhou Yu without mentioning the boats: "Kongming does's seem to need bamboo, feathers, glue, or other materials. He seems to have something else in mind." Puzzled, Zhou Yu said, "Let's see what he has to say after three days have gone by."

Lu Su quietly placed at Kongming's disposal all he had requested. But neither on the first day nor on the second did Kongming make any move. On the third day at the fourth watch he secretly sent for Lu Su. "Why have you called me here?" Su asked. "Why else? To go with me to fetch the arrows," Kongming replied. "From where?" inquired Lu Su. "Ask no questions," said Kongming. "Let's go; you'll see." He ordered the boats linked by long ropes and set out for the north shore.

That night tremendous fogs spread across the heavens, and the river mists were so thick that even face-to-face people could not see each other. Kongming urged his boats on into the deep fog. The rhapsody "Heavy Mists Mantling the Yangzi" describes it well:

> Vast the river! Wide and farflung! West, it laps the mountains Mang and E. South, it grips the southern shires. North, it girdles the nine rivers, gathers their waters, and carries them into the sea, its surging waves rolling through eternity.
>
> Its depths hold monsters and strange forms: the Lord of the Dragons, the Sea Thing, the river goddesses, the Ocean Mother, ten-thousand-span whales, and the nine-headed centipede. This redoubt of gods and spirits, heroes fight to hold.
>
> At times the forces of yin and yang that govern nature fail, and day and darkness seem as one, turning the vast space into a fearful monochrome. Everywhere the fog, stock-still. Not even a cartload can be spotted. But the sound of gong or drum carries far.
>
> At first, a visible gloom, time for the wise leopard of the southern hills to seclude itself. Gradually darkness fills the expanse. Does it want the North Sea leviathan itself to lose its way? At last it reaches the very sky and mantles the all-upbearing earth. Grey gloomy vastness. A shoreless ocean. Whales hurtle on the waves. Dragons plunge and spew mist.
>
> It is like the end of early rains, when the cold of latent spring takes hold: everywhere, vague, watery desert and darkness that flows and spreads. East, it blankets the shore of Chaisang. South, it blocks the hills of Xiakou. A thousand warjunks, swallowed between the river's rocky steeps, while a single fishing boat boldly bobs on the swells.

Unit 6
Kongming Borrows Cao Cao's Arrows Through a Ruse; Huang Gai Is Flogged Following a Secret Plan (excerpt)

In so deep a fog, the deep-domed heavens have gone dark. The countenance of dawn is dull: the day becomes a murky twilight; the reddish hills, aquamarine jade. Great Yu, who first controlled the floods, could not with all his wisdom sound its depths. Even clear-eyed Li Lou could not use his measures, despite his keen vision.

Let the water god calm these waves. Let the god of elements put away his art. Let the sea creatures and those of land and air be gone. For now the magic isle of Penglai is cut off, and the gates of the polar stars are shrouded.

The roiling, restless fog is like the chaos before a storm, swirling streaks resembling wintry clouds. Serpents lurking there can spread its pestilence, and evil spirits can havoc wreak, sending pain and woe to the world of men, and the storms of wind and sand that plague the border wastes. Common souls meeting it fall dead. Great men observe it and despair. Are we returning to the primal state that preceded form itself—to undivided Heaven and earth?

By the fifth watch Kongming's little convoy was nearing Cao Cao's river base. The vessels advanced in single file, their prows pointed west. The crews began to roar and pound their drums. Lu Su was alarmed. "What if they make a sally?" he asked. Kongming smiled and replied, "I'd be very surprised if Cao Cao plunged into this fog. Let's pour the wine and enjoy ourselves. We'll go back when the fog lifts."

As the clamor reached Cao Cao's camp, the new naval advisers Mao Jie and Yu Jin sent reports at once. Cao Cao issued an order: "The fog has made the river invisible. This sudden arrival of enemy forces must mean an ambush. I want absolutely no reckless movements. Let the archers and crossbowmen, however, fire upon the enemy at random." He also sent a man to his land headquarters calling for Zhang Liao and Xu Huang to rush an extra three thousand crossbowmen to the shore. By the time Cao's order reached Mao Jie and Yu Jin, their men had already begun shooting for fear the southerners would penetrate their camp. Soon, once the marksmen from the land camp had joined the battle, ten thousand men were concentrating their shots toward the river. The shafts came down like rain.

Kongming ordered the boats to reverse direction and press closer to shore to receive the arrows while the crews continued drumming and shouting. When the sun climbed, dispersing the fog, Kongming ordered the boats to hurry homeward. The straw bundles bristled with arrow shafts, for which Kongming had each crew shout in unison: "Thanks to the prime minister for the arrows!" By the time this was reported to Cao Cao, the light craft, borne on swift currents, were twenty *li* downriver, beyond overtaking. Cao Cao was left with the agony of having played the fool.

Kongming said to Lu Su, "Each boat has some five or six thousand arrows. So without costing the Southland the slightest effort, we have gained over one hundred thousand arrows, which tomorrow we can return to Cao's troops—a decided convenience to us!" "Master, you are indeed supernatural," Lu Su said. "How did you know there would be such a fog today?" "A military commander is a mediocrity," Kongming explained, "unless he is versed in the patterns of the heavens, recognizes the advantages of the terrain, knows the interaction of prognostic signs, understands the changes in weather, examines the maps of deployment, and is clear about the balance of forces. Three days ago I calculated today's fog. That's why I took a chance on the three-day limit. Zhou Yu gave me ten days to finish the job, but neither materials nor workmen. He plainly meant to kill me for laxity. But my fate is linked to heaven. How could Zhou Yu have succeeded?" Respectfully, Lu Su acknowledged Kongming's superior powers.

When the boats reached shore, five hundred men sent by Zhou Yu had already arrived to transport the arrows. Kongming directed them to take the arrows—upward of one hundred thousand of them—from the boats and to deliver them to the chief commander's tent. Meanwhile, Lu Su explained in detail to Zhou Yu how Kongming had acquired them. Zhou Yu was astounded. Then, with a long sigh of mingled admiration and despair, he said, "Kongming's godlike machinations and magical powers of reckoning are utterly beyond me!" A poet of later times left these lines in admiration:

> That day the river-shrouding fogs
> Melted all distance in a watery blur.
> Like driving rain or locusts Cao's arrows came:
> Kongming had humbled the Southland commander.

Kongming entered the camp. Zhou Yu came out of his tent and greeted him with cordial praise: "Master, we must defer to your superhuman powers of reckoning." "A pretty subterfuge of common cunning," Kongming replied, "not worth your compliments." Zhou Yu invited Kongming into his tent to drink. "Yesterday," Zhou Yu said, "Lord Sun urged us to advance. But I still lack that unexpected stroke that wins the battle. I appeal to you for instruction." "I am a run-of-the-mill mediocrity," replied Kongming. "What kind of unique stratagem could I offer you?" "Yesterday I surveyed Cao's naval stations," Zhou Yu continued. "They are the epitome of strict order, all according to the book, invulnerable to any routine attack. I have one idea, but it may not be workable. Master, could you help me to decide?"

"Refrain from speaking for a moment, Chief Commander," Kongming said. "We'll write on our palms to see whether we agree or not." Zhou Yu was delighted to oblige. He called for brush and ink, and, after writing on his own masked hand, passed the brush to Kongming, who wrote on his own. Then the two men shifted closer to one another, opened their hands, and laughed. The same word was on each: fire. "Since our views coincide," said Zhou Yu, "my doubts are resolved. Protect our secret." "This is our common cause," answered Kongming. "Disclosure is unthinkable. My guess is that even though Cao Cao has twice fallen victim to my fires, he will not be prepared for this. It may be your ultimate weapon, Chief Commander." After drinking they parted. None of the commanders knew of their plan.

Unit 6
Kongming Borrows Cao Cao's Arrows Through a Ruse; Huang Gai Is Flogged Following a Secret Plan (excerpt)

Notes on the Text

1. **yin and yang**

   The school of Yin and Yang thought was one of the philosophical schools of thought during the Warring States period. This school is often mentioned side by side with the school of the Five Processes or Five Phases. In Chinese philosophy, yin and yang ("dark-bright", "negative-positive") describe how seemingly opposite or contrary forces may actually be complementary, interconnected, and interdependent in the natural world, and how they interrelate to one another.

2. **Great Yu**

   Great Yu, also called Yu the Great, was a legendary ruler in ancient China famed for his introduction of flood control and his upright moral character, inaugurating dynastic rule in China by founding the Xia Dynasty. Traditional stories say that Yu sacrificed a great deal to control the floods. For example, his hands were said to be thickly callused, and his feet were completely covered with callus. In a folktale, Yu had only been married four days when he was given the task of fighting the floods. He said goodbye to his wife, saying that he did not know when he would return. During the thirteen years of flooding, he passed by his own family's doorstep three times, but never did he step inside his own home.

3. **the magic isle of Penglai**

   The magic isle of Penglai is said to be a fabled abode of immortals in Shandong Province. It has been regarded as one of the three magic isles (the other two are Fangzhang and Yingzhou) where immortals inhabit in Chinese fairytales.

Glossary

ambush /ˈæmbʊʃ/	*n.* the act of hiding and waiting for sb. and then making a surprise attack on them e.g.: *They were lying in ambush waiting for the aid convoy.*
convoy /ˈkɒnvɔɪ/	*n.* a group of vehicles or ships travelling together, especially when soldiers or other vehicles travel with them for protection e.g.: *A United Nations aid convoy loaded with food and medicine finally got through to the besieged town.*
cordial /ˈkɔːdiəl/	*adj.* pleasant and friendly e.g.: *The government wisely maintained cordial relations with the Russians.*
elated /iˈleɪtɪd/	*adj.* very happy and excited because of sth. good that has happened, or will happen be elated at/by sth. e.g.: *I was elated by the prospect of the new job ahead.*

girdle /ˈgɜːdl/   *v.* to surround sth.

e.g.: *A chain of volcanoes girdles the Pacific.*

havoc /ˈhævək/   *v.* If one thing plays havoc with another or wreaks havoc on it, it prevents it from continuing or functioning as normal, or damage it.

e.g.: *Continuing strikes are beginning to play havoc with the national economy.*

laxity /ˈlæksəti/   *n.* the quality of not being strict, severe or careful enough about work, rules or standards of behaviour

e.g.: *the moral laxity of today's society*

levity /ˈlevəti/   *n.* the treatment of a serious matter with humour or lack of due respect

e.g.: *The joke provided a moment of levity in an otherwise dreary meeting.*

monochrome /ˈmɒnəkrəʊm/   *n.* black, white and shades of grey

e.g.: *an artist who works in monochrome*

murky /ˈmɜːki/   *adj.* 1. (of a liquid) not clear; dark or dirty with mud or another substance

e.g.: *She gazed into the murky depths of the water.*

     2. (of air, light, etc.) dark and unpleasant because of smoke, fog, etc.

e.g.: *a murky night*

plunge /plʌndʒ/   *v.* 1. to fall or jump suddenly from a high place

e.g.: *Her car plunged off a bridge.*

     2. to fall or drop suddenly in amount, value, etc.

e.g.: *The president's approval rating has plunged to 20 percent.*

plunge in/into e.g.: *The nurse grabbed his arm and plunged the needle in.*

subterfuge /ˈsʌbtəfjuːdʒ/   *n.* a secret, usually dishonest way of behaving

e.g.: *Journalists often use subterfuge to obtain material for stories.*

summon /ˈsʌmən/   *v.* 1. to order sb. to appear in court

e.g.: *He was summoned to appear before the magistrates.*

     2. to order sb. to come to you

summon sb. to sth. e.g.: *In May 1688 he was urgently summoned to London.*

tardy /ˈtɑːdi/   *adj.* slow to act, move or happen; late in happening or arriving

be tardy in doing sth. e.g.: *The law is often tardy in reacting to changing attitudes.*

Unit 6
Kongming Borrows Cao Cao's Arrows Through a Ruse; Huang Gai Is Flogged Following a Secret Plan (excerpt)

While Reading

I. Please fill in the blanks with the words in the parentheses with the appropriate part of speech.

1. Your report last week was unfair. It was based upon wholly unfounded and totally _____ allegations. (justification)
2. He overextended himself when he accepted the special _____, but he knew that a brave fighter should never shrink from danger. (assign)
3. When the thief was caught making off with a gold watch on the table, he refused to make any _____ of his guilt. (acknowledge)
4. The German Company has _____ that it will be laying off thousands of workers later this year, but a series of shocking _____ is still around the corner. (disclose)
5. I don't know how the errors managed to avoid _____ for so long, but it's time for us to do some _____ work to find out the truth. (detect)
6. In the US, it typically brings beneficial precipitation to the arid Southwest, less _____ weather across the North, and a reduced risk of Florida wildfires. (winter)
7. In striving to be "real men", they live higher-risk lifestyles, driven by internalized messages of competition, _____, control, emotional suppression, and independence. (vulnerable)
8. The fact that he and his boss went to the same college was purely _____, and he did not plan to explain for this _____. (coincide)
9. The collected images are authentic and original in the truest sense. These magnificently _____ portraits of Earth encourage us all to learn more about our complex world. (engage)
10. She knew their truce would not last. Finally, there would be a _____ of another fight. When the day of _____ came, they would have to face some unpleasant truths. (reckon)

II. Please choose one word or phrase that best completes the sentence.

1. Even after years of close acquaintance you could still be _____ by his sentimentality.
   A. taken after   B. taken up with
   C. taken in   D. taken along
2. The two disputing countries decided not to _____ arms.
   A. appeal to   B. appeal from
   C. appeal without   D. appeal for
3. After my parents went for a holiday, the whole house was put _____ without any supervision.
   A. under my suspicion   B. at my disposal
   C. on duty   D. at random

4. Recent reports found that lodging with a student of a different race may decrease prejudice and compel students to _____ more ethnically diverse friendships.
   A. engage in   B. engage into
   C. engage with   D. engage for
5. If all goes well, Frankenstein will not be the best metaphor for synthetic biologists; they may be more like Pandora opening her box—but releasing the hope without the _____.
   A. happiness   B. joy
   C. doubt   D. woe
6. The music suddenly _____ and quickened into an exciting rhythm.
   A. swelled   B. increased
   C. strengthen   D. boosted

III. Translation

1. Please translate the following from English into Chinese.
   1) godlike machinations and magical powers of reckoning
   2) to convey one's felicitations to somebody
   3) a pretty subterfuge of common cunning   4) to divulge the truth
   5) a run-of-the-mill mediocrity   6) with all respect
   7) There is no levity in the army.   8) to suffer maximum punishment
   9) to have good use for something   10) to be versed in the patterns of the heavens
   11) to recognize the advantages of the terrain   12) One's fate is linked to heaven.

2. Please translate the following from Chinese into English.
   1）按兵不动   2）措办军务
   3）有失听教   4）害人
   5）辩解   6）大雾漫天
   7）突袭   8）失色
   9）应敌   10）误事
   11）定罪   12）看阵图

3. Please translate each sentence with at least one key word or its derivative.
   Key Words: spoil, disperse, agony, oblige, submit
   1）暴风雨越来越猛烈。最终，我被迫弃车徒步前行。
   2）祖父母每次来访都忍不住要宠溺孙辈。
   3）在那一年的痛苦和接下来整整一年的悲恸中，我生活中的一切都停止了。
   4）一时无法恢复运行的，轨道交通线路运营单位应当组织乘客疏散和换乘。
   5）我心里难过地想：这风暴是故意来破坏我的快乐的，它的一切恶意都是针对我的。
   6）如果那时我答应他们的要求，他们就不会坚持那些指控了。

Unit 6
Kongming Borrows Cao Cao's Arrows Through a Ruse; Huang Gai Is Flogged Following a Secret Plan (excerpt)

7）警方下令驱散聚集在那座建筑旁的人群。
8）他笨拙地摔倒了，痛苦地抱住右膝躺在地上。
9）我们打电话给三位经济学家咨询如何消除赤字，他们坦率地给予了答复。
10）绝望之际，史密斯夫人只好同意在其右膝上做手术以减轻疼痛。

After Reading

I. Please make a sentence with the words and expressions you have learnt from the text.

1. to favor with:
2. to seclude oneself:
3. to refrain from:
4. to hoodwink:
5. to take in:

II. Paragraph Writing

1. Please write a paragraph of around 150 words about the main characteristics of the three major roles Zhuge Liang, Zhou Yu and Lu Su in the story.

2. Please write a paragraph of around 100 words with the following words and expressions you have learnt from the text. Make sure that the paragraph you have written is grammatically correct and coherent.

> surge; mantle; shire; deep-domed heaven; murky; swell; blanket

Original Edition in Chinese

用奇谋孔明借箭　献密计黄盖受刑（节选）

却说鲁肃领了周瑜言语，径来舟中相探孔明。孔明接入小舟对坐。肃曰："连日措办军务，有失听教。"孔明曰："便是亮亦未与都督贺喜。"肃曰："何喜？"孔明曰："公瑾使先生来探亮知也不知，便是这件事可贺喜耳。"唬得鲁肃失色，问曰："先生何由知之？"孔明曰："这条计只好弄蒋干。曹操虽被一时瞒过，必然便省悟，只是不肯认错耳。今蔡、张两人既死，江东无患矣，如何不贺喜？吾闻曹操换毛玠、于禁为水军都督，则这两个手里，好歹送了水军性命。"鲁肃听了，开口不得，把些言语，支吾了半晌，别孔明而回。孔明嘱曰："望子敬在公瑾面前，勿言亮先知此事。恐公瑾心怀妒忌，又要寻事害亮。"鲁肃应诺而去，回见周瑜，把上项事只得实说了。瑜大惊曰："此人决不可留。吾决意斩之。"肃劝曰："若杀孔明，却被曹操笑也。"瑜曰："吾自有公道斩之，教他死而无怨。"肃曰："何以公道斩之？"瑜曰："子敬休问，来日便见。"

　　次日，聚众将于帐下，教请孔明议事。孔明欣然而至。坐定，瑜问孔明曰："即日将与曹军交战，水路交兵，当以何兵器为先？"孔明曰："大江之上，以弓箭为先。"瑜曰："先生之言，甚合愚意。但今军中正缺箭用，敢烦先生监造十万枝箭，以为应敌之具。此系公事，先生幸勿推却。"孔明曰："都督见委，自当效劳。敢问十万枝箭何时要用？"瑜曰："十日之内，可完办否？"孔明曰："操军即日将至，若候十日，必误大事。"瑜曰："先生料几日可完办？"孔明曰："只消三日，便可拜纳十万枝箭。"瑜曰："军中无戏言。"孔明曰："怎敢戏都督？愿纳军令状：三日不办，甘当重罚。"瑜大喜，唤军政司当面取了文书，置酒相待曰："待军事毕后，自有酬劳。"孔明曰："今日已不及，来日造起。至第三日，可差五百小军，到江边搬箭。"饮了数杯，辞去。鲁肃曰："此人莫非诈乎？"瑜曰："他自送死，非我逼他。今明白对众要了文书，他便两胁生翅，也飞不去。我只分付军匠人等，教他故意迟延，凡应用物件，都不与齐备。如此必然误了日期。那时定罪，有何理说？公今可去探他虚实，却来回报。"

　　肃领命，来见孔明。孔明曰："吾曾告子敬，休对公瑾说，他必要害我。不想子敬不肯为我隐讳，今日果然又弄出事来。三日内如何造得十万箭？子敬只得救我。"肃曰："公自取其祸，我如何救得你？"孔明曰："望子敬借我二十只船，每船要军士三十人，船上皆用青布为幔，各束草千余个，分布两边。吾别有妙用。第三日，包管有十万枝箭。只不可又教公瑾得知。若彼知之，吾计败矣。"肃应诺，却不解其意。回报周瑜，果然不提起借船之事，只言孔明并不用箭竹翎毛胶漆等物，自有道理。瑜大疑曰："且看他三日后如何回覆我。"

　　却说鲁肃私自拨轻快船二十只，各船三十余人，并布幔束草等物尽皆齐备，候孔明调用。第一日，却不见孔明动静；第二日亦只不动。至第三日四更时分，孔明密请鲁肃到船中。肃问曰："公召我来何意？"孔明曰："特请子敬同往取箭。"肃曰："何处去取？"孔明曰："子敬休问，前去便见。"遂命将二十只船，用长索相连，径望北岸进发。

　　是夜大雾漫天。长江之中雾气更甚，对面不相见。孔明促舟前进，果然是好大雾。前人有篇《大雾垂江赋》曰：

　　　　大哉长江！西接岷峨，南控三吴，北带九河。汇百川而入海，历万古以扬波。至若龙伯、海若、江妃、水母，长鲸千丈，天蜈九首，鬼怪异类，咸集而有。盖夫鬼神之所凭依，英雄之所战守也。时也阴阳既乱，昧爽不分。讶长空之一色，忽大雾之四屯。虽舆薪而莫睹，惟金鼓之可闻。初若溟濛，才隐南山之豹；渐而充塞，欲迷北海之鲲。然后上接高天，下垂厚地；渺乎苍茫，浩乎无际。鲸鲵出水而腾波，蛟龙潜渊而吐气。又如梅霖收溽，春阴酿寒，溟溟漠漠，浩

Unit 6
Kongming Borrows Cao Cao's Arrows Through a Ruse; Huang Gai Is Flogged Following a Secret Plan (excerpt)

浩漫漫。东失柴桑之岸，南无夏口之山。战船千艘，俱沉沦于岩壑；渔舟一叶，惊出没于波澜。甚则穹昊无光，朝阳失色。返白昼为昏黄，变丹山为水碧。虽大禹之智，不能测其浅深；离娄之明，焉能辨乎咫尺。于是冯夷息浪，屏翳收功，鱼鳖遁迹，鸟兽潜踪；隔断蓬莱之岛，暗围阊阖之宫。恍惚奔腾，如骤雨之将至；纷纭杂沓，若寒云之欲同。乃能中隐毒蛇，因之而为瘴疠；内藏妖魅，凭之而为祸害。降疾厄于人间，起风尘于塞外。小民遇之夭伤，大人观之感慨。盖将返元气于洪荒，混天地为大块。

当夜五更时候，船已近曹操水寨。孔明教把船只头西尾东一带摆开，就船上擂鼓呐喊。鲁肃惊曰："倘曹兵齐出，如之奈何？"孔明笑曰："吾料曹操于重雾中必不敢出。吾等只顾酌酒取乐，待雾散便回。"

却说曹寨中听得擂鼓呐喊，毛玠、于禁二人慌忙飞报曹操。操传令曰："重雾迷江，彼军忽至，必有埋伏，切不可轻动。可拨水军弓弩手乱箭射之。"又差人往旱寨内唤张辽、徐晃，各带弓弩军三千，火速到江边助射。比及号令到来，毛玠、于禁怕南军抢入水寨，另差弓弩手，在寨前放箭。少顷，旱寨内弓弩手亦到，约一万余人，尽皆向江中放箭，箭如雨发。孔明教把船吊回，头东尾西，逼近水寨受箭，一面擂鼓呐喊。待至日高雾散，孔明令收船急回。二十只船，两边束草上，排满箭枝。孔明令各船上军士齐声叫曰："谢丞相箭。"比及曹军寨内报知曹操时，这里船轻水急，已放回二十余里，追之不及。曹操懊悔不已。

却说孔明回船，谓鲁肃曰："每船上箭约五六千矣。不费江东半分之力，已得十万余箭，明日即将来射曹军，却不甚便？"肃曰："先生真神人也，何以知今日如此大雾？"孔明曰："为将而不通天文，不识地利，不知奇门，不晓阴阳，不看阵图，不明兵势，是庸才也。亮于三日前已算定今日有大雾，因此敢任三日之限。公瑾教我十日完办，工匠料物都不应手，将这一件风流罪过，明白要杀我。我命系于天，公瑾焉能害我哉！"鲁肃拜服。

船到岸时，周瑜已差五百军在江边等候搬箭。孔明教于船上取之，可得十余万枝。都搬入中军帐交纳。鲁肃入见周瑜，备说孔明取箭之事。瑜大惊，慨然叹曰："孔明神机妙算，吾不如也！"后人有诗赞曰：

一天浓雾满长江，远近难分水渺茫。
骤雨飞蝗来战舰，孔明今日伏周郎。

少顷，孔明入寨见周瑜。瑜下帐迎之，称羡曰："先生神算，使人敬服。"孔明曰："诡谲小计，何足为奇。"

瑜邀孔明入帐共饮。瑜曰："昨吾主遣使来催督进军，瑜未有奇计，愿先生教我。"孔明曰："亮乃碌碌庸才，安有妙计！"瑜曰："某昨观曹操水寨，极其严整有法，非等闲可攻。思得一计，不知可否。先生幸为我一决之。"孔明曰："都督且休言。各自写于手内，看同也不同。"瑜大喜，教取笔砚来，先自暗写了，却送与孔明。孔明亦暗写了。两个移近坐榻，各出掌中之字，互相观看，皆大笑。原来周瑜掌中字，乃一"火"字，孔明掌中亦一"火"字。瑜曰:"既我两人所见相同,更无疑矣。幸勿漏泄。"孔明曰:"两家公事,岂有漏泄之理。吾料曹操虽两番经我这条计,然必不为备。今都督尽行之可也。"饮罢分散,诸将皆不知其事。

Text B

C. H. Brewitt-Taylor's Version

K'ung-Ming "Borrows" Some Arrows: Huang Kai Accepts a Punishment (excerpt)

The gossip Lu Su departed on his mission and found K'ung-ming seated in his little craft.

"There has been so much to do that I have not been able to come to listen to your instructions," said Lu Su.

"That is truly so," said K'ung-ming, "and I have not yet congratulated the Commander-in-Chief."

"What have you wished to congratulate him upon?"

"Why Sir, the matter upon which he sent you to find out whether I knew about it or not. Indeed I can congratulate him on that."

Lu Su turned pale and gasped, "But how did you know, Master?"

"The ruse succeeded well thus played off on Chiang Kan. Ts'ao has been taken in this once, but he will soon rise to it. Only he will not confess his mistake. However, the two men are gone and your country is freed from a grave anxiety. Do you not think that a matter for congratulation? I hear Mao Chieh and Yu Chin are the new admirals, and in their hands lie both good and evil for the fate of the fleet."

Lu Su was quite dumbfounded; he stayed a little time longer passing the time in making empty remarks, and then took his leave. As he was going away K'ung-ming cautioned him against letting Chou Yu know that his new rival had guessed his ruse. "I know he is jealous and he only seeks some chance to do me harm."

Lu Su promised; nevertheless he went straight to his chief and related the whole thing just as it happened.

"Really he must be got rid of," said Chou Yu, "I have quite decided to put the man out of the way."

"If you slay him, will not Ts'ao Ts'ao laugh at you?"

"Oh, no; I will find a legitimate way of getting rid of him so that he shall go to his death without resentment."

Unit 6
Kongming Borrows Cao Cao's Arrows Through a Ruse; Huang Gai Is Flogged Following a Secret Plan (excerpt)

"But how can you find a legitimate way of assassinating him?"

"Do not ask too much. You will see presently."

Soon after all the officers were summoned to the main tent and K'ung-ming's presence was desired. He went contentedly enough. When all were seated Chou Yu suddenly addressed K'ung-ming, saying, "I am going to fight a battle with the enemy soon on the water: what weapons are the best?"

"On a great river arrows are the best," said K'ung-ming.

"Your opinion and mine agree. But at the moment we are short of them. I wish you would undertake to supply about a hundred thousand arrows for the naval fight. As it is for the public service you will not decline, I hope!"

"Whatever task the Commander-in-Chief lays upon me I must certainly try to perform," replied K'ung-ming. "May I enquire by what date you require the hundred thousand arrows?"

"Could you have them ready in ten days?"

"The enemy will be here very soon; ten days will be too late," said K'ung-ming.

" In how many days do you estimate the arrows can be ready?"

"Let me have three days; then you may send for your hundred thousand."

"No joking, remember," said the General. "There is no joking in war time."

"Dare I joke with the Commander-in-Chief? Give me a formal military order and if I have not completed the task in three days I will take my punishment."

Chou Yu, secretly delighted, sent for the secretaries and prepared the commission then and there. Then he drank to the success of the undertaking and said, "I shall have to congratulate you most heartily when this is accomplished."

"This day is not to count," said K'ung-ming. "On the third from tomorrow morning send five hundred small boats to the river side to convey the arrows."

They drank a few more cups together, and then K'ung-ming took his leave. After he had gone, Lu Su said, "Do you not think there is some deceit about this?"

"I think he has signed his own death warrant," said Chou. "Without being pressed in the least he asked for a formal order in the face of the whole assembly. If he grew a pair of wings he could not escape. Only I will just order the workmen to delay him as much as they can, and not supply him with materials, so that he is sure to fail. And then, when the certain penalty is incurred, who can criticize? You can go and enquire about it all and keep me informed."

So off went Lu Su to seek K'ung-ming, who at once reproached him with having blabbed about the former business, "He wants to hurt me, as you know, and I did not think you could not keep my secret. And now there is what you saw today and how do you think I can get a hundred thousand arrows made in three days? You will simply have to rescue me."

"You brought the misfortune on yourself and how can I rescue you?" said Lu.

"I look to you for the loan of a score of vessels, manned each by thirty men. I want blue cotton screens and bundles of straw lashed to the sides of the boats. I have good use for them. On the third day I have undertaken to deliver the fixed number of arrows. But on no account must you let Chou Yu know, or my scheme will be wrecked. "

Lu Su consented and this time he kept his word. He went to report to his chief as usual, but he said nothing about the boats. He only said K'ung-ming was not using bamboo or feathers or glue or varnish, but has some other way of getting arrows.

"Let us await the three days' limit," said Chou Yu, puzzled though confident.

On his side Lu Su quietly prepared a score of light swift boats, each with its crew and the blue screens and bundles of grass complete and, when these were ready, he placed them at K'ung-ming's disposal. His friend did nothing on the first day, nor on the second. On the third day at the middle of the fourth watch, K'ung-ming sent a private message asking Lu Su to come to his boat.

"Why have you sent for me, Sir?" asked Lu Su.

"I want you to go with me to get those arrows."

"Whither are you going?"

"Do not ask: You will see."

Then the twenty boats were fastened together by long ropes and moved over to the north bank. The night proved very foggy and the mist was very dense along the river, so that one man could scarcely see another. In spite of the fog K'ung-ming urged the boats forward.

There is a poem on these river fogs: —

> Mighty indeed is the Yangtse River!
> Rising far in the west, in the mountains of Omei and Min,
> Ploughing its way through Wu, east flowing, resistless,
> Swelled by its nine tributary streams, rolling down from the far north,
> Aided and helped by a hundred rivulets swirling and foaming,
> Ocean receives it at last welcoming, joyful, its waters.
> Therein abide sea-nymphs and water gods,
> Enormous whales a thousand fathoms long,
> Nine-headed monstrous beasts yclept *t'ien-wu*,
> Demons and uncouth creatures wondrous strange.
> In faith it is the home and safe retreat
> Of devils black, and sprites, and wondrous growths,
> And eke the battle ground of valiant men.
> At times occur strange strife of elements,
> When darkness strives on light's domains t'encroach,
> Whereat arises in the vaulted dome of blue
> White wreaths of fog that toward the center roll.
> Then darkness falls, too dense for any torch
> T'illumine; only clanging sounds can pass.

Unit 6
Kongming Borrows Cao Cao's Arrows Through a Ruse; Huang Gai Is Flogged Following a Secret Plan (excerpt)

The fog at first appears, a vaporous wreath
Scarce visible. But thickening fast, it veils
The southern hills, the Painted leopard's home.
And spreads afar, until the northern sea
Leviathans are mazed and lose their course.
And denser yet it touches on the sky,
And spreads a heavy mantle o'er the earth.
Then, wide as is the high pitched arch of heaven,
Therein appears no single rift of blue.
Now mighty whales lead up their wives to sport
Upon the waves, the sinuous dragons dive
Deep down and, breathing, swell the heaving sea,
The earth is moist as with the early rains,
And spring's creative energy is chilled.
Both far and wide and high the damp fog spreads,
Great cities on the eastern bank are hid,
Wide ports and mountains in the south are lost,
Whole fleets of battle ships, a thousand keels,
Hide in the misty depths; frail fishing boats
High riding on a wave are seen—and lost.
The gloom increases and the domed sky
Grows dark and darker as the sun's light fails.
The daylight dies, dim twilight's reign begins,
The ruddy bills dissolve and lose their hue.
The skill of matchless Yu would fail to sound
The depth and height; and Li Lou's eye, though keen,
Could never pierce this gloom. Now is the time,
O sea and river gods, to use your powers.
The gliding fish and creeping water folk
Are lost; there is no track for bird or beast.
Fair P'englai Isles are hidden from our sight,
The lofty gates of heaven have disappeared.
Nature is blurred and indistinct, as when
A driving rain storm hurries o'er the earth.
And then, perhaps, within the heavy haze
A noisome serpent vents his venom foul
And plagues descend, or impish demons work
Their wicked wills.

Ills fall on humans but do not stay,
Heaven's cleansing breath sweeps them away,
But while they last the mean ones cry,
The nobler suffer silently.
The greatest turmoil is a sign
Of quick return to state benign.

The little fleet reached Ts'ao Ts'ao's naval camp about the fifth watch and orders were given to form line lying prows west, and then to beat the drums and shout.

"But what shall we do if they attack us?" exclaimed Lu Su.

K'ung-ming replied with a smile, "I think the fleet will not venture out in this fog; go on with your wine and let us be happy. We will go back when the fog lifts."

As soon as the shouting from the river was heard by those in the camp the two commanders ran off to report to their chief, who said, "Coming up in a fog like this means that they have prepared an ambush for us. Do not go out, but get all the force together and shoot at them."

He also sent orders to the soldier camps to despatch six companies of archers and crossbowmen to aid the marines.

The naval forces were then lined up on the bank to prevent a landing. Presently the soldiers arrived and a legion and more men were shooting down into the river, where the arrows fell like rain. By and bye K'ung-ming ordered the boats to turn round so that their prows pointed east and to go closer in so that many arrows might hit them.

The drums were kept beating till the sun was high and the fog began to disperse, when the boats got under way and sailed down stream. The whole twenty boats were bristling with arrows on both sides. As they left, all the crews derisively shouted, "We thank you, Sir Minister, for the arrows."

They told Ts'ao Ts'ao, but by the time he came the light boats helped by the swift current were a long way down river and pursuit was impossible. Ts'ao Ts'ao saw that he had been duped and was very sorry, but there was no help for it.

On the way down K'ung-ming said to his companion, "Every boat must have five or six thousand arrows and so, without the expenditure of an ounce of energy, we must have more than ten myriad arrows, which tomorrow can be shot back again at Ts'ao Ts'ao's army to his great inconvenience."

"You are really superhuman," said Lu Su. "But how did you know there would be a thick fog today?"

"One cannot be a leader without knowing the workings of heaven and the ways of earth. One must understand the secret gates and the inter-dependence of the elements, the mysteries of tactics and the value of forces. It is but an ordinary talent. I calculated three days ago that there would be a fog today and so I set the limit at three days. Chou Yu would give me ten days, but

Unit 6
Kongming Borrows Cao Cao's Arrows Through a Ruse; Huang Gai Is Flogged Following a Secret Plan (excerpt)

neither artificers nor materials, so that he might find occasion to put me to death as I knew, but my fate lies with the Supreme and how could Chou Yu harm me?"

Lu Su could not but agree. When the boats arrived half a company were in readiness on the bank to carry away the arrows. K'ung-ming bade them go on board the boats, collect them and bear them to the tent of the Commander-in-Chief. Lu Su went to report that the arrows had been obtained and told Chou Yu by what means.

Chou Yu was amazed and sighed sadly, saying, "He is better than I, his methods are more than human."

> Thick lies the fog on the river,
> Nature is shrouded in white,
> Distant and near are confounded,
> Banks are no longer in sight.
> Fast fly the pattering arrows,
> Stick in the boats of the fleet.
> Now can full tale be delivered,
> K'ung-ming is victor complete.

When, shortly after his return, K'ung-ming went to the tent of the Commander-in-Chief he was welcomed by Chou Yu, who came forward to greet him, saying, "Your superhuman predictions compel one's esteem."

"There is nothing remarkable in that trifling trick," replied he.

Chou Yu led him within and wine was brought.

Chou Yu said, "My lord sent yesterday to urge me to advance, but I have no master plan ready; I wish you would assist me, Master."

"But where should I, a man of poor, everyday ability, find such a plan as you desire?"

"I saw the enemy's naval camp just lately and it looked very complete and well organized. It is not an ordinary place to attack. I have thought of a plan, but I am not sure it will answer. I should be happy if you would decide for me."

"General," replied K'ung-ming, "do not say what your plan is but each of us will write in the palm of his hand and see whether our opinions agree."

So pen and ink were sent for and Chou Yu first wrote on his own palm, and then passed the pen to K'ung-ming who also wrote. Then getting close together on the same bench each showed his hand to the other, and both burst out laughing, for both had written the same word, "Fire."

"Since we are of the same opinion," said Chou Yu, "there is no longer any doubt. But our intentions must be kept secret."

"Both of us are public servants and what would be the sense of telling our plans? I do not think Ts'ao Ts'ao will be on his guard against this although he has had two experiences. You may put your scheme into force."

They finished their wine and separated. Not an officer knew a word of the general's plans.

Notes on the Text

1. About the text

The present text is taken from *Romance of the Three Kingdoms* translated by C. H. Brewitt-Taylor, published by Tuttle Publishing in 2002.

2. C. H. Brewitt-Taylor

Charles Henry Brewitt-Taylor (1857–1938), was a long time official in the Imperial Maritime Customs Service in China and a sinologist best known for his translation of *Romance of the Three Kingdoms*, published in 1925.

Unit 7

The Cadaver Demon Three Times Mocks Tripitaka Tang; The Holy Monk in Spite Banishes Handsome Monkey King (excerpt)

Reading Guide

This text is an excerpt from the 27th episode "The Cadaver Demon Three Times Mocks Tripitaka Tang; The Holy Monk in Spite Banishes Handsome Monkey King" of *The Journey to the West* translated and edited by Anthony C. Yu. This is the first full-length English version of *The Journey to the West*, which was published by the University of Chicago Press between 1977 and 1983. The four-volume book was highly praised by scholars when it came into being, and Prof. Yu was awarded the "Ryan Award" for good publication by the University of Chicago Press in 1984. According to David Frederick, senior editor of the University of Chicago Press, around 16,000 first volumes of the first edition have been sold in over three decades, with around 8,000 second, third and fourth volumes sold respectively. In 2012, the revised version of *The Journey to the West* was published by the Press, and it soon became well-received at Amazon.com.

This excerpt is a well-known episode from *The Journey to the West*, which fully depicts the characteristics of Tripitaka and his three disciples, namely Pilgrim, Eight Rules and Sha Monk. Pilgrim's "fiery eyes and diamond pupils" are best at identifying all kinds of monsters. The cadaver demon wants to eat a piece of Tripitaka's flesh, so she disguises herself as a beautiful girl. However, Pilgrim sees through her trick, and smashes the demon with his iron rod mercilessly. Eight Rules is gossipy and concupiscent. Tripitaka is easily influenced by his disciple Eight Rules, and banishes Pilgrim who does nothing wrong. Sha Monk is least depicted in this episode as the description of his words and behavior is relatively little. Anthony C. Yu highly emphasizes the representation of the appearance and inner world of the characters. Furthermore, the Chinese poems, perfectly translated in the English version, are worth reading and pondering.

Before Reading

I. Preview Requirements: Please make a preparatory research on the background information, key words and phrases of this text.

1. Do research on the translator Anthony C. Yu.
2. Read some materials related to Buddhism, especially Xuan Zang's contribution to the prevalence of Buddhism in the Tang Dynasty.
3. Get to know some major ideas on Taoism, especially the influence of Taoism in the Tang Dynasty.
4. Underline the new words in the text and make some study on them such as *arouse, behold, errand, zealous, grumble,* and *snout*.
5. Learn the useful expressions in the text such as *call out, be liable to, resort to, be wary of, redeem one's vow, talk nonsense, fall into one's trap,* and *be indebted to*.

II. Preview Questions: Please answer some questions about the understanding of the main content of the text.

1. What is the writing style of the text? Exposition, description, narration or argumentation?
2. What is the story about? Could you please describe the most impressive scene in the text?
3. What is the clue of the text? What kind of danger did Tripitaka and his disciples face?
4. Which character impressed you most? Please list some words or phrases that were used to describe that character.
5. What kind of trick did evil spirits usually use to cheat people?
6. For what reasons did Tripitaka give for expelling Pilgrim? Were his reasons sound?
7. Suppose you were Pilgrim, how could you make Tripitaka believe that those figures were actually a monster?
8. How do you evaluate Tripitaka and his disciples? Could they complete their journey to the West without Pilgrim? Please give your evidence and examples.
9. Please compare Pilgrim with a Western hero such as Harry Potter. What are their similarities and differences?
10. What are the major differences between Eastern and Western mythologies? Consider their origins, images of gods, functions and so on.

Text A

Anthony C. Yu's Version

The Cadaver Demon Three Times Mocks Tripitaka Tang; The Holy Monk in Spite Banishes Handsome Monkey King (excerpt)

……

Dear monster! She lowered her dark wind into the field of the mountain, and, with one shake of her body, she changed into a girl with a face like the moon and features like flowers. One cannot begin to describe the bright eyes and the elegant brows, the white teeth and the red lips. Holding in her left hand a blue sandstone pot and in her right a green porcelain vase, she walked from west to east, heading straight for the Tang Monk.

> *The sage monk resting his horse on the cliff*
> *Saw all at once a young girl drawing near:*
> *Slender hands hugged by gently swaying green sleeves;*
> *Tiny feet exposed beneath a skirt of Hunan silk.*
> *Perspiring her face seemed flower bedewed;*
> *Dust grazed her moth-brows like willows held by mist.*
> *And as he stared intently with his eyes,*
> *She seemed to be walking right up to his side.*

When Tripitaka saw her, he called out, "Eight Rules, Sha Monk, just now Wukong said that this is an uninhabited region. But isn't that a human being who is walking over there?" "Master," said Eight Rules, "you sit here with Sha Monk. Let old Hog go take a look." Putting down his muckrake and pulling down his shirt, our Idiot tried to affect the airs of a gentleman and went to meet her face to face. Well, it was as the proverb says:

> *You can't determine the truth from afar.*
> *You can see clearly when you go near.*

The girl's appearance was something to behold!

> *Ice-white skin hides jadelike bones;*
> *Her collar reveals a milk-white bosom.*

Willow brows gather dark green hues;
Almond eyes shine like silver stars.
Her features like the moon are coy;
Her natural disposition is pure.
Her body's like the willow-nested swallow;
Her voice's like the woods' singing oriole.
A half-opened haitong caressed by the morning sun.
A newly bloomed peony displaying her charm.

When Idiot saw how pretty she was, his worldly mind was aroused and he could not refrain from babbling. "Lady Bodhisattva!" he cried. "Where are you going? What's that you are holding in your hands?" This was clearly a fiend, but he could not recognize her! The girl immediately answered him, saying, "Elder, what I have in the blue pot is fragrant rice made from wine cakes, and there's fried wheat gluten in the green vase. I came here for no other reason than to redeem my vow of feeding monks." When Eight Rules heard these words, he was very pleased. Spinning around, he ran like a hog maddened by plague to report to Tripitaka, crying, "Master! 'The good man will have Heaven's reward!' Because you are hungry, you ask Elder Brother to go beg for some vegetarian food. But we really don't know where that ape has gone to pick his peaches and have his fun! If you eat too many peaches, you are liable to feel a bit stuffed and gaseous anyway! Take a look instead. Isn't that someone coming to feed the monks?" "Coolie, you're just clowning!" said an unbelieving Tang Monk. "We've been traveling all this time and we haven't even run into a healthy person! Where is this person who's coming to feed the monks?" "Master," said Eight Rules, "isn't this the one?"

When Tripitaka saw the girl, he jumped up and folded his hands. "Lady Bodhisattva," he said, "where is your home? What sort of family is yours? What kind of vow have you made that you have to come here to feed the monks?" This was clearly a fiend, but our elder could not recognize her either! When that monster heard the Tang Monk asking after her background, she at once resorted to falsehood. With clever, specious words, she tried to deceive her interrogator, saying, "Master, this mountain, which turns back serpents and frightens wild beasts, bears the name of White Tiger. My home is located due west of here. My parents, still living, are frequent readers of sūtras and keen on doing good works. They have fed liberally the monks who come to us from near and far. Because my parents had no son, they prayed to the gods, and I was born. They would have liked to marry me off to a noble family, but, wary of helplessness in their old age, they took in a son-in-law instead, so that they would be cared for in life and death." Hearing this, Tripitaka said, "Lady Bodhisattva, your speech is rather improper! The sage classic says, 'While father and mother are alive, one does not travel abroad; or if one does, goes only to a proper destination.' If your parents are still living, and if they have taken in a husband for you, then your man should have been the one sent to redeem your vow. Why do you walk about the

Unit 7

The Cadaver Demon Three Times Mocks Tripitaka Tang; The Holy Monk in Spite Banishes Handsome Monkey King (excerpt)

mountain all by yourself? You don't even have an attendant to accompany you. That's not very becoming of a woman!"

Smiling broadly, the girl quickly tried to placate him with more clever words. "Master," she said, "my husband is at the northern fold of this mountain, leading a few workers to plow the fields. This happens to be the lunch I prepared for them to eat. Since now is the busy season of farm work, we have no servants; and as my parents are getting old, I have to run the errand myself. Meeting you three distant travelers is quite by accident, but when I think of my parents' inclination to do good deeds, I would like very much to use this rice as food for monks. If you don't regard this as unworthy of you, please accept this modest offering."

"My goodness! My goodness!" said Tripitaka. "I have a disciple who has gone to pick some fruits, and he's due back any moment. I dare not eat. For if I, a monk, were to eat your rice, your husband would scold you when he learns of it. Will it then not be the fault of this poor monk?" When that girl saw the Tang Monk refuse to take the food, she smiled even more seductively and said, "O Master! My parents, who love to feed the monks, are not even as zealous as my husband. For his entire life is devoted to the construction of bridges and the repairing of roads, in reverence for the aged and pity for the poor. If he heard that the rice was given to feed Master, his affection for me, his wife, would increase manyfold." Tripitaka, however, simply refused to eat, and Eight Rules on one side became utterly exasperated. Pouting, our Idiot grumbled to himself, "There are countless priests in the world, but none is more wishy-washy than this old priest of ours! Here's ready-made rice, and three portions to boot! But he will not eat it. He has to wait for that monkey's return and the rice divided into four portions before he'll eat." Without permitting further discussion, he pushed over the pot with one shove of his snout and was about to begin.

Look at our Pilgrim! Having picked several peaches from the mountain peak in the south, he came hurtling back with a single somersault, holding the alms bowl in his hand. When he opened wide his fiery eyes and diamond pupils to take a look, he recognized that the girl was a monster. He put down the bowl, pulled out his iron rod, and was about to bring it down hard on the monster's head. The elder was so aghast that he pulled his disciple back with his hands. "Wukong," he cried, "whom have you come back to hit?"

"Master," said Pilgrim, "don't regard this girl in front of you as a good person. She's a monster, and she has come to deceive you."

"Monkey," said Tripitaka, "you used to possess a measure of true discernment. How is it that you are talking nonsense today? This Lady Bodhisattva is so kind that she wants to feed me with her rice. Why do you say that she's a monster?"

"Master," said Pilgrim with a laugh, "how could you know about this? When I was a monster back at the Water-Curtain Cave, I would act like this if I wanted to eat human flesh. I would change myself into gold or silver, a lonely building, a harmless drunk, or a beautiful woman. Anyone feeble-minded enough to be attracted by me I would lure back to the cave. There I would enjoy him as I pleased, by steaming or boiling. If I couldn't finish him off in one meal,

I would dry the leftovers in the sun to keep for rainy days. Master, if I had returned a little later, you would have fallen into her trap and been harmed by her." That Tang Monk, however, simply refused to believe these words; he kept saying instead that the woman was a good person.

"Master," said Pilgrim, "I think I know what's happening. Your worldly mind must have been aroused by the sight of this woman's beauty. If you do have the desire, why not ask Eight Rules to cut some timber and Sha Monk to find us some grass. I'll be the carpenter and build you a little hut right here where you can consummate the affair with her. We can each go our own way then. Wouldn't that be the thing to do? Why bother to undertake such a long journey to fetch the scriptures?" The elder, you see, was a rather tame and gentle person. He was so embarrassed by these few words that his whole bald head turned red from ear to ear.

As Tripitaka was struck dumb by his shame, Pilgrim's temper flared again. Wielding his iron rod, he aimed it at the monster's face and delivered a terrific blow. The fiend, however, had a few tricks of her own. She knew the magic of Releasing the Corpse. When she saw Pilgrim's rod coming at her, she roused her spirit and left, leaving behind the corpse of her body struck dead on the ground. Shaking with horror, the elder mumbled, "This ape is so unruly, so obdurate! Despite my repeated pleadings, he still takes human life without cause." "Don't be offended, Master," said Pilgrim, "just come see for yourself what kind of things are in the pot." Sha Monk led the elder near to take a look. The fragrant rice made from wine cakes was nowhere to be found; there was instead a potful of large maggots with long tails. There was no fried wheat gluten either, but a few frogs and ugly toads were hopping all over the place. The elder was about to think that there might be thirty percent truthfulness in Pilgrim's words, but Eight Rules would not let his own resentment subside. He began to cast aspersions on his companion, saying, "Master, this woman, come to think of it, happens to be a farm girl of this area. Because she had to take some lunch to the fields, she met us on the way. How could she be deemed a monster? That rod of Elder Brother is quite heavy, you know. He came back and wanted to try his hand on her, not anticipating that one blow would kill her. He's afraid that you might recite that so-called Tight-Fillet Spell, and that's why he's using some sort of magic to hoodwink you. It's he who has caused these things to appear, just to befuddle you so that you won't recite the spell."

This single speech of Eight Rules, alas, spelled disaster for Tripitaka! Believing the slanderous suasion of our Idiot, he made the magic sign with his hand and recited the spell. At once Pilgrim began to scream, "My head! My head! Stop reciting! Stop reciting! If you've got something to say, say it." "What do I have to say?" asked the Tang Monk. "Those who have left the family must defer to people every time, must cherish kindness in every thought. They must

> *Keep ants out of harm's way when they sweep the floor,*
> *And put shades on lamps for the love of moths.*

And you, you practice violence with every step! Since you have beaten to death this innocent

Unit 7
The Cadaver Demon Three Times Mocks Tripitaka Tang; The Holy Monk in Spite Banishes Handsome Monkey King (excerpt)

commoner, what good would it do even if you were to go acquire the scriptures? You might as well go back." "Master," said Pilgrim, "where do you want me to go back to?" The Tang Monk said, "I don't want you as my disciple." "If you don't want me as your disciple," said Pilgrim, "I fear that you may not make it on your way to the Western Heaven." "My life is in the care of Heaven," said the Tang Monk. "If it's ordained that I should be food for the monster, even if I were to be steamed or boiled, it's all right with me. Furthermore, do you think really that you have the power to deliver me from the great limit? Go back quickly!" "Master," said Pilgrim, "it's all right for me to go back, but I have not yet repaid your kindness." "What kindness have I shown you?" asked the Tang Monk. When the Great Sage heard this, he knelt down immediately and kowtowed, saying, "Because old Monkey brought great disruption to the Celestial Palace, he incurred for himself the fatal ordeal of being clamped by Buddha beneath the Mountain of Two Frontiers. I was indebted to the Bodhisattva Guanyin who gave me the commandments, and to Master who gave me freedom. If I don't go up to the Western Heaven with you, it will mean that I

> *Knowing kindness without repaying am no princely man.*
> *Mine will be forever an infamous name.*"

Now the Tang Monk, after all, is a compassionate holy monk. When he saw Pilgrim pleading so piteously with him, he changed his mind and said, "In that case, I'll forgive you this time. Don't you dare be unruly again. If you work violence again as before, I'll recite this spell over and over twenty times." "You may recite it thirty times," said Pilgrim, "but I won't hit anyone again." Helping the Tang Monk to mount the horse, he then presented the peaches that he picked. The Tang Monk indeed ate a few of the peaches on the horse to relieve his hunger momentarily.

Notes on the Text

1. Tripitaka

In Sanskrit, tripitaka refers to "three baskets"; one of the most common and best known of the organizing schema of the Indian Buddhist canon. These three baskets were the Sutrapitaka (basket of discourses), Vinayapitaka (basket of disciplinary texts) and Abhidharmapitaka (basket of "higher dharma" or "treatises").

2. Bodhisattva

In Sanskrit, it refers to "enlightenment being". The term is typically glossed to mean "a being who has resolved to become a Buddha".

3. Sūtra

In a Buddhist context, it can be translated as "discourse", "sermon", or "scripture"; a sermon said to be delivered by the Buddha or delivered with his sanction.

4. Tight-Fillet Spell

To control Pilgrim, Bodhisattva Guanyin teaches Tripitaka Tight-Fillet Spell. Every time when Tripitaka recites this kind of spell, Pilgrim will feel hurt by the tight fillet around his head, and has to follow Tripitaka's direction.

Glossary

aghast /əˈgɑːst/ — *adj.* filled with horror and surprise when you see or hear sth.
aghast at sth. e.g.: *He stood aghast at the sight of so much blood.*

behold /bɪˈhəʊld/ — *v.* to look at or see sb./sth.
e.g.: *Her face was a joy to behold.*

consummate /kənˈsʌmət/ — *v.* to make a marriage or romantic relationship complete by having sex
e.g.: *The marriage was never consummated.*

discernment /dɪˈsɜːnmənt/ — *n.* the ability to show good judgment about the quality of sb./sth.
e.g.: *He shows great discernment in his choice of friends.*

exasperated /ɪgˈzæspəreɪtɪd/ — *adj.* extremely annoyed, especially if you cannot do anything to improve the situation
e.g.: *She was becoming exasperated with all the questions they were asking.*

feeble-minded /ˌfiːblˈmaɪndɪd/ — *adj.* weak and unable to make decisions
e.g.: *Unable to face the threatening future, the feeble-minded woman took her own life.*

hoodwink /ˈhʊdwɪŋk/ — *v.* to trick sb.
hoodwink sb. into doing sth. e.g.: *She had been hoodwinked into buying a worthless necklace.*

hurtle /ˈhɜːtl/ — *v.* to move very fast in a particular direction
e.g.: *A runaway car came hurtling towards us.*

obdurate /ˈɒbdjərət/ — *adj.* refusing to change your mind or your actions in any way.
e.g.: *Some members of the committee are likely to prove obdurate on this matter.*

placate /pləˈkeɪt/ — *v.* to make sb. feel less angry about sth.
e.g.: *The concessions did little to placate the students.*

seductively /sɪˈdʌktɪvli/ — *adv.* in a way that is intended to make someone feel attracted to you and want to have sex with you
e.g.: *She once posed seductively for a men's magazine.*

wield /wiːld/ — *v.* 1. to have and use power, authority, etc.

Unit 7
The Cadaver Demon Three Times Mocks Tripitaka Tang; The Holy Monk in Spite Banishes Handsome Monkey King (excerpt)

           e.g.: *She wields enormous power within the party.*
            2. to hold sth., ready to use it as a weapon or tool
           e.g.: *He was wielding a large knife.*
wishy-washy /ˈwɪʃi wɒʃi/ *adj.* 1. not having clear or firm ideas or beliefs
           e.g.: *He's just a wishy-washy liberal.*
            2. not bright in colour
           e.g.: *a wishy-washy blue*

While Reading

I. Please fill in the blanks with the words in the parentheses with the appropriate part of speech.

1. She was among the most _____ of women, and the suffering of the Cubans aroused her _____. (compassion)
2. As a Christian, you must obey the Ten _____, or you will be severely punished by the God. (command)
3. When she was delivering an important speech, she was so nervous that there was a _____ pause in her speech. (moment)
4. "Food Service is a reliable, _____ supplier to many companies throughout Europe and puts the utmost attention to its customer care." the spokesperson said. (trust)
5. With its beautiful natural light and mild climate, Hollywood would attract _____ movie-makers to come. (count)
6. The Prime Minister made a statement closely approximate to a _____, which aroused a fierce political controversy. (false)
7. The two nations have been arguing over control of _____ islands in the Caribbean Sea. (inhabit)
8. When she heard of such a ridiculous rumor that her parents had betrayed the country, her eyes were flinty and _____. (believe)
9. When realizing that the car ran out of petrol, she stopped the car at a petrol station and told the _____ to fill it up. (attend)
10. The House resolution calls the commission's report irredeemably biased and _____ of further consideration or legitimacy and urges the Obama administration, which has already condemned it, to strongly oppose its endorsement by the United Nations. (worth)

II. Please choose one word or phrase that best completes the sentence.

1. If the storm continues, we'll have to _____ the lifeboat.
  A. call in   B. call out
  C. call up   D. call round

2. Roosevelt either did not _____ the scandal or refused to credit what he heard.
   A. learn of
   B. learn about
   C. learn from
   D. learn by heart

3. Once a product is downloaded, it is your responsibility not to lose, destroy, or damage it, and Apple shall not _____ you if you do so.
   A. be subject to
   B. be prone to
   C. be liable to
   D. be apt to

4. You are more likely to _____ trouble if the data is password-protected or encrypted.
   A. run into
   B. run out
   C. run after
   D. run up

5. You should also _____ low-fat and fat-free foods (with the exception of dairy products), because food companies often compensate for the lack of fat by adding more sugar.
   A. be aware of
   B. be wary of
   C. be particular about
   D. be typical of

6. This girl is fortunate enough to have her mother as her _____ friend, so she can share everything with her mother.
   A. chest
   B. breast
   C. heart
   D. bosom

III. Translation

1. Please translate the following from English into Chinese.

1) almond eyes
2) the air of a gentleman
3) to feed the monks
4) to take in a son-in-law
5) the fragrant rice
6) the busy season of farm work
7) fried wheat gluten
8) to do good deeds
9) to talk nonsense
10) to redeem one's vow

2. Please translate the following from Chinese into English.

1）月貌花容
2）吉人自有天相
3）报恩
4）回心转意
5）权且充饥
6）旷野无人
7）战战兢兢
8）火眼金睛

3. Please translate each sentence with at least one key word or its derivative.

Key Words: plead, mount, defer, offend, scold

1）每周存点钱，你会惊喜地发现你的积蓄在快速增长。
2）他打断了别人的谈话，同样非常得罪人。
3）当他看到弟弟哀求的表情，心一下子就软了下来。

Unit 7
The Cadaver Demon Three Times Mocks Tripitaka Tang; The Holy Monk in Spite Banishes Handsome Monkey King (excerpt)

4）当我还是个小毛孩的时候，我从来没有骑过马，我爸爸却让我骑上马，在他身边飞驰，一点也不担心我。

5）她考试作弊被抓住，她的父母恳求再给她一次机会。

6）别理那孩子，你越是责骂他，他越是来劲调皮捣蛋。

7）如果所有其他办法都不奏效，我就采取强硬手段。

8）即便这些决定不能立刻得到政治上的支持，我也绝不会推迟执行这些决定。

9）每当我表现不乖的时候，就会挨父母的一顿训斥。

10）出于对老板的尊重，我拒绝讨论这件事。

After Reading

I. Please make a sentence with the words and expressions you have learnt from the text.

1. to exasperate:
2. to shove:
3. to be aghast at:
4. to cast aspersions on:
5. to be indebted to:

II. Paragraph Writing

1. Please write a paragraph of around 150 words about the main characteristics of the five major roles Tripitaka, Pilgrim, Eight Rules, Sha Monk, and Lady White Bone in the story.

2. Please write a paragraph of around 100 words with the following words and expressions you have learnt from the text. Make sure that the paragraph you have written is grammatically correct and coherent.

> bloom; charm; caress; graze; ice-white skin; perspire; slender

Original Edition in Chinese

尸魔三戏唐三藏　圣僧恨逐美猴王（节选）

……

　　好妖精，停下阴风，在那山凹里摇身一变，变作个月貌花容的女儿，左手提着一个青砂罐儿，右手提着一个绿磁瓶儿，从西向东而来。三藏见了，叫八戒，沙僧："悟空才说这里旷野无人，你看那里不走出一个人来了？"八戒道："等老猪去看看来。"那呆子放下钉钯，摆摆摇摇，充作个斯文气象，一直迎着那女子。真是个：

柳眉舒翠黛，杏眼闪银星。
月样容仪俏，天然性格清。
体似燕藏柳，声如莺啭林。
半放海棠笼晓日，才开芍药弄春晴。

　　那八戒一见，就动了凡心，叫道："女菩萨，往那里去？手里提着是甚么东西？"那女子连声答应道："长老，我这青罐里是香米饭，绿瓶里是炒面筋。特来此处无他故，因还誓愿要斋僧。"八戒闻言，满心欢喜。急抽身就跑了个猪颠风，报与三藏道："师父，吉人自有天相！师父叫师兄去化斋，那猴子不知那里摘桃儿耍子去了。桃子吃多了，有些嘈人。你看那不是个斋僧的来了？"唐僧道："我们走了这向，好人也不曾遇着一个，斋僧的从何而来？"八戒道："师父，这不到了！"三藏一见，连忙起身合掌道："女菩萨，你府上何处？有甚愿心，来此斋僧？"那妖精道："师父，此山叫做蛇回兽怕的白虎岭，正西下面是我家。我父母看经好善，丈夫更是个善人，一生好修桥补路，供佛斋僧。今幸有缘，遇着师父，敢将此饭奉上，权当一斋。"三藏也还在踌躇，怎当八戒馋虫拱动，他把个罐子提过来，正要动口。

　　只见那行者一个筋斗点将回来，睁火眼金睛观看，认得那女子是个妖精，放下钵盂，掣铁棒当头就打，唬得个长老用手扯住道："悟空，你走来打谁？"行者道："师父，你面前这个女子，莫当做个好人，他是个妖精，要来骗你哩！"三藏道："你这个猴头，这女菩萨有此善心，将这饭要斋我等，你怎么说他是个妖精？"行者笑道："师父，你那里认得。老孙在水帘洞内做妖魔时，若想人肉吃，便是这等变化迷人。我若来迟，你定遭他毒手。"唐僧那里肯信，只说是个好人。行者道："师父，我知道你见他那等容貌，必然动了凡心。若果有此意，就在这里搭个窝铺，你与他圆房成事，我们大家散火，却不是好？何必又取甚经去！"那长老原是个软善的人，吃他这句言语，羞得个满面通红。

　　行者又发起性来，掣铁棒望妖精劈头一下。那怪物有些手段，使个解尸法，真身预先走了，把一个假尸首打死在地下。唬得个长老战战兢兢，口中作念道："这猴着然无礼，无故伤人性命。"行者道："师父，你且来看看这瓶罐里是甚东西。"长老近前一看，那里是甚香米饭和面筋，却是一罐子长尾蛆，几个癞虾蟆满地乱跳。长老却有三分儿信了，怎禁猪八戒气不忿，在旁漏唆嘴道："这个女子是此间农妇，却怎么栽他是妖怪。哥哥把他打杀了；怕你念甚么《紧箍儿咒》，故意的使个障眼法儿，变做这样东西，演幌你眼哩！"

三藏自此一言，就是晦气到了，果然信那呆子撺掇，手中捻诀，口里念咒。行者就叫："头疼，头疼，莫念，莫念！有话便说。"唐僧道："有甚话说！出家人时时要行方便，念念不离善心。你怎么无故打死平人，取将经来何用？你回去罢。"行者道："师父，你教我回那里去？"唐僧道："我不要你做徒弟。"行者道："你不要我做徒弟，只怕你西天路去不成。"唐僧道："我命在天，终不然你救得我大限？你快回去！"行者道："师父，我回去便也罢了，只是不曾报得你的恩哩！"唐僧道："我与你有甚恩？"那大圣闻言，连忙跪下叩头道："老孙因大闹天宫，致下了伤身之难，被我佛压在两界山，幸观音菩萨与我受戒，幸师父救脱吾身。若不与你同上西天，显得我知恩不报非君子，万古千秋作骂名。"原来这唐僧是个慈悯的圣僧，他见行者哀告，却也回心转意道："既如此说，且饶你这一次，再休无礼。如再仍前作恶，这咒儿颠倒就念二十遍！"行者却才伏侍唐僧上马，又将摘来桃子奉上。唐僧在马上也吃了几个，权且充饥。

Text B

W.J.F. Jenner's Version

The Corpse Fiend Thrice Tricks Tang Sanzang; The Holy Monk Angrily Dismisses the Handsome Monkey King (excerpt)

......

The splendid evil spirit stopped its negative wind in a hollow and changed itself into a girl with a face as round as the moon and as pretty as a flower. Her brow was clear and her eyes beautiful; her teeth were white and her lips red. In her left hand she held a blue earthenware pot and in her right a green porcelain jar. She headed east towards the Tang Priest.

> *The holy monk rested his horse on the mountain,*
> *And suddenly noticed a pretty girl approaching.*
> *The green sleeves over her jade fingers lightly billowed;*
> *Golden lotus feet peeped under her trailing skirt.*
> *The beads of sweat on her powdered face were dew on a flower;*
> *Her dusty brow was a willow in a mist.*
> *Carefully and closely he watched her*
> *As she came right up to him.*

"Pig, Friar Sand," said Sanzang when he saw her, "don't you see somebody coming although Monkey said that this was a desolate and uninhabited place?" "You and Friar Sand stay sitting here while I go and take a look." The blockhead laid down his rake, straightened his tunic, put on the airs of a gentleman, and stared at the girl as he greeted her. Although he had not been sure from a distance, he could now see clearly that the girl had

> *Bones of jade under skin as pure as ice,*
> *A creamy bosom revealed by her neckline.*
> *Her willow eyebrows were black and glossy,*
> *And silver stars shone from her almond eyes.*
> *She was as graceful as the moon,*
> *As pure as the heavens.*
> *Her body was like a swallow in a willow-tree,*
> *Her voice like an oriole singing in the wood.*
> *An opening peony displaying her Charm,*
> *She was wild apple-blossom enmeshing the sun.*

When the idiot Pig saw how beautiful she was his earthly desires were aroused, and he could not hold back the reckless words that came to his lips. "Where are you going, Bodhisattva," he said, "and what's that you're holding?" Although she was obviously an evil fiend he could not realize it. "Venerable sir," the girl replied at once, "this blue pot is full of tasty rice, and the green jar contains fried gluten-balls. I've come here specially to fulfil a vow to feed monks." Pig was thoroughly delighted to hear this. He came tumbling back at breakneck speed and said to Sanzang, "Master, 'Heaven rewards the good'. When you sent my elder brother off begging because you felt hungry, that ape went fooling around somewhere picking peaches. Besides, too many peaches turn your stomach and give you the runs. Don't you see that this girl is coming to feed us monks?" "You stupid idiot," replied Sanzang, who was not convinced, "we haven't met a single decent person in this direction, so where could anyone come from to feed monks?" "What's she then, master?" said Pig.

When Sanzang saw her he sprang to his feet, put his hands together in front of his chest, and said, "Bodhisattva, where is your home? Who are you? What vow brings you here to feed monks?" Although she was obviously an evil spirit, the venerable Sanzang could not see it either. On being asked about her background by Sanzang, the evil spirit immediately produced a fine-sounding story with which to fool him. "This mountain, which snakes and wild animals won't go near, is called White Tiger Ridge," she said. "Our home lies due west from here at the foot of it. My mother and father live there, and they are devout people who read the scriptures and feed monks from far and near. As they had no son, they asked Heaven to bless them. When I was born they wanted to marry me off to a good family, but then they decided to find me a husband

Unit 7

The Cadaver Demon Three Times Mocks Tripitaka Tang; The Holy Monk in Spite Banishes Handsome Monkey King (excerpt)

who would live in our home to look after them in their old age and see them properly buried." "Bodhisattva, what you say can't be right," replied Sanzang. "The *Analects* say, 'When father and mother are alive, do not go on long journeys; if you have to go out, have a definite aim.' As your parents are at home and have found you a husband, you should let him fulfil your vow for you. Why ever are you walking in the mountains all by yourself, without even a servant? This is no way for a lady to behave." The girl smiled and produced a smooth reply at once: "My husband is hoeing with some of our retainers in a hollow in the north of the mountain, reverend sir, and I am taking them this food I've cooked. As it's July and all the crops are ripening nobody can be spared to run errands, and my parents are old, so I'm taking it there myself. Now that I have met you three monks from so far away, I would like to give you this food as my parents are so pious. I hope you won't refuse our paltry offering." "It's very good of you," said Sanzang, "but one of my disciples has gone to pick some fruit and will be back soon, so we couldn't eat any of your food. Besides, if we ate your food your husband might be angry with you when he found out, and we would get into trouble too." As the Tang Priest was refusing to eat the food, the girl put on her most charming expression and said, "My parents' charity to monks is nothing compared to my husband's, master. He is a religious man whose lifelong pleasure has been repairing bridges, mending roads, looking after the aged, and helping the poor. When he hears that I have given you this food, he'll love me more passionately than ever." Sanzang still declined to eat it. Pig was beside himself. Twisting his lips into a pout, he muttered indignantly, "Of all the monks on earth there can't be another as soft in the head as our master. He won't eat ready-cooked food when there are only three of us to share it between. He's waiting for that ape to come back, and then we'll have to split it four ways." Without allowing any more discussion he tipped the pot towards his mouth and was just about to eat.

At just this moment Brother Monkey was somersaulting back with his bowl full of the peaches he had picked on the southern mountain. When he saw with the golden pupils in his fiery eyes that the girl was an evil spirit, he put the bowl down, lifted his cudgel, and was going to hit her on the head when the horrified Sanzang held him back and said, "Who do you think you're going to hit?" "That girl in front of you is no good," he replied. "She's an evil spirit trying to make a fool of you." "In the old days you had a very sharp eye, you ape," Sanzang said, "but this is nonsense. This veritable Bodhisattva is feeding us with the best of motives, so how can you call her an evil spirit?" "You wouldn't be able to tell, Master," said Monkey with a grin. "When I was an evil monster in the Water Curtain Cave I used to do that if I wanted a meal of human flesh. I would turn myself into gold and silver, or a country mansion, or liquor, or a pretty girl. Whoever was fool enough to be besotted with one of these would fall in love with me, and I would lure them into the cave, where I did what I wanted with them. Sometimes I ate them steamed and sometimes boiled, and what I couldn't finish I used to dry in the sun against a rainy day. If I'd been slower getting here, Master, you'd have fallen into her snare and she'd have finished you off." The Tang Priest refused to believe him and maintained that she was a good person. "I know you, Master," said Monkey. "Her pretty face must have made you feel randy. If that's the way you feel, tell Pig to fell a few trees and send Friar Sand look off to for some grass. I'll be the carpenter, and well build you a hut here that you and the girl can use as your bridal chamber. We can all go our own ways. Wouldn't marriage be a worthwhile way of living? Why bother plodding on to fetch some scriptures or other?" Sanzang, who had always been such a soft and virtuous man, was unable to take this. He was so embarrassed that he blushed from his shaven pate to his ears.

While Sanzang was feeling so embarrassed, Monkey flared up again and struck at the evil spirit's face. The fiend, who knew a trick or two, used a magic way of abandoning its body: when it saw Monkey's cudgel coming it braced itself and fled, leaving a false corpse lying dead on the ground. Sanzang shook with terror and said to himself, "That monkey is utterly outrageous. Despite all my good advice he will kill people for no reason at all." "Don't be angry, Master," said Monkey. "Come and see what's in her pot." Friar Sand helped Sanzang over to look, and he saw that so far from containing tasty rice it was full of maggots with long tails. The jar had held not gluten-balls but frogs and toads, which were now jumping around on the ground. Sanzang was now beginning to believe Monkey. This was not enough, however, to prevent a furious Pig from deliberately making trouble by saying, "Master, that girl was a local countrywoman who happened to meet us while she was taking some food to the fields. There's no reason to think that she was an evil spirit. My elder brother was trying his club out on her, and he killed her by mistake. He's deliberately trying to trick us by magicking the food into those things because he's afraid you'll recite the Band-tightening Spell. He's fooled you into not saying it."

This brought the blindness back on Sanzang, who believed these trouble-making remarks and made the magic with his hand as he recited the spell. "My head's aching, my head's aching," Monkey said. "Stop, please stop. Tell me off if you like." "I've nothing to say to you," replied Sanzang. "A man of religion should always help others, and his thoughts should always be virtuous. When sweeping the floor you must be careful not to kill any ants, and to spare the moth you should put gauze round your lamp. Why do you keep murdering people? If you are going to kill innocent people like that there is no point in your going to fetch the scriptures. Go back!" "Where am I to go back to?" Monkey asked. "I won't have you as my disciple any longer," said Sanzang. "If you won't have me as your disciple," Monkey said, "I'm afraid you may never reach the Western Heaven." "My destiny is in Heaven's hands," replied Sanzang. "If some evil spirit is fated to cook me, he will; and there's no way of getting out of it. But if I'm not to be eaten, will you be able to extend my life? Be off with you at once." "I'll go if I must," said Monkey, "but I'll never have repaid your kindness to me." "What kindness have I ever done you?" Sanzang asked. Monkey knelt down and kowtowed. "When I wrecked the Heavenly Palace," he said, "I put myself in a very dangerous position, and the Buddha crushed me under the Double Boundary Mountain. Luckily the Bodhisattva Guanyin administered the vows to me, and you, Master, released me, so if I don't go with you to the Western Heaven I'll look like a 'scoundrel who doesn't return a kindness, with a name that will be cursed for ever'." As Sanzang was a compassionate and holy monk this desperate plea from Monkey persuaded him to relent. "In view of what you say I'll let you off this time, but don't behave so disgracefully again. If you are ever as wicked as that again I shall recite that spell twenty times over." "Make it thirty if you like," replied Monkey. "I shan't hit anyone else." With that he helped Sanzang mount the horse and offered him some of the peaches he had picked. After eating a few the Tang Priest felt less hungry for the time being.

Notes on the Text

1. **About the text**

   The present text is taken from *Journey to the West* translated by W. J. F. Jenner, published by Foreign Languages Press in 2011.

2. **W. J. F. Jenner**

   W.J.F. Jenner (born in 1940) is an English sinologist, specializing in Chinese history and culture, and translator of Chinese literature. From 1958 to 1962, he studied sinology at Oxford, and wrote his dissertation about the history of Luoyang in the 5th and 6th century. He translated the well-known Chinese classic novel *Journey to the West*, Lu Xun's work *Selected Poems*, Ding Ling's work *Miss Sophie's Diary and Other Stories*, and so on.

Unit 8

Pursuing the Dream

Reading Guide

    This text is excerpted from Scene 12 "Pursuing the Dream" in *The Peony Pavilion*, translated by Cyril Birch. Cyril Birch is a translator and the Professor of Chinese and Comparative Literature at the University of California, Berkeley. Written in 1598 by Tang Xianzu, *The Peony Pavilion* is one of the most memorable love stories in Chinese literary canon and a masterpiece of Ming drama. Its heroine, Bridal Du, is a cloistered girl who dreams of love, then dies pining for her dream suitor. Returning to earth in ghostly form, she is restored to life through the devotion of a young scholar. *The Peony Pavilion* not only presents a love story, but also tackles psychological and social issues. It gives a panoramic view of the 16th century Chinese society. The play has a dramatic personae of social strata, ranking from the emperor to the farmers, from high-ranking officials to rascals, from foreign merchants to Tartar invaders, from nuns to prostitutes. Imagination runs from the human world to the underworld. *The Peony Pavilion* was not introduced to Europe until the early 20th century. H. Acton translated one scene of the play into English in 1939. The first complete English translation was done by Cyril Birch and published by Indiana University Press in 1980.

    This excerpt is a well-known and representative episode from *The Peony Pavilion*, which depicts the change of Bridal Du's mood from being excited to chase her lover, the young scholar Liu Mengmei in the garden to being melancholy for suddenly discovering that the love was only in a dream, and to finally being hopeless and longing for death. This episode is worth reading because of its penetrating depiction of a maid's yearning for love. Cyril Birch has captured all the elegance, lyricism, and subtle, earthy humor of this panoramic tale of romance and Chinese society.

Unit 8
Pursuing the Dream

Before Reading

I. Preview Requirements: Please make a preparatory research on the background information, key words and phrases of this text.
1. Do research on the translator Cyril Birch.
2. Do research on Romanticism. Try to define Romanticism and find out its main characteristics. Find out about Romanticism and the representative romantic literary works in English literature.
3. Do research on the feudal ethical codes, especially Cheng and Zhu Neo-Confucianism. Try to find out what influence they had on women in the Ming and Qing Dynasties.
4. Do research on the three waves of feminist movements in the Western world.
5. Please make a comparison between Bridal Du in *Peony Pavilion* and Juliet in *Romeo and Juliet*.
6. Do research on Kunqu Opera of China.
7. Find and study the new words in the text such as *bind, envision, despair, fragile,* and *turmoil*.
8. Learn the useful expressions in the text such as *make a pretense of, ponder on, let off, in exchange for, in charge of, in response, at will, at play, fold away, prop up, lure into, chance by, drag behind, moan for, keep company with,* and *twist and turn.*

II. Preview Questions: Please answer some questions about the understanding of the main content of the text.
1. What did the Madam forbid Bridal Du to do according to Fragrance's monologue at the beginning of this episode? Why did the Madam ask Fragrance to make a vow?
2. Did Bridal Du have a good sleep last night? Why or why not?
3. When Fragrance told Bridal Du that it was the Madam's order that Bridal Du should eat an early breakfast, how did Bridal Du respond? What can we learn about her through her response?
4. When Fragrance went away after serving the breakfast, where did Bridal Du go in such a hurry and what for? How did she find the scene there?
5. What barriers did Bridal Du have to overcome to pursue her dream in the garden? What did this imply about Bridal Du?
6. When Fragrance left the garden, what did Bridal Du do in the garden? How did she find the scene like the peony pavilion and the buds of peony in the garden at first and at last? What brought about the sudden change in her mood?
7. At the climax of this episode, Bridal Du counted it a great fortune to be buried beside the flowering apricot and wished that she could choose to live or die at will like the flowers and herbs. Was she talking about life or death only?

8. What did Bridal Du grieve when she found her lover in the dream was nowhere to be found? What atmosphere did the birdcall help to create?
9. Was Fragrance able to understand Bridal Du's joy and sorrow? What can we know about the conditions of the maids at that time through the role of Fragrance? How do you describe the differences between Bridal Du and Fragrance?
10. How did Bridal Du's attitude toward her own situation change throughout this episode?
11. What does "Pursuing the Dream" imply about Bridal Du's attitude toward love? Is it passive or active? What role does this episode play in the whole story of *The Peony Pavilion*?

Text A

Cyril Birch's Version

Pursuing the Dream

SPRING FRAGRANCE:
I Wash the sleep from your eyes, prop up your hair
 with pins bound in rhino hide.
 Rising early to serve milady
 sleepily stumble
 by the closet
 through the boudoir
 past the painted screen.

 Miss Fragrance, an [as] it please [pleases] you,
 milady's maid alway;
 but a tomcat of a tutor
 hindered the mice at play
 till my mistress, stirred by the Songs,
 found an auspicious day
 and dragging me behind her
 to the garden made her way.
 Now Madam finds her snoozing,
 asks what the matter be,
 scolds our dear young lady,
 then takes it out on me.
 What can I say but "sorry,

no more of such liberty"

—but will Madam let me off

without solemn vow? Not she!

VOICE *(from offstage)*:

And what sort of a vow did you have to make, Fragrance?

FRAGRANCE:

"If I trouble my mistress again

may I never find a man of my own."

A crow in charge of a phoenix

—what can I do but moan?

Nightlong my mistress tosses,

greets the dawn with a groan,

mumbling away to herself

while bright the day has grown.

VOICE :

Hurry up with the young mistress' breakfast!

FRAGRANCE:

Word from the kitchen: breakfast's ready.

Tea for milady—forward—steady!

BRIDAL DU *(enters)*:

IIa Curves of arching hills—

the paint wears from my brows.

What made my fragile limbs

twist and turn all night beneath the coverlet?

Why so weary? No late moon gazing

kept me from my rest.

Is it concern for falling blossoms

draws my dawn thoughts to the garden?

A hazy dream of petal-scented love

threw my maiden thoughts into a turmoil

A wakeful night, watching the flickering lamp,

scolding my maid, whom nothing could arouse.

Yesterday, a random spring stroll—who was it I met in my dream? So close we were, so loving, I was sure this was my life's true love. Now, when I quietly ponder on what passed, my spirits sink and I despair. Ah, pity me, pity me! *(She grieves)*

FRAGRANCE *(enters with breakfast tray)*:
   "Grains of rice the rare parrot pecked off,"
   tea in a "partridge-speckled bowl."
Please to eat your breakfast.
BRIDAL:
   What mind have I for that!
   IIb Morning toilet just completed,
   mirror stand not yet folded away,
   all seems flat and flavorless;
   how am I to swallow this?
FRAGRANCE:
   Madam's orders, you are to eat an early breakfast.
BRIDAL:
   You use my mother as a threat
   against one who truly starves!
Tell me, how are people really supposed to eat?
FRAGRANCE:
   Three meals a day.
BRIDAL:
   Ha! What strength have I to lift this bowl?
   I can make only a pretense of eating
—take it away and eat it yourself.
FRAGRANCE:
   Give me the breakfast leftovers
   and keep your paint and rouge.
                              (Exit)
BRIDAL:
   Fragrance has left me. Ah Heaven, how stately were the pools and pavilions where yesterday my dream took place. How I long for that bygone dream in exchange for this new-found sorrow! Pursuing my thoughts through endless twistings, all night I lay sleepless. Now I can seize my chance to give Fragrance the slip and search the garden alone. *(She grieves)* Ah, for me, truly,
   in dreams "no fluttering side by side
   of splendid phoenix wings,
   between hearts the one minute thread
   from root to tip of the magic horn.1" [①]
                    (She begins to walk)
Here is the garden. Luckily the gate is wide open and the gardener is nowhere to be seen.

See how the ground is carpeted with fallen petals!

IIIa Never till now did spring so stir the heart.
High and low over the plastered walls
no place but springtime longings dance and fly.
(She stumbles)

Oh, the hawthorn catching at my skirt—
like my heart, it will not let me leave.

And this little meander of a stream! Can it be that

IIIb faery lovers trace again
the source of the Peach Blossom Spring?
Here too flying petals fleck the ripples.
The Lord of Heaven need pay the florist nothing,
but for us below, what grief for fallen blossoms
as springtime passes unfulfilled!

FRAGRANCE *(enters)*:
By going off for breakfast I lost my young mistress. I have sought her everywhere—ah, so here you are.

IVa So graceful a pose
beneath the trailing apricot branches.
But what brings you
so early to the garden all alone?

BRIDAL:
Before the gilded porticoes,
in deep shade spying on nesting swallows—
aimless steps have carried me to these wonders.

FRAGRANCE:
But should your mother chance by,
what a start to find an empty boudoir—
"Where does my daughter wander,
where does my daughter wander?"

BRIDAL *(annoyed)*:
IVb If she did find out

I suppose she'd call it "youthful fancy."

FRAGRANCE:
>A bit too fancy—keep it plain.

BRIDAL:
>How they bully me,
>turning a simple garden
>into a forbidden paradise.

FRAGRANCE:
>If I may be so bold—
this was the mistress' orders—
>spring should be met with a busy needle,
>stronger incense, an active writing brush.

BRIDAL:
>What else did she tell you?

FRAGRANCE:
>In this deserted garden
>hobgoblins and trolls abound:
>back now to small secluded court,
>back now to small secluded court!

BRIDAL:
>I understand. Be sure to find my mother now, and tell her I shall follow immediately.

FRAGRANCE:
>Wild flowers by the step recognize their mistress,
>but "the parrot irked by the cage knows how to scold."

(Exit)

BRIDAL:
>Now that my maid is gone I can pursue my dream.
> V Rock garden above the pool,
>>path by tree-peony pavilion.
>>Buds of peony inset along the balustrade,
>>strand by strand willows hover,
>>string by string elm seeds dangle—
>>offerings of coins to mourn the spring!

Ah, but what a story there is to tell of yesterday, when the young scholar sought a poem on his willow branch, before he forced our union of delight!
> VI Of whose house was this youth whose sudden visit
>>lured secluded maid deep into garden?
>>And then—though words must falter—
>>he touched my face;

    such loving pains he took
    and I, I moved my lips
    wishing to speak.
How pleasing I found him, my young scholar,
 VII though ours no loving bond from former life,
    nor all my life had I ever glimpsed his face.
    Can it be in my next life he is fated to appear,
    in this life only a dream?
    So like to life was this young scholar
    who took my life into his arms. ②
How my longings stir to recall that moment!
VIII Against the weathered rock
    he leaned my wilting body,
    then as he laid my jade limbs down
    "smoke issued from jade in warmth of sun." ③
    By balustrade
    past swing
    there I spread the folds of my skirt,
    a covering for earth
    for fear of the eyes of Heaven.
    Then it was we knew
    perfect mystery
    of joy ineffable.
And when my dream had reached the summit of delight, there came flower petals scattering down!
 IX Tense in his eagerness
    he put his lips to the fragrance of my shoulder
    while I with thoughtful ease responded to him.
    Soon the bright mirror of my mind was clouded
    to envision such an event,
    such a sweet melting.
    Ha! Falling from air, red shadows,
    petals torn from heart of flower!
    Was I fettered by my own dreaming spirit?
Alas, I seek and seek, but nothing remains. The pavilion of the tree peonies, the peony balustrade, how can they stand so chill and lonely, no sign of human presence? How sad they make me! (*She weeps*)
 X So wild a place, no other hut or kiosk near,

  so hard to seek, eyes misty with love.
  Under clear white sun and bright blue sky,
  how can I grasp what happened in a dream?
  For a flash it is there before me,
  I linger, circling, doubting,
  but here, here he crushed my gold bracelet to the ground!
Should I see him again,
  could it be false?

 XI Somehow I can picture him before me.
  Slowly, slowly he appears,
  then lightly, lightly fades.
  But gone not far—
  before clouds disperse and rain dries away,
  he will return among flowers, beneath willows.
  From yesterday to today
  before my eyes as in my heart,
  the couch of love transforms upon the instant.

Let me linger another moment. (She looks up) Why! In a place where no one comes, suddenly I find a great flowering apricot, beautiful with its thick clusters of fruit.

 XII How can its fragrance spread so clear,
  its shade like a parasol reach full around?
  Thriving in this third month of spring
  "when rich rain swells the red to bursting,"
  its leaves shine glossy green,
  its full round fruit hide bitter heart.
  Here shaded from the sun
  I may find again a dream of Luofu.④

So be it: I am so drawn to this flowering apricot, I should count it a great good fortune to be buried here beside it when I die.

XIII My heart is strangely drawn
  to this apricot's side.
  Just as we please ourselves
  which flower or herb we most love,
  ah, could we only live or die at will,
  then who would moan for bitter pain?
  Let me commit my fragrant spirit,
  though rains be dank and drear,
  to keep company with this apricot's roots.

       (She sinks wearily to the ground)

FRAGRANCE *(enters)*:
    Off by spring pavilion she "hunts for kingfisher feathers."
    To freshen the noontime court, her maid adds
    incense to the burner.
So, my young mistress is tired from her stroll and is drowsing under this flowering apricot.
XIVa How has your garden roaming
    brought you to rest against this apricot's side?

BRIDAL:
    I raised my eyes,
    its branches filled my vision,
    and heartache overcame me.

                      (She weeps)

BRIDAL, FRAGRANCE:
    What reason for this grief,
    what cause for secret tears?

FRAGRANCE:
    What is troubling you, mistress?

BRIDAL:
XIVb Spring bade adieu,
    we gazed, but found no word to say
    and I, I too
    would snap a sprig of willow
    to question Heaven's will
    but now, now I must grieve
    that I could make no poem in response.

FRAGRANCE:
    What does this riddle mean?

BRIDAL, FRAGRANCE:
    What reason for this grief,
    what cause for secret tears?

FRAGRANCE:
    Let's go now.

BRIDAL *(moving away, then pausing)*:
XIVc Slower, before we leave
    let me still linger a while.

                    (Offstage, a birdcall)

    Listen, the late-spring cuckoo
    "better go back" he calls.

Must I choose

if I would come to this garden again

between short sleep of dream

and longer sleep of death?

BRIDAL, FRAGRANCE:

What reason for this grief,

what cause for secret tears?

FRAGRANCE:

Here we are, now come with me to see your mother.

BRIDAL:

SO, SO.

XV Half in a swoon I am brought to painted walkways

to inquire after the health of my lady mother.

Ah, Bridal, Bridal,

"the blossoming branch mocks her who sleeps alone."

Envoi:

BRIDAL:

Where to seek him

who at Wuling found faery love?

FRAGRANCE:

Affections of a wanderer

so soon out of mind.

BRIDAL:

Time after time to come

when dreams of spring arise,

FRAGRANCE:

sad thoughts of what might have been

forever bind the heart.

Notes from the Original Text:

① Quotation from Li Shangyin (about 812—858), the first word only changed from "body" to "dream"; translation by A. C. Graham. The "magic horn" is the unicorn's.

② The original includes the word "life" (*sheng*) in every line: for the playwright, *sheng* has basic philosophical implications.

③ A magical transformation alluded to in Li Shangyin's poem "The Patterned Lute".

④ Allusion to a Tang story (traditionally attributed to Liu Zongyuan, whom our hero claims as his ancestor) of a man who woke from drinking to find himself beneath a flowering apricot which the day before had been a beautiful woman.

Unit 8
Pursuing the Dream

Notes on the Text

1. Boudoir

Boudoir is a maid's bedroom, where the maid lives and eats, practices needlework and studies poems and etiquettes. In the ancient times, the maid in the house was forbidden to go outside unless she was to greet her relatives, worship the Buddha or appreciate the lantern in Double Seven Day. The girls walking in the street were usually of low social status like the servant girls.

2. Phoenix

Phoenix is referred to as the king of birds in Chinese culture. It is an important element in Chinese culture, which symbolizes auspiciousness and harmony.

3. Young scholar

Before the Song Dynasty, the young scholars were mostly from families of higher social classes like landlords or bureaucratic families because of the high cost of education. However, there were examples of those young scholars who were of humble births, wishing to change their destiny through taking the imperial examinations. There were many ways for young scholars to make a living. For example, if they succeeded in the imperial examination, it was highly likely that they served as imperial officials; if they didn't, they could teach in the old-style private schools, sell their paintings, be private advisers and so on.

4. Heaven

Heaven here refers to the place where the gods live. "Questioning Heaven" shows people's desperate wish to get some enlightenment from the supernatural powers.

5. Wuling

Wuling is described as a secluded heavenly place embodying beauty, peace and harmony in a well-known essay *Peach Blossom Spring* written by Tao Yuanming in the Eastern Jin Dynasty.

Glossary

auspicious /ɔːˈspɪʃəs/ *adj.* showing signs that sth. is likely to be successful in the future
e.g.: *His career as a playwright had an auspicious start.*

bracelet /ˈbreɪslət/ *n.* a piece of jewellery worn around the wrist or arm
e.g.: *A gold bracelet dangled from his left wrist.*

bully /ˈbʊli/ *v.* to frighten or hurt a weaker person; to use your strength or power to make sb. do sth.
bully sb. into sth./into doing sth. e.g.: *I won't be bullied into signing anything.*

despair /dɪˈspeə(r)/ *v.* to lose hope or be without hope
e.g.: *He began to despair of ever finding a job.*

disperse /dɪˈspɜːs/ *v.* 1. to move apart and go away in different directions; to make sb./sth.

		do this
		e.g.: *The crowd dispersed quickly.*
		2. to spread or to make sth. spread over a wide area
		e.g.: *The seeds are dispersed by the wind.*
envision /ɪnˈvɪʒn/		*v.* to imagine what a situation will be like in the future, especially a situation you intend to work towards
		e.g.: *They envision an equal society, free of poverty and disease.*
fetter /ˈfetə(r)/		*v.* (*literary*) to restrict sb.'s freedom to do what they want
		e.g.: *The black mud fettered her movements.*
fragile /ˈfrædʒaɪl/		*adj.* 1. easily broken or damaged
		e.g.: *fragile glass/bones*
		2. not strong and likely to become ill/sick
		e.g.: *Her father is now 86 and in fragile health.*
grieve /griːv/		*v.* to feel very sad, especially because sb. has died
		grieve for/over sb./sth. e.g.: *They are still grieving for their dead child.*
incense /ˈɪnsens/		*n.* a substance that produces a pleasant smell when you burn it, used particularly in religious ceremonies
		e.g.: *The musty aroma of incense made her head swim.*
ineffable /ɪnˈefəbl/		*adj.* (*formal*) too great or beautiful to describe in words
		e.g.: *The beauty of a sunset is ineffable.*
irk /ɜːk/		*v.* (*literary*) to annoy or irritate sb.
		e.g.: *Her flippant tone irked him.*
lure /lʊə(r)/		*v.* to persuade or trick sb. to go somewhere or to do sth. by promising them a reward
		lure sb. into e.g.: *The child was lured into a car but managed to escape.*
meander /miˈændə(r)/		*n.* a curve of a river or stream
		e.g.: *At least he had remembered "broad meander valley", while looking at this map.*
moan /məʊn/		*v.* 1. to make a long deep sound, usually expressing unhappiness, suffering or sexual pleasure
		e.g.: *The injured man was lying on the ground, moaning.*
		2. (*informal*) to complain about sth. in a way that other people find annoying
		moan (on) about sth. (to sb.) e.g.: *What are you moaning on about now?*
mock /mɒk/		*adj.* to laugh at sb./sth. in an unkind way, especially by copying what they say or do
		e.g.: *He's always mocking my French accent.*
ponder /ˈpɒndə(r)/		*v.* (*formal*) to think about sth. carefully for a period of time

		ponder about/on/over sth. e.g.: *She pondered over his words.*
secluded /sɪˈkluːdɪd/		*adj.* 1. (of a place) quiet and private; not used or disturbed by other people
		e.g.: *a secluded garden/beach/spot*
		2. without much contact with other people
		e.g.: *He is incommunicado in a secluded cottage in Wales.*
snap /snæp/		*v.* 1. to break sth. suddenly with a sharp noise; to be broken in this way
		e.g.: *The wind had snapped the tree into two.*
		2. to speak or say sth. in an impatient, usually angry, voice
		snap at sb./sth. e.g.: *I was tempted to snap back angrily at him.*
turmoil /ˈtɜːmɔɪl/		*n.* a state of great anxiety and confusion
		e.g.: *His statement threw the court into turmoil.*
weary /ˈwɪəri/		*adj.* 1. very tired, especially after you have been working hard or doing sth. for a long time
		e.g.: *She suddenly felt old and weary.*
		2. (*formal*) no longer interested in or enthusiastic about sth.
		weary of sth./of doing sth. e.g.: *Students soon grow weary of listening to a parade of historical facts.*

While Reading

I. Please fill in the blanks with the words in the parentheses with the appropriate part of speech.

1. She resorted to stealing food out of _____. (desperate)
2. People need time to _____ after the death of a loved one. (grief)
3. There were throes of love within her, of aspiration, of an _____ delight in being. (ineffability)
4. This building plan makes a _____ of the government's environmental policy. (mock)
5. They enjoyed ten days of peace and _____. (seclude)
6. He was _____ of the constant battle between them. (wear)
7. Countries which prefer to rely on America are happy to maintain the _____. (pretend)
8. People have to move to other areas in _____ of work. (pursue)
9. Her father was a quiet man with _____ manners. (grace)
10. The old man turned off the wireless, and went on listening _____ to his wife. (affection)

II. Please choose one word or phrase that best completes the sentence.

1. He went down to the shore of the sea, and began to _____ what he should do.
   A. ponder on   B. give up
   C. fold away   D. let off

2. We forget that they are our brothers and sisters and treat them as objects that can be destroyed _____.
   A. at heart
   B. at will
   C. at first
   D. at play

3. We _____ a parent to care for us, to forgive our errors, to save us from our childish mistakes.
   A. moan for
   B. allow for
   C. long for
   D. answer for

4. I am _____ sustaining the first-aid centre with blood plasma.
   A. in response to
   B. in exchange for
   C. in honor of
   D. in charge of

5. There is one thing that people can't _____ from you, and that is your wisdom.
   A. take out
   B. take away
   C. take in
   D. take on

6. They waited for an impossible dream to turn real, for a demon to _____ an angel.
   A. turn into
   B. turn around
   C. turn over
   D. turn out

III. Translation

1. Please translate the following from English into Chinese.

1) to mumble away to oneself
2) solemn vow
3) to twist and turn all night
4) to throw one's maiden thoughts into a turmoil
5) to stir the heart
6) a young scholar
7) former life
8) strand by strand
9) no sign of human presence
10) a bright blue sky
11) for a flash
12) to linger a while

2. Please translate the following from Chinese into English.

1）乌鸦管的（得）凤凰
2）如遇平生
3）一日三餐
4）寻思展（辗）转
5）梦无彩凰双飞翼
6）心有灵犀一点通
7）残红满地
8）小庭深院
9）生生死死随（遂）人愿
10）罢了
11）系心肠
12）眼连天

3. Please translate each sentence with at least one key word or its derivative.

Key Words: lure, drag, snap, envision, moan

1）她经不起金钱的引诱，被拉下水了。

2）他抓住她的手臂把她拖进房间。
3）我们中又有谁从未因受到感动而去抓拍地平线上的夕阳、流动的河流以及春天的花朵？
4）这些发明能够使资本家无法想象的事情成为可能。
5）很多人抱怨停车难的问题。
6）尽管经济萧条，但是一些电影大片还是让美国的影迷们在圣诞节期间走进了电影院。
7）如果不喜欢自己的生活，靠自己去改变。果真能做到，就会发生你预想中的改变。
8）即使是一个错误都可以拖累你的生活，你可以想象一下坏习惯能带来多大的危害。
9）当我走进房间，我看到室友坐在地板上呻吟。
10）他啪的一声把那根树枝折断了。

After Reading

I. Please make a sentence with the words and expressions you have learnt from the text.

1. to make a pretense of:
2. to keep company with:
3. to envision:
4. to spy on:
5. to ponder on:

II. Paragraph Writing

1. Please write a paragraph of around 150 words about the main characteristics of the two major roles Fragrance and Bridal Du in the story.

2. Please write a paragraph of around 100 words of Bridal Du's monologue in the garden with the following words and expressions you have learnt from the text. Make sure that the paragraph you have written is grammatically correct and coherent.

> turmoil; recall; scatter; seek; linger

Original Edition in Chinese

寻 梦

【夜游宫】（贴上）腻脸朝云罢盥，倒犀簪斜插双鬟。侍香闺起早，睡意阑珊；衣桁前，妆阁畔，画屏间。

　　伏侍千金小姐，丫鬟一位春香。请过猫儿师父，不许老鼠放光。侥幸《毛诗》感动，小姐吉日时良。拖带春香遣闷，后花园里游芳。谁知小姐瞌睡，恰遇着夫人问当。絮了小姐一会，要与春香一场。春香无言知罪，以后劝止娘行。夫人还是不放，少不得发咒禁当。（内介）春香姐，发个甚咒来？（贴）敢再跟娘胡撞，教春香即世里不见儿郎。虽然一时抵对，乌鸦管的凤凰？一夜小姐焦躁，起来促水朝妆。由他自言自语，日高花影纱窗。（内介）快请小姐早膳。（贴）报道官厨饭热，且去传递茶汤。（下）

【月儿高】（旦上）几曲屏山展，残眉黛深浅。为甚衾儿里不住的柔肠转？这憔悴非关爱月眠迟倦，可为惜花，朝起庭院？

　　忽忽花间起梦情，女儿心性未分明。无眠一夜灯明灭，分煞梅香唤不醒。昨日偶尔春游，何人见梦。绸缪顾盼，如遇平生。独坐思量，情殊怅恍。真个可怜人也。（闷介）（贴捧茶食上）香饭盛来鹦鹉粒，清茶擎出鹧鸪斑。小姐早膳哩。（旦）咱有甚心情也！

【前腔】梳洗了才匀面，照台儿未收展。睡起无滋味，茶饭怎生咽？（贴）夫人分付，早饭要早。（旦）你猛说夫人，则待把饥人劝。你说为人在世，怎生叫做吃饭？（贴）一日三餐。（旦）咳，甚瓯儿气力与擎拳！生生的了前件。

　　你自拿去吃便了。（贴）受用余杯冷炙，胜如剩粉残膏。（下）（旦）春香已去。天呵，昨日所梦，池亭俨然。只图旧梦重来，其奈新愁一段。寻思展转，竟夜无眠。咱待乘此空闲，背却春香，悄向花园寻看。（悲介）哎也！似咱这般，正是：梦无彩凤双飞翼，心有灵犀一点通。（行介）一径行来，喜的园门洞开，守花的都不在。则这残红满地呵！

【懒画眉】最撩人春色是今年。少甚么低就高来粉画垣，原来春心无处不飞悬。（绊介）哎，睡荼䕷抓住裙衩线，恰便是花似人心好处牵。

　　这一湾流水呵！

Unit 8
Pursuing the Dream

【前腔】为甚呵玉真重溯武陵源？也则为水点花飞在眼前。是天公不费买花钱，则咱人心上有题红怨。咳，辜负了春三二月天。

（贴上）吃饭去，不见了小姐，则得一径寻来。呀，小姐，你在这里！

【不是路】何意婵娟，小立在垂垂花树边。才朝膳，个人无伴怎游园？（旦）画廊前，深深蓦见衔泥燕，随步名园是偶然。（贴）娘回转，幽闺窄地教人见，那些儿闲串？那些儿闲串？
【前腔】（旦作恼介）哇，偶尔来前，道的咱偷闲学少年。（贴）咳，不偷闲，偷淡。（旦）欺奴善，把护春台都猜做谎桃源。（贴）敢胡言，这是夫人命，道春多刺绣宜添线，润逼炉香好腻笺。（旦）还说甚来？（贴）这荒园垒，怕花妖木客寻常见。去小庭深院，去小庭深院！

（旦）知道了。你好生答应夫人去，俺随后便来。（贴）"闲花傍砌如依主，娇鸟嫌笼会骂人。"（下）
（旦）丫头去了，正好寻梦。

【忒忒令】那一答可是湖山石边，这一答似牡丹亭畔。嵌雕阑芍药芽儿浅，一丝丝垂杨线，一丢丢榆荚钱。线儿春甚金钱吊转！

呀，昨日那书生将柳枝要我题咏，强我欢会之时，好不话长！

【嘉庆子】是谁家少俊来近远，敢迤逗这香闺去沁园？话到其间腼腆。他捏这眼，奈烦也天；咱嗽这口，待酬言。
【尹令】那书生可意呵，咱不是前生爱眷，又素乏平生半面。则道来生出现，乍便今生梦见。生就个书生，恰恰生生抱咱去眠。

那些好不动人春意也。

【品令】他倚太湖石，立着咱玉婵娟。待把俺玉山推倒，便日暖玉生烟。捱过雕阑，转过秋千，掯着裙花展。敢席着地，怕天瞧见。好一会分明，美满幽香不可言。

梦到正好时节，甚花片儿吊下来也！

【豆叶黄】他兴心儿紧咽咽，呜着咱香肩。俺可也慢掂掂做意儿周旋。等闲间把一个照人儿昏善，那般形现，那般软绵。忑一片撒花心的红影儿，吊将来半天。敢是咱梦魂儿厮缠？

咳！寻来寻去，都不见了！牡丹亭，芍药阑，怎生这般凄凉冷落，杳无人迹？好不伤心也！（泪介）

【玉交枝】是这等荒凉地面，没多半亭台靠边，好是咱眯瞜色眼寻难见。明放着白日青天，猛教人抓不到魂梦前。霎时间有如活现，打方旋再得俄延，呀，是这答儿压黄金钏匾。

要再见那书生呵，

【月上海棠】怎赚骗，依稀想像人儿见。那来时茌苒，去也迁延。非远，那雨迹云踪才一转，敢依花傍柳还重现。昨日今朝，眼下心前，阳台一座登时变。

再消停一番。（望介）呀，无人之处，忽然大梅树一株，梅子磊磊可爱。

【二犯幺令】偏则他暗香清远，伞儿般盖的周全。他趁这，他趁这春三月红绽雨肥天，叶儿青。偏迸着苦仁儿里撒圆。爱煞这昼阴便，再得到罗浮梦边。

罢了，这梅树依依可人，我杜丽娘若死后，得葬于此，幸矣。

【江儿水】偶然间心似缱，梅树边。这般花花草草由人恋，生生死死随人愿，便酸酸楚楚无人怨。待打并香魂一片，阴雨梅天，守的个梅根相见。（倦坐介）

（贴上）佳人拾翠春亭远，侍女添香午院清。咳，小姐走乏了，梅树下眈。

【川拨棹】你游花院，怎靠着梅树偃？（旦）一时间望，一时间望眼连天，忽忽地伤心自怜。（泣介）（合）知怎生情怅然，知怎生泪暗悬？

（贴）小姐甚意儿？

【前腔】（旦）春归人面，整相看无一言，我待要折，我待要折的那柳枝儿问天，我如今悔不与题笺。（贴）这一句猜头儿是怎言？（合前）

（贴）去罢。（旦作行又住介）

【前腔】为我慢归休，缓留连。（内鸟啼介）听，听这不如归春暮天，难道我再，难道我再到这亭园，则挣的个长眠和短眠！（合前）

（贴）到了，和小姐瞧奶奶去。（旦）罢了。

【意不尽】软咍咍刚扶到画阑偏，报堂上夫人稳便。咱杜丽娘呵，少不得楼上花枝也则是照独眠。

（旦）武陵何处访仙郎？
（贴）只怪游人思易忘。
（旦）从此时时春梦里，
（贴）一生遗恨系心肠。

Text B

Wang Rongpei's Version

Seeking the Dream

(Enter Chunxiang)

Chunxiang:

*(To the tune of **Yeyougong**)*
  I wash my face at early dawn
  And put on hairpins in the morn.
  I serve the miss from morn till night
  With drowsy eyes in candlelight:
  Before the wardrobe,
  Beside the dressing-table,
  Between the painted screens.

I'm Chunxiang, maid to serve Miss Du. Miss Du has a tutor, who is like a cat watching over the mice. It happens that she was affected by the *Book of Poetry* and thus chose an auspicious day to have a walk in the back garden to while away the time. Miss Du was just dozing off when the madam dropped in. She scolded Miss Du and laid the blame on me. I kept silent and then promised never to do that again, but the madam would not let me off and I had to vow and swear.

Voice Within:

What did you vow and swear, Sister Chunxiang?

Chunxiang:

"If I should make trouble again," I said, " I would never be able to get married." Although I answered like that, how can a crow control a phoenix? Miss Du tossed and turned all night. She got up early this morning and urged me to fetch water for her to make up. She has been talking to herself all the time till now the sun is shining over the flowers and windows.

Voice Within:

Hurry up! It's time for Miss Du to have breakfast.

Chunxiang:

"*The cook has word for me*

To fetch the soup and tea."

(Exit Chunxiang)

(Enter Du Liniang)

Du Liniang:

*(To the tune of **Yueergao**)*

Like arching hills on painted screens,

My brows are drawn by various means.

Why couldn't quilts conceal my care?

The moon is not the thing I'd stare.

Isn't it the fallen bloom

That draws me from my room?

"*Among the flowers rose a dream*

That drove my thoughts to riotous stream.

I stayed awake with candlelight,

To watch my maid sleep well all night."

A random spring stroll yesterday brought me face to face with someone in the dream. I fixed my eyes on him as if he had been my true lover. When I sit alone thinking over the dream, I feel depressed. How piteous I am!

(In a depressed mood)

(Enter Chunxiang with tea and food)

Chunxiang:

"*The tray contains pearl-like rice*

And fragrant tea of costly price."

Breakfast is ready, Mistress.

Du Liniang:

I'm not in a mood for breakfast.

(To the previous tune)

I have just washed and done my face

And left the glass not yet in place.

I see life as a total waste;

How can I have a pleasant taste?

Chunxiang:

Orders from Madam that you have an early breakfast.

Du Liniang:

For you to use my mother's word

To push a hungry soul appears absurd.

Do you know how people eat to keep alive?

Chunxiang:

Three meals a day.

Du Liniang:

Alas,

    Not strong enough to hold the bowl,

    I've had enough as a hungry soul.

Take the breakfast away and have it by yourself.

Chunxiang:

    "*I would prefer the leftover food*

    To paints and rough that is no good."

    (*Exit Chunxiang*)

Du Liniang:

Chunxiang is gone at last. Oh heavens, the lake and the pavilion in yesterday's dream were real enough. I tried to relive the old dream but new disappointment ensued. I tossed and turned all night without a moment's sleep. Now that Chunxiang is gone, I'll take this opportunity to sneak into the garden and have a look.

    (*In a sad mood*)

Oops, I feel as if

    "*The dream displays no phoenix on the wing,*

    But links the yearning hearts with one tough string."

    (*Walks*)

Here's the garden. As luck has it, the gate is left open and the gardener is not here. How the ground is scattered with fallen petals!

    (*To the tune of **Lanhuamei***)

    This spring has strongly stirred my heart.

    High above the garden walls,

    The blooms and branches stretch and dart.

    (*Stumbles*)

    Oh, the raspberries are pulling at my skirt,

    As if they tried to grasp my heart and flirt.

How the streamlet flows!

    (*To the previous tune*)

    Why should lovers try to find the same old place?

    The blooms and streams must have left trace.

    For flowers, the heavens need not pay a cent

    But people cried o'er fallen petals

    As lovely spring thus came and went.

(*Enter Chunxiang*)

Chunxiang:
When I came back from breakfast, I lost sight of Miss Du. I have to look for her here and there. Oh, here you are, mistress!

(*To the tune of **Bushilu***)

How comes my pretty mistress stands

By plum trees with a twig in hands?

What brings you to this zone

So early in the morn alone?

Du Liniang:

On the corridor,

I saw the swallows build a nest

And followed them without a rest.

Chunxiang:

If Madam comes to you

And finds you out of view,

She'll say, "Where's she fooling around?

Where's she fooling around?"

Du Liniang:

(*Feigns to be annoyed*)

(*To the previous tune*)

I came here all by chance,

But you suggest I seek after leisure.

Chunxiang:
Well, you're not seeking after leisure, but after pleasure.

Du Liniang:

Don't treat me as a child

And say the garden's wild.

Chunxiang:

I dare not be so bold,

But Madam gave the order that

You do more needlework in spring

And scent the paper twofold.

Du Liniang:
What else did she say?

Chunxiang:

This garden is a haunted place,

With ghosts and demons all apace.

> Back to your secluded chambers!
>
> Back to your secluded chambers!

Du Liniang:

Yes, I see. You go first and make promise for me to my mother and I'll be back in no time.

Chunxiang:

> "*Wild flowers lie unstirred*
>
> *While caged birds utter foul word.*"
>
> *(Exit Chunxiang)*

Du Liniang:

Now that Chunxiang is gone, it's time for me to see my dream.

> *(To the tune of **Teteling**)*
>
> Here the lakeside rocks are piles,
>
> With Peony Pavilion lying wild.
>
> There the peonies dot the way;
>
> The twigs of willows sway;
>
> The elm fruits dangling from the trees
>
> Are mourning in the springtime breeze!

Oh, this is the place where the scholar asked me to write a poem in the name of willow twigs and forced me to make love with him. It's a long, long story!

> *(To the tune of **Jiaqingzi**)*
>
> Who was the handsome man
>
> That lured me through the garden tour?
>
> I felt shamed for sure.
>
> He stroked me, my eyes blurred;
>
> I tried to speak, but without a word.
>
> *(To the tune of **Yinling**)*

How enticing the scholar is!

> In my previous life I had not been his wife
>
> And never saw him in this life.
>
> In my afterlife I shall be his wife
>
> And dream appears first in this life.
>
> Overcome by his enticing charms,
>
> I left myself in his strong arms.

What a splendid moment!

> *(To the tune of **Pinling**)*
>
> He leaned against the rocks and stones;
>
> I stood beside him with faint groans.
>
> He pulled me softly to the ground,

Permeated with springtime warmth around.
Above the fence,
Across the swing,
My skirt spread out from hence.
We lay on grass and faced the sky,
But what if heavens should spy?
It was eternal time
That we enjoyed life's prime.

At the best time of the dream, some petals dropped from the flowers!

(*To the tune of* **Douyehuang**)
He grew much bolder
And kissed my shoulder.
I played with him in little haste,
But soon became less graced,
Soft and tender
With a sensual taste.
But floral rains that gleam
Bewildered me in my sweet dream.

Alas, here and there I seek my dream, but I've found nothing. The Peony Pavilion, the rose grove, how can they be so desolate! How can they be so lifeless! How the sight breaks my heart!

(*Weeps*)

(*To the tune of* **Yujiaozhi**)
In a place forlorn,
Without pavilions far and near,
How is it that I can neither see nor hear?
In the broad daylight,
I fail to find the dreamland sight.
The visions flash before my eye
And would not linger though I try.
Well, it's here that we meet and sigh.

Oh that I see my man again!

(*To the tune of* **Yueshanghaitang**)
How can I explain
Why he appears again?
How he comes at leisured pace;
There he leaves without a trace.
He is not far away—

Before the rain and cloud disperse,
Behind the blooms I see him stay.
At this time yesterday,
On this very spot,
I was transformed and went astray.
I'll stay here for another moment.

(*Looks around*)

Why! In this lonely place where no one comes, a huge plum tree stands before me, hanging with lovely fruits.

(*To the tune of* **Erfanyaoling**)

How can its fragrance spread
And its leaves crown like a shed?
When plums are ripe and rain is clean,
The vernal leaves are thriving green.
How can the plum contain a bitter heart?
I love the shade provided by the tree,
For in my dream I'll play another part.

Well, the plum tree is lovely indeed. After my death, I would be lucky enough if I could be buried underneath.

(*To the tune of* **Jiangershui**)

All of a sudden my heart is drawn
Toward this plum tree by the lawn.
If I were free to pick my bloom or grass,
If I were free to choose to live or die,
I would resign to fate without a sigh.
I'll risk my life
And weather raging storms
To be your faithful wife.

(*Sits down on the ground wearily*)

(*Enter Chunxiang*)

Chunxiang:

"*She tours the garden in spring days;*
Her maid burns incense in court maze."

Well, Miss Du is dosing off under the plum tree as she is tired from the garden tour.

(*To the tune of* **Chuanbozhao**)

How does the plum tree allure
You to end the garden tour?

Du Liniang:
 When I gaze,

 When I gaze at the endless skies,

 Woe and sorrow moist my eyes.

 (*In tears*)

Du Liniang, Chunxiang:
 Who knows from where the woe arises?

 Who knows from where the tear arises?

Chunxiang:
 What's weighing on your mind, mistress?

Du Liniang:
 (*To the previous tune*)

 How absurd

 That we gazed without a word!

 I should have held,

 I should have held the twig and yelled.

 Now I regret,

 Now I regret that not a word he did get.

Chunxiang:
 What is the riddle you have set?

Du Liniang, Chunxiang:
 Who knows form where the woe arises?

 Who knows from where the tear arises?

Chunxiang:
We'd better go back now.

Du Liniang:
 (*Starts to move but stops again*)

 (*To the previous tune*)

 Spring, stay a while

 And linger in exile.

 (*Birds sing within*)

 Listen,

 Listen to the cuckoo's song.

 Is it true that I can only come—

 Come here to see the plum—

 In dream or death that will prolong?

Du Liniang, Chunxiang:
 Who knows from where the woe arises?

  Who knows from where the tear arises?

Chunxiang:

Here we are. Let's go and see Madam, mistress.

Du Liniang:

Not now.

  (*To the tune of **Yibujin***)
  I dragged my weary steps to my own room,
  About to greet my mom,
  But I alone sleep with bedside bloom.

Du Liniang:

Where on earth can fairy love be found?

Chunxiang:

The tourist's zeal can hardly be profound.

Du Liniang:

In dreams my man will show up off and on;

Chunxiang:

Eternal woe will ne'er be dead and gone.

Notes on the Text

1. About the text

The present text is taken from *The Peony Pavilion* translated by Wang Rongpei, published by Shanghai Foreign Language Education Press in 2003.

2. Wang Rongpei

Wang Rongpei (1942—2017) is a great educator, translator, and lexicologist. He graduated from the Foreign Language Department of Fudan University as a post graduate and started teaching. In 1996, Wang began to translate *The Peony Pavilion*, the most famous work of Tang Xianzu and then started a 20-year journey of translating all the dramatic works by Tang Xianzu. In 2014, *The Complete Dramatic Works of Tang Xianzu* was published by Shanghai Foreign Language Education Press and appeared in the New York Book Fair in 2015, which drew wide attention. The whole translation of *The Peony Pavilion* was collected by the library of Manchester University and other overseas libraries.

Unit 9

The Rejected Suit

Reading Guide

  This text is excerpted from Scene 22 "The Rejected Suit" in *The Peach Blossom Fan*, translated by Chen Shih-Hsiang and Harold Acton with Cyril Birch. At Acton's suggestion, Professor Chen, who had been researching early Chinese poetry, collaborated with him in translating *The Peach Blossom Fan* in the 1950s as a means of continuing their shared study of classical Chinese literature. The manuscript draft of *The Peach Blossom Fan* was left unfinished because of Professor Chen's untimely death in 1971. Cyril Birch, Professor Chen's colleague at the University of California Berkeley, undertook to complete the final seven scenes and revised the draft throughout. *The Peach Blossom Fan* was first published by University of California Press in 1976, with an introduction by Acton. A most recent version of the book is republished by the New York Review of Books in 2015, with a new introduction by Judith T. Zeitlin, a renowned American scholar of Chinese literature. Dylan Suher of the literary magazine *Asymptote* (a Taiwan-based online literary magazine dedicated to translations of world literature) described *The Peach Blossom Fan* as "The greatest masterpiece of the literature of political disappointment", and remarked that the play contains "some of the most elegant Chinese ever written—a density of poetic expression that rivals Shakespeare's"[①].

  This excerpt presents one of the climatic scenes in *The Peach Blossom Fan*, where Fragrant Princess (Li Hsiang-chün) knocked her head against the ground when forced to marry Master Ts'ao, leaving blood spots on the fan which was given by her beloved Hou Fang-yü. After that, Yang Wen-ts'ung, a painter and poet, drew a branch of peach blossoms with Fragrant Princess's blood on the fan and the fan was sent to Hou to show Fragrant Princess's determination and persistent love. As Judith T. Zeitlin states in the introduction, the author K'ung Shang-jen "transforms it (the peach blossom fan) into a dynamic microcosm of the romance between

---

① https://www.asymptotejournal.com/criticism/kung-shang-jen-the-peach-blossom-fan/

Fragrant Princess and Hou as intertwined with the fate of the Ming Dynasty". The profound meaning of the romance and the symbolic meaning of the fan are worth further pondering.

Before Reading

I. Preview Requirements: Please make a preparatory research on the background information, key words and phrases of this text.

1. Do research on the three translators Chen Shih-Hsiang, Harold Acton and Cyril Birch.
2. Do research on Southern Drama and its characteristics.
3. Do research on the historical context of *The Peach Blossom Fan,* especially the decline of the Ming Dynasty.
4. Find and study the new words in the text such as *avenge, azure, commotion, inscribe, implore* and *preside.*
5. Learn the useful expressions in the text such as *marry into, out of the question, beat off, talk things over,* and *thrust on.*

II. Preview Questions: Please answer some questions about the understanding of the main content of the text.

1. What is the most impressive scene in the text?
2. Wherein does the conflict lie in this text?
3. What is the character of Fragrant Princess? How does her character bear on the interpretation of the story?
4. Why did Fragrant Princess reject her marriage with Master Ts'ao? Do you think she was reasonable?
5. What is the importance of the physical actions in the story? How did they offer clues to the feelings and attitudes of the characters? Consider, for instance, how Fragrant Princess reacts to Mistress Li and Yang's attempt to dress her up as a bride.
6. What is the significance of the fact that Fragrant Princess knocked her head on the ground by way of protest? Does the fact of the blood help develop the plot?
7. What is Fragrant Princess's attitude towards love? How do you assess the value of her attitude?
8. What do you think of the romance between Fragrant Princess and Hou Fang-yü?
9. What is the dominant emotion of the text?
10. As two well-known Chinese legendary dramas, do *The Peach Blossom Fan* and *The Peony Pavilion* share certain similarities? Consider their background, social conflicts, and images.

Text A

Chen Shih-Hsiang, Harold Acton & Cyril Birch's Version

The Rejected Suit

(*Steward and young servant enter holding lanterns inscribed "The Prime Minister." Others carry clothes, silver, and a litter.*)

All (*recite*):

The Old Matchmaker has not been sent down from the moon, But the Go-between Star has been seen here below.

Steward:

Fragrant Princess must be compelled to marry by order of the Prime Minister. Let us make haste.

Young Servant:

I have heard that there are both a mother and daughter living in the Old House. How can we tell them apart?

Yang (*entering quickly*):

Wait a minute, you two. I shall accompany you.

Steward (*greeting him*):

If Your Excellency will be so kind, there will certainly be no mistake.(*They walk on.*)

Steward and Yang (*reciting*):

The moon beams on the azure river,

The frost gleams on the wooden bridge.

Here we are. Let us knock at the door. (*They knock.*)

Maid (*entering*):

As soon as I close the back door I have to open the front one, like the master of a posting station. Who's there?

Steward:

Open quickly.

Maid:

Mercy on us! Lanterns, torches, a litter, horses, and attendants. Is Your Honour Yang holding a parade?

Yang:

Fie, run and call your mistress.

Maid (*loudly*):

Madam, His Honour Yang is here.

Unit 9
The Rejected Suit

Li Chen-li (*entering*):

    Where has your Honour been banqueting this evening?

Yang:

    I have come from the Prime Minister to bring you glad tidings.

Li:

    Please explain.

Yang:

    A very high official has asked to marry your daughter. (*Sings*):

    Behold the gorgeous litter,

    See the garments glitter,

    The servants how they pour

    In brocade outside the door!

    Behold the silver crowns

    And the rich embroidered gowns!

Li:

    Who sent them here? Why weren't we told in advance?

Yang (*sings*):

    Don't you see the lanterns, pair by pair,

    Bearing the insignia

    Of the Prime Minister himself?

Li:

    Is it the Prime Minister who wants to marry her?

Yang:

    No. (*sings*):

    Her lot will be to offer cups of jade

    To Master Ts'ao, Director of Supplies,

    The Prime Minister's close kinsman.

Li:

    We have already rejected this T'ien's proposal. Why should we be pestered again?

Servant (*arriving with silver, says to Mistress Li*):

    Are you the Fragrant Princess? Please take this gift of money.

Li:

    I must run upstairs and talk things over.

Steward (*appears and says*):

    This is the Prime Minister's command. There's no time for discussion. Take the money and come to the litter at once.

Yang (*to Steward*):

    She will never dare refuse. You wait outside. I'll look after the money while she gets ready.

Steward and Servant:
> Let us find a couple of wenches and have some fun.
> (*Exeunt. Mistress Li, Yang, and maid go upstairs with the clothes and the money.*)

Yang (*calling*):
> Fragrant Princess, are you asleep?

Fragrant Princess:
> What is all the hubbub about?

Li:
> Have you no idea?

Fragrant Princess (*to Yang*):
> Does your Honour wish to hear me sing?

Li:
> This is no occasion for music. (*Sings*):
> In a violent rush,
> They thrust nuptial gifts upon us,
> Resolved to ravish my daughter from me.
> How can we escape their grasp?
> Will no substitute suffice?

Fragrant Princess:
> This is terrible. I'm frightened to death. What cursed fiend is threatening me now?

Li:
> It is the same T'ien Yang, and the Prime Minister is backing his efforts. (*Sings*):
> How hapless is the fate of a singing-girl!
> At any moment blown away
> Like a poor willow catkin.

(*To Yang*): Your Honour has been so kind to us in the past. Why are you so cruel now?

Yang:
> I am blameless in this matter. On hearing that you had rejected T'ien Yang, the Prime Minister lost his temper and sent fierce retainers to enforce his will. I was afraid they might treat you roughly, so I came along to protect you.

Li:
> Please continue to be kind and think of some way to save us.

Yang:
> To my mind, three hundred silver *taels* are nothing to sneeze at. Nor does it seem beneath Fragrant Princess's dignity to marry the Director of Military Supplies. Besides, how can she resist two such powerful officials?

Li:

Perhaps Your Honour is right. In the circumstances, I don't see how we can persist in our refusal. Dear daughter, please be reasonable. It would be wiser to pack and go along with them.

Fragrant Princess (*angrily*):

How can you even suggest such a thing, Mother? When I married my lord Hou, His Honour Yang was the matchmaker, and you presided over the nuptial ceremony. The token of my solemn vow is still in my keeping. (*She fetches the fan and says*): My lord wrote this poem as a pledge. Your Honour has seen it. Have you forgotten? (*Sings*):

Our vow is sacred;
I shall devote my whole life to my lord.
My heart will never change,
Fixed as the poem on this silken fan.
Had we been together only a single night,
Our love will last forever.

Yang:

But Master Hou came to grief and had to fly. Now nobody knows where he is. If he does not return in three years' time, will you wait for him all your life?

Fragrant Princess:

I'll wait for him three years, ten years, a hundred years. Never shall I marry this T'ien Yang.

Yang:

Mercy, what a temper! You are behaving as you did when you refused the trousseau, scattering your hairpins, tearing your dress, and cursing old Juan.

Fragrant Princess:

Both Juan and T'ien belonged to the eunuch Wei's clique. Having refused Juan's bribe, why should I embrace T'ien Yang?

Voices from backstage:

It is getting late. Make haste and enter the litter. We have strict orders to carry you to the boat.

Li:

Dear daughter, pray consider your future. Think of the security you will enjoy at T'ien's house.

Fragrant Princess:

That means nothing whatever to me. I am determined to keep my chastity for my lord. (*Sings*):

I would rather freeze and starve

Than leave this tower.

Li:

As things are, I cannot let her have her way. Your Honour, please set the gifts down while we help her to get dressed. (*Mistress Li tries to dress Fragrant Princess's hair, and Yang attempts to help her on with a gown. Fragrant Princess struggles and beats them off with her fan.*)

Yang:

How fierce. She uses her love-token as a murderous sword.

Li:

Let us try to get her dressed and carry her downstairs. (*Yang attempts to carry her.*)

Fragrant Princess (*crying*):

Even if I die, I shall not leave this room. (*She falls to the ground wailing, and knocks her head against it till she faints.*)

Li:

Alas, alas! Do rouse yourself, dear daughter. You have ruined your fair complexion.

(*To Yang*): Look, she has bled so much that she has stained her fan. (*She hands the fan to a maid, saying*): We shall have to put her to bed. (*The maid carries Fragrant Princess out.*)

Voices from backstage:

It is now the third watch of night. After grabbing the money, you will not come to the litter. We shall put you under arrest.

Yang (*calls downstairs*):

Wait a minute, steward. It is very distressing for a mother and daughter to part. Don't be too rough with them!

Li:

Now that my daughter has fainted, with all this commotion outside I don't know where to turn or what to do.

Yang:

Remember the power of the Prime Minister. If you provoke him further, resentment may drive him to extremes. Then your life as well as your daughter's will be in danger.

Li:

I implore Your Honour to save us.

Yang:

I can see no way out unless we attempt a makeshift.

Li:

Please explain.

Yang:

For a singing-girl to marry into an honourable family is generally considered a piece of good luck. T'ien's rank is superior, and his family is rich. Since Fragrant Princess will not have him, I think you should take her place.

Li: (*shocked*):

But that is out of the question. Besides, how could I ever bear to leave my daughter?

Yang:

If they come to arrest you, you will have to bear the wrench.

Li (*stupefied*):

So be it then. Let Fragrant Princess keep to her room, I shall have to go. But it isn't safe. I fear they will recognize me.

Yang:

I shall maintain that you are Fragrant Princess. Nobody will dare contradict me.

Li:

Then I shall have to dress myself up as a bride. (*She proceeds to do so, calling backstage*): Dear daughter, I beg you to take care of yourself. I am going in your stead. Keep the three hundred silver *taels* for me. Don't squander them recklessly. (*Sings*):

Red lanterns light the street below;

Out in the night, a bitter wind will blow.

Once swept away, the flower may not return.

Steward and Young Servant (*entering with litter and lanterns*):

Hurrah, at last the bride appears. Please step into the litter.

Li (*to Yang*):

Farewell, Your Honour.

Yang:

Take care of yourself on the journey. We are bound to meet again.

Li:

I hope Your Honour will spend the night here and look after my unhappy daughter.

Yang:

I promise to do so.

Li (*entering the litter, sings*):

Henceforth my friends early and late

May but glance at me from the road.

It is hard to step out of the gate,

Once inside an official's abode.

I got to my uncertain fate

Lacking all knowledge of my mate. (*Exit.*)

Yang (*laughing*):

    Now Mistress Li will be married into a respectable family, and Fragrant Princess will keep her chastity. Brother Juan is avenged, and the Prime Minister's prestige is saved. All's well that ends well, thanks to my brilliant plan! But the parting of mother and daughter was sad to witness. (*Sings*):

    A hurried switch of partners in the night,
    A melancholy song as parting nears.
    Now in the tower of swallows, sore distress,
    And only the pillow's chill to soothe her fears.

Notes on the Text

The Old Matchmaker

There is a saying in Chinese that marriages are made in heaven and prepared on the moon. The Old Matchmaker ties together the feet of future marriage partners with a red thread. Once people are tied together, there is no way that they could avoid marriage.

Glossary

avenge /əˈven(d)ʒ/   *v.* to inflict harm in return for (an injury or wrong done to oneself or another)

e.g.: *He promised to avenge the terrible wrongs done to them, and they responded enthusiastically.*

azure /ˈæzjʊə/   *adj.* bright blue in colour like a cloudless sky

e.g.: *Thin streaks of cloud trailed across an azure sky.*

commotion /kəˈməʊʃ(ə)n/   *n.* a state of confused and noisy disturbance

e.g.: *They set off firecrackers to make a lot of commotion.*

implore /ɪmˈplɔː/   *v.* to beg someone earnestly or desperately to do sth.

implore sb. to do sth. e.g.: *He implored her to change her mind.*

insignia /ɪnˈsɪgnɪə/   *n.* a distinguishing badge or emblem of military rank, office, or membership of an organization

e.g.: *He noticed my military insignia and asked if I was going to Saudi Arabia for the Gulf War.*

nuptial /ˈnʌpʃ(ə)l/   *adj.* relating to marriage or weddings

e.g.: *While I'm not going on an actual Wedding Tour this year, my nuptial calendar is, as always, quite full.*

pester /ˈpestə/   *v.* to trouble or annoy (someone) with frequent or persistent requests or interruptions

pester sb. for sth. e.g.: *Beggars pestered him for money.*

	pester sb. with sth. e.g.: *She constantly pestered him with telephone calls.*
preside /prɪˈzaɪd/	*v.* 1. be in the position of authority in a meeting or other gathering
	preside at e.g.: *The Prime Minister will preside at an emergency cabinet meeting.*
	2. be in charge of (a place or situation)
	preside over e.g.: *Johnson has presided over eight matches since Beck's dismissal.*
soothe /suːð/	*v.* 1. to make (a person who is distressed, anxious, etc.) quiet or calm; to calm or comfort
	e.g.: *A shot of brandy might soothe his nerves.*
	2. to make (pains, aches, etc.) less severe or painful; to ease
	e.g.: *This will help to soothe your sunburn.*
stupefy /ˈstjuːpɪfaɪ/	*v.* 1. to dull the mind or senses of sb.
	stupefy sb. with sth. e.g.: *Surgeons would attempt to stupefy the patient with alcohol, opium, or morphia, but with little effect.*
	2. to overcome sb. with astonishment; to amaze
	e.g.: *The amount they spend on clothes would appall their parents and stupefy their grandparents.*
suffice /səˈfaɪs/	*v.* be enough or adequate
	e.g.: *Two examples should suffice to prove the contention.*
tael /teɪl/	*n.* a unit of weight used in China and East Asia, of varying amount between one to two and a half ounces
	e.g.: *The garden's building project lasted 10 years and cost Gu more than 10,000 taels of silver.*
token /ˈtəʊkən/	*n.* a thing serving as a visible or tangible representation of a fact, quality, feeling, etc.
	e.g.: *I wanted to offer you a small token of my appreciation.*
wail /weɪl/	*v.* 1. to cry or complain (about sth.) in a loud (usu. shrill) voice
	wail about/over sth. e.g.: *There's no use wailing about/over mistakes made in the past.*
	2. to express one's grief at the loss or death of sb.
	wail for sb. e.g.: *She was wailing for her lost child.*

While Reading

I. Please fill in the blanks with the words in the parentheses with the appropriate part of speech.

1. There are no other _____ reasons or interest which justify this being given permission for a further appeal. (compel)
2. There is a brooding _____ in his black and white photography. (melancholy)
3. Andrew and Lisa separated in 2011 after six years of _____ and formally divorced in 2017. (marry)
4. You couldn't be more _____, Alex. You've utterly misread the situation. (mistake)
5. The bird struggled to break loose and flied higher and higher regardless of the girl's _____ in tears. (implore)
6. The extent to which some persons can go on reading without having any clear idea of what they read is _____ amazing! (stupefy)
7. He saw himself as a Master of the Universe, a(n) _____ of wrongs. (avenge)
8. These _____ are not just in another language; they do not seem to offer names or dates at all. (inscribe)
9. I felt my heart begin to pound a bit faster, and took a _____ drink from my water glass to dispel my anxiety. (haste)
10. Staff have to go through the _____ and anxiety-provoking process of applying for their own jobs. (dignity)

II. Please choose one word or phrase that best completes the sentence.

1. Marriages are sometimes arranged by families, as each family is seeking to _____ another family of at least equal, if not superior, wealth and social standing.
   A. marry with   B. marry into
   C. marry to   D. marry

2. Screaming at someone in public is _____, but it sounds like not everyone feels the same way.
   A. beneath my dignity   B. behind my dignity
   C. beside my dignity   D. under my dignity

3. Who wants to _____ after being physically subdued and humiliated?
   A. talk things on   B. talk things about
   C. talk things over   D. talk things with

4. Being a diplomat's wife _____ multiple roles _____ her and often she has to burn the proverbial midnight oil to catch up on unfinished work on the canvas.
   A. thrusts…on   B. thrusts…with
   C. thrusts…over   D. thrusts…about

5. The question remains: how should museum curators and historians interpret those trophies of cultural imperialism that remain _____?
   A. on their keeping   B. within their keeping
   C. with their keeping   D. in their keeping
6. During his illness Colm was never able to leave the house and going to school was _____ for him.
   A. out of question   B. out of the question
   C. out of problem   D. out of the problem

III. Translation

1. Please translate the following from English into Chinese.
   1) the Old Matchmaker   2) the Go-between Star
   3) to bring glad tidings   4) nuptial gifts
   5) the parting of mother and daughter 6) to scatter one's hairpins
   7) to keep one's chastity   8) to attempt a makeshift
   9) to step into the litter   10) to take care of oneself on the journey

2. Please translate the following from Chinese into English.
   1）好好将息   2）妆新人
   3）夜已三更   4）定盟之物
   5）不干我事   6）花容
   7）同乡至戚   8）绣衣
   9）这断不能。   10）后会有期

3. Please translate each sentence with at least one key word or its derivative.
   Key Words: preside, suffice, attend, soothe, implore
   1）我恳请大家保持冷静，并保证你们在一个安全的地方。
   2）主席应当主持所有的董事会会议，并且应当在票数相同的情况下，投出具有决定性的一票。
   3）到餐室喝杯茶，跟同事闲聊15分钟可能会缓解午间危机（mid-day crisis）的症状。
   4）对于贫穷的西部城市来说，每年几亿欧元的资金已经足够了。
   5）虽然因为你的口音问题我没怎么听懂，但是你的语气很抚慰人心，我感觉好多了。
   6）今天上午他的确去听讲了，可是不知怎的他似乎心不在焉。
   7）可能会有一笔抚恤金，数目不算很大，但足够给她姐姐颐养天年。
   8）总统有六名警卫员时时刻刻在他左右保卫他。
   9）现在是领导世界经济的国际组织进行机构改革的时候了。
   10）于是它奋力挣脱，不顾女孩流着泪苦苦哀求，愈飞愈高。

After Reading

I. Please make a sentence with the words and expressions you have learnt from the text.

1. to avenge:
2. to ravish:
3. to wail for:
4. by the same token:
5. to pester sb. for sth.:

II. Paragraph Writing

1. Please write a paragraph of around 150 words sketching the character of Fragrant Princess and her attitude towards love.

2. Please write a paragraph of around 100 words with the following words and expressions you have learnt from the text. Make sure that the paragraph you have written is grammatically correct and coherent.

> azure; blameless; reject; thrust; blow away

Original Edition in Chinese

守 楼

（外、小生拿内阁灯笼、衣、银跟轿上）天上从无差月老，人间竟有错花星①。（外）我们奉老爷之命，硬娶香君，只得快走。（小生）旧院李家母子两个，知他谁是香君。（末急上呼介）转来同我去罢。（外见介）杨姑老爷肯去，定娶不错了。（同行介）月照青溪水，霜沾长板桥。来此已是，快快叫门。（叫门介）（杂扮保儿上）才关后户，又开前庭；迎官接客，卑职驿丞②。（问介）那个叫门？（外）快开门来。（杂开门惊介）呵呀！灯笼火把，轿马人夫，杨老爷来夸官③了。（末）唉！快唤贞娘出来。（杂大叫介）妈妈出来，杨老爷到门了。（小旦急上问介）

老爷从那里赴席回来么？（末）适在马舅爷相府，特来报喜。（小旦）有什么喜？（末）有个大老官来娶你令爱哩。（指介）

【渔家傲】你看这彩轿青衣④门外催，你看这三百花银，一套绣衣。（小旦惊介）是那家来娶，怎不早说？（末）你看灯笼大字成双对，是中堂⑤阁内。（小旦）就是内阁老爷自己娶么？（末）非也。漕抚田公，同乡至戚，赠个佳人捧玉杯。

（小旦）田家亲事，久已回断，如何又来歪缠？（小生拿银交介）你就是香君么，请受财礼。（小旦）待我进去商量。（外）相府要人，还等你商量；快快收了银子，出来上轿罢。（末）他怎敢不去，你们在外伺候，待我拿银进去，催他梳洗。（末接银，杂接衣，同小旦作进介）（小生、外）我们且寻个老表子燥脾去。（俱暂下）（小旦、末、杂作上楼介）（末唤介）香君睡下不曾？（旦上）有甚紧事，一片吵闹。（小旦）你还不知么？（旦见末介）想是杨老爷要来听歌。（小旦）还说甚么歌不歌哩。

【剔银灯】忙忙的来交聘礼，凶凶的强夺歌妓；对着面一时难回避，执着名别人谁替。（旦惊介）唬杀奴也！又是那个天杀的？（小旦）还是田仰，又借着相府的势力，硬来娶你。堪悲，青楼薄命，一霎时杨花乱吹。

（小旦向介末）杨老爷从来疼俺母子，为何下这毒手？（末）不干我事，那马瑶草知你拒绝田仰，动了大怒，差一班恶仆登门强娶。下官怕你受气，特为护你而来。（小旦）这等多谢了，还求老爷始终救解。（末）依我说三百财礼，也不算吃亏；香君嫁个漕抚，也不算失所；你有多大本事，能敌他两家势力？（小旦思介）杨老爷说的有理，看这局面，拗不去了。孩儿趁早收拾下楼罢！（旦怒介）妈妈说那里话来！当日杨老爷作媒，妈妈主婚，把奴嫁与侯郎，满堂宾客，谁没看见。现收着定盟之物。（急向内取出扇介）这首定情诗，杨老爷都看过，难道忘了不成？

【摊破锦地花】举案齐眉⑥。他是我终身倚，盟誓怎移。宫纱扇现有诗题，万种恩情，一夜夫妻。（末）那侯郎避祸逃走，不知去向；设若三年不归，你也只顾等他么？（旦）便等他三年；便等他十年；便等他一百年；只不嫁田仰。（末）呵呀！好性气，又像摘翠脱衣骂阮圆海的那番光景了。（旦）可又来，阮、田同是魏党，阮家妆奁尚且不受，倒去跟着田仰么？（内喊介）夜已深了，快些上轿，还要赶到船上去哩。（小旦劝介）傻丫头！嫁到田府，少不了你的吃穿哩。（旦）呸！我立志守节，岂在温饱。忍寒饥，决不下这翠楼梯。

（小旦）事到今日，也顾不得他了。（叫介）杨老爷放下财礼，大家帮他梳头穿衣。（小旦替梳头，末替穿衣介）（旦持扇前后乱打介）（末）好利害，一柄诗扇，倒像一把防身的利剑。（小旦）草草妆完，抱他下楼罢。（末抱介）（旦哭介）奴家就死不下此楼。（倒地撞头晕卧介）（小旦惊介）呵呀！我儿苏醒，竟把花容，碰了个稀烂。（末指扇介）你看血喷满地，连这诗扇都溅坏了。（拾扇付杂介）（小旦唤介）保儿，扶起香君，且到卧房安歇罢。（杂扶旦下）（内喊介）夜已三更了，诓去银子，不打发上轿；我们要上楼拿人哩。（末向楼下介）管家略等一等；他母子难舍，其实可怜的。（小旦急介）孩儿碰坏，外边声声要人，这怎么处？（末）那宰相势力，你是知道的，这番羞了他去，你母子不要性命了。（小旦怕介）求杨老爷救俺则个。（末）没奈何，且寻个权宜之法罢！（小旦）有何权宜之法？（末）娼家从良，原是好事，况且嫁与田府，不少吃穿，香君既没造化，你倒替他享受去罢。（小旦急介）这断不能。一时一霎，叫我如何舍得。（末怒介）明日早来拿人，看你舍得不舍得。（小旦呆介）也罢！叫香君守着楼，我去走一遭儿。（想介）不好，不好，只怕有人认得。（末）我说你是香君，谁能辨别。（小旦）既是这等，少不得又妆新人了。（忙打扮完介）（向内叫介）香君我儿，好好将息，我替你去了。（又嘱介）三百两银子，替我收好，不要花费了。（末扶小旦下楼介）

【麻婆子】（小旦）下楼下楼三更夜，红灯满路辉；出户出户寒风起，看花未必归。（小生、外打灯抬轿上）好，好，新人出来了，快请上轿。（小旦别末介）别过杨老爷罢。（末）前途保重，后会有期。（小旦）老爷今晚且宿院中，照管孩儿。（末）自然。（小旦上轿介）萧郎从此路人窥⑦，侯门再出岂容易。（行介）舍了笙歌队，今夜伴阿谁。

（俱下）（末笑介）贞丽从良，香君守节，雪了阮兄之恨，全了马舅之威！将李代桃⑧，一举四得，倒也是个妙计。（叹介）只是母子分别，未免伤心。
匆匆夜去替娥眉，一曲歌同易水悲⑨；
燕子楼中人卧病，灯昏被冷有谁知。

注释：
① 花星：旧时江湖术士推算星命时的一种术语。本是表示婚姻的征兆，对妇女而言，主有男女风情的纠葛。
② 驿丞：掌管驿站的官，经常要迎官接客。
③ 夸官：士子考中进士或官员升迁时，排列鼓乐仪仗游街，称为夸官。
④ 青衣：指奴仆。古时奴婢一般穿青衣。
⑤ 中堂：唐代在中书省设政事堂，是宰相办事的地方，后人因此称宰相为中堂。
⑥ 举案齐眉：形容夫妻相敬。东汉时梁鸿的妻子孟光每次吃饭都举案齐眉，表示对丈夫的尊敬。
⑦ 萧郎从此路人窥：李贞丽引唐代崔郊的故事来说明自己这一入田府，恐怕再难出来。萧郎，唐代对美好男子的通称。
⑧ 将李代桃：乐府《鸡鸣》篇："桃生露井上，李树生桃傍。虫来啮桃根，李树代桃僵。"后人用李代桃僵来表示代人受罪或顶替做某事。
⑨ 一曲歌同易水悲：借用战国荆轲和燕太子丹在易水分别的故事来形容李香君母子分别之情景。

Text B

Xu Yuanchong & Frank M. Xu's Version

Fragrant in Her Bower

(*Enter a messenger of Prime Minister Ma and an attendant following a palankeen.*)

Messenger:

The go-between will do no wrong under the sky;

A beauty-seeker may have no discerning eye.

By order of Prime Minister Ma, we are going to take a bride, so we must make haste.

Attendant:

In Lee's Bower the mother is said as fair as the daughter.

How can we distinguish one from the other?

(*Enter Yang Wencong in haste.*)

Yang:

Come back! I shall go with you.

Messenger (*Saluting Yang*):

Since Secretary Yang condescends to go with us, we are sure to make no mistake.

(*They walk together.*)

Yang:

The clear stream is steeped in moonlight;

The wooden bridge is covered with frost white.

Here is Lee's Bower. Let us knock at the door. (*Knocking.*)

(*Enter a Maid Servant.*)

Maid:

I have just closed the door;

Again I come to the fore.

Who is knocking?

Messenger:

Open the door!

Maid (*Startled on opening the door*):

Ah! Lanterns and torches, palankeen and footmen! It is Secretary Yang coming.

Yang:

Tell Mother Lee to come down.

Maid:

Will you please come down, Mother Chaste! Here comes Secretary Yang. (*Enter Mother Lee in haste.*)

Lee (*Saluting Yang*):

Are you coming back from a feast, Secretary Yang?

Yang:

I am coming on behalf of Prime Minister Ma to congratulate you.

Lee:

For what?

Yang:

A high official will ask your daughter's hand.

(*Pointing to three hundred pieces of gold and singing to the tune of* **Fisherman's Pride**):

Here are three hundred pieces of gold, what's more,
A sumptuous palankeen with footmen at your door.

Lee (*Startled*):

Which high official? Why not inform us beforehand?

Yang:

Have you not seen the characters on the lantern? We are coming from the mansion of the Prime Minister.

Lee:

Is the high official the prime minister himself?

Yang:

No, the prime minister would send a beautiful maid
To Secretary Tian for holding his cup of jade.

Lee:

We have already refused Tian. Why is he coming again?

Messenger (*Giving her the gold*):

Are you Fragrant? Please take the engagement money.

Lee:

I shall go in to consult with her.

Messenger:

The prime minister is waiting. How can you waste time in consultation? Take the money and mount the palankeen please.

Yang:

We shall not delay long. You may wait outside. I take the money and go in to hasten her. (*Yang takes the gold, the maid takes the embroidered dress, and Mother Lee goes upstairs with them.*)

Messenger & Attendant:

Let us go to see another songstress.

(*Exeunt*)

(*Mother Lee and Yang go upstairs with the maid.*)

Yang (*Calling*):

Fragrant, have you gone to bed or not yet?

(*Enter Fragrant.*)

Fragrant:

What noise! Is there anything unexpected?

Lee:

You have not yet heard it?

Fragrant (*Saluting Yang*):

Are you coming here to hear songs, Secretary Yang?

Lee:

How can we have time to hear songs?

(*Singing to the tune of* ***A Silver Lamp***):

They come in haste to send us gold

And force you to wed a man old.

What with their power could we do?

Who might go with them if not you?

Fragrant:

It is again that old villain. He has frightened me to death.

Lee:

It's Tian relying on Prime Minister Ma's power

To force you to go to his bower.

What grief for flowerlike beauty to be blown

Away like willow down!

(*To Yang*) You are always kind to us. How can you allow Tian to do so?

Yang:

This is beyond my power. Prime Minister Ma is angry at your refusal to Tian, so he orders his lackeys to take Fragrant by force. I come with them only to prevent them from using violence.

Lee:

We should be grateful to you for that, but I hope you will help us to the end.

Yang:

In my opinion three hundred pieces of gold is not a small sum of money, and Secretary Tian is not an unworthy match for Fragrant. Besides, do you think you are in a position to oppose the prime minister and his favorite secretary?

Lee (*Meditating*):

What you say is right. We can by no means oppose the authorities. My dear daughter, I think you cannot but go with them.

Fragrant (*Angry*):

How can you say that, dear mother? Have you forgotten that it was you who gave my hand to Master Hou, and Secretary Yang also attended the wedding? Here is the token of our love.

(*Taking out the fan.*) Secretary Yang, you did read the poem on the fan. How could all this be forgotten?

(*Singing to the tune of* **Embroidered Flowers**):
We are vowed man and wife;
I will rely on him throughout my life.
And I will keep my vow;
The verse is still on the fan now.
One night we were made man and wife,
We are married all through our life.

Yang:

But Master Hou, to escape the disaster, has fled far away and no one knows where. Would you wait for him if he did not come back for three years?

Fragrant:

I will wait for him not only three years, but ten years or even a hundred years. But I will never give my hand to Secretary Tian.

Yang:

Ah! What a strong character! You play the same part as you rejected Ruan's dowry by taking off the embroidered dress and the jade hairpin.

Fragrant:

You need not tell the old tale. Both Ruan and Tian belong to Eunuch Wei's party. How can I accept Tian's gold?

Voice within:

It is late in the night. Will the bribe come out and sit in the palankeen at once? It will be a long way for us to go back by boat.

Lee:

My unwise daughter, why will you not go to Tian's mansion where you will have more than enough to eat and to dress?

Fragrant:

I am determined to be true to Master Hou. How could I care for food and dress?
It is nor hunger nor cold for which I care.
I am determined not to go there.

Lee:

We have no time to lose. I can no longer wait for you to change your mind. (*To Yang*) Secretary Yang, would you please leave the gold here. Let us help her put on her wedding dress. (*Lee tries to comb her hair and Yang to put the wedding dress on her.*)

(*Fragrant brandishes the fan to strike whoever comes near her.*)

Yang:

How angry she is! The word on the fan seems sharper than the sword.

Lee:

Now she is hastily dressed. Let us hasten her downstairs.

(*Yang tries to carry her down.*)

Fragrant (*Weeping*):

I would rather die than go there. (*Falling on the floor with her head knocked on the corner stone and fainting away.*)

Lee (*Startled*):

Alas! Wake up, my dear daughter! How can you destroy your flowerlike face in such a way!

Yang (*Pointing to the fan*):

Even the poetic fan is stained with blood.

(*Picking up the fan and giving it to the maid.*)

Lee:

Maid, help to raise her and lay her on bed!

(*The maid helps her to rise.*)

Voice within:

It is midnight now. You have taken the gold. Why not come down and ride in the palankeen? Should we go upstairs and help you to come down?

Yang (*To the lackey*):

Wait a little bit longer. It is pitiable to see the daughter torn away from the mother.

Lee (*Anxious*):

Fragrant is badly hurt and the lackey is pressing us. What can I do?

Yang:

You know the authority of the prime minister. What will he not do if he feels himself offended! Would he not take your life and your daughter's?

Lee:

Would you please save us?

Yang:

We must think of a way out.

Lee:

What way?

Yang:

It is not a bad thing for your daughter to be married again. You need not worry about your meals and dress if she were wedded with Secretary Tian. Since your daughter is not willing to share such fortune, would you go in her place?

Lee (*Anxious*):

That will not do. How can I leave my daughter and my bower!

Yang:

If they seize you by force, could you say you would not leave your bower?

Lee (*Stupefied*):

What can I do but leave the bower to Fragrant? I cannot but go to Tian's mansion instead of my daughter. (*Thinking over*) What if they find I am not Fragrant?

Yang:

If I say you are what we want, who could tell mother from daughter?

Lee:

In that case, what can I do but disguise myself as an old new bride.

(*Busy in making up and dressing up.*)

(*To Fragrant*) My dear daughter, I cannot but go in your stead, but you must repose yourself. As for the three hundred pieces of gold, you must keep them in safety. Do not spend them without my permission.

(*Yang helps her go downstairs.*)

(*Singing to the tune of* **A Pock Marked Woman**):

I go downstairs late at midnight.

With red lanterns the road is bright.

The cold wind blows when I leave my bower.

Could I come back when there is no more flower?

(*Enter the messenger and the attendant with the palankeen.*)

Messenger:

Well, at last comes the bride. Would you please mount the palankeen?

Lee (*To Yang*):

Goodbye, Secretary Yang.

Yang:

Heaven bless you. I will see you later.

Lee:

Would you please stay in my bower for one night and take care of my daughter?

Yang:

You need not tell me that.

(*Lee mounts the palankeen.*)

Lee:

The gallant is no longer a lord I adore.

Could it be easy to come out of a mansion's door?

I have left my bower of music bright

To accompany a new lord tonight. (*Exit.*)

Yang (*Smiling*):

The mother wed, the daughter in the bower.

Ruan is revenged and Ma has shown his power,

One stone has killed four birds. What an ingenious intriguer!

(*Sighing*)

But it would break my heart

To see mother and daughter part.

One takes the other's place on this night long.

The river would be grieved to hear their farewell song.

The daughter lies in bed ill in the Swallow's Bower.

Who knows by dim lamplight in cold quilt her sad hour!

Notes on the Text

1. About the text

The present text is taken from *Peach Blooms Painted with Blood* translated by Xu Yuanchong and Frank M. Xu, published by China International Press and Zhonghua Book Company in 2012.

2. Xu Yuanchong

Born in Nanchang City, Jiangxi Province in 1921, he graduated from the Southwest Associated University and université de Paris. Mr. Xu is a professor of literary translation at Peking University. His English publications include *On Chinese Verse in English Rhyme* and *Vanished Springs* prefaced by C. N. Yang, the 1959 Nobel Prize winner for physics. In addition to *Songs of the Immortals* published by Penguin Books, he has translated many Chinese literary classics into English or French, such as *Book of Poetry*, *Elegies of the South*, *300 Tang Poems*, *300 Song Lyrics*, *Selected Poems of Li Bai*, *Poems and Lyrics of Su Dongpo*, *Romance of Western Bower* and *The Selected Poems of Mao Zedong*. He has also translated some world literary classics, such as Gustave Flaubert's *Madame Bovary*, into Chinese. Prof. Xu won the Lifetime Achievement Award in Translation conferred by the Translator Association of China (TAC) in 2010.

Unit 10

The Painted Skin

Reading Guide

    This text, "The Painted Skin", is one of the tales in *Strange Tales from a Chinese Studio*, translated by Herbert A. Giles. As a collection of supernatural-themed tales compiled from ancient Chinese folk stories by Pu Songling, *Strange Tales from a Chinese Studio* has been considered a masterpiece of the eerie and fantastic. It consists of a collection of three hundred, for the greater part, brief stories, anecdotes, terse sketches, events of interest, and moral examples. Written in a brilliant style which in its brevity recalls the classical language, and seasoned with covert literary allusions, it has not only been eagerly devoured by the literary gourmands of China, but has also become very popular among the masses. Professor Herbert A. Giles's translation embodies 164 stories, the best contained in the original.[①]

    The author Pu Songling (1640—1715) was born in a poor family in Zibo City, Shandong Province. He took the academic degree—the Xiucai degree at the age of 19, but he did not succeed in acquiring a higher academic degree—the Gongsheng degree until he was 71 years old. He spent the bulk of his life working as a private tutor, and collected the stories that were later published to great acclaim as *Strange Tales from a Chinese Studio*. To some extent, his loss of social status is the world's gain. "The Painted Skin" is one of his most fabulous stories, in which a hideous ghost wearing the painted skin of a beauty cheats a young scholar Wang, and tears out his heart. The ghost is finally stricken by a Taoist priest, takes off the painted skin, reappears as its original form, and becomes a dense column of smoke curling up from the ground. This story is metaphorical and enlightening.

---

    ① Laufer, B. "Reviewed Work: *Strange Stories from a Chinese Studio* by Herbert A. Giles." *The Journal of American Folklore*, Vol. 39, No. 151(Jan-Mar., 1926), 86-90.

Unit 10
The Painted Skin

Before Reading

I. Preview Requirements: Please make a preparatory research on the background information, key words and phrases of this text.
1. Do research on the translator Herbert A. Giles.
2. Do research on the Tuttle Publishing, and get to know some translations of Chinese classics published by this publishing company.
3. Do research on the role of Taoist priests in the Qing Dynasty, and think about why Taoist priests were so popular among the masses at that time. How does Taoism differ from Confucianism?
4. Find and study the new words in the text such as *acquiesce, smite, startle, bewitch, entreat, prostrate,* and *allude*.
5. Learn the useful expressions in the text such as *consent to, throw aside, drive away, peep out, get away, drop off,* and *apply to*.

II. Preview Questions: Please answer some questions about the understanding of the main content of the text.
1. What is your impression of *Strange Tales from a Chinese Studio*? Have you ever read some other stories in this book? What are they, if any?
2. Is there any relation between Pu Songling's failure in the Chinese Imperial Exam and the creation of *Strange Tales from a Chinese Studio*? What ideas does Pu Songling try to convey in this book?
3. What is this story about? Do you find it horrifying or shocking? Is there anything unique about the story compared with other supernatural-themed tales?
4. What do you think of Wang? Why did he decide to hide this beauty in his study? What kind of human weakness did Wang reveal? Please find examples and evidence from the text.
5. What's the personality of Wang's wife? Do you regard her as a virtuous wife? Do you think her personality contributes to Wang's tragedy?
6. What kind of trick did the devil use to fool people? Why could she succeed all the time? What is the metaphorical meaning of the devil?
7. What is the symbolic meaning of the maniac in the story? Do you find he has something in common with Diogenes? Do you consider him as a beggar, madman, philosopher or immortal? Why?

Text A

Herbert A. Giles's Version

The Painted Skin

At T'ai-yüan there lived a man named Wang. One morning he was out walking when he met a young lady carrying a bundle and hurrying along by herself. As she moved along with some difficulty,① Wang quickened his pace and caught her up, and found she was a pretty girl of about sixteen. Much smitten, he inquired whither she was going so early, and no one with her. "A traveller like you," replied the girl, "cannot alleviate my distress; why trouble yourself to ask?" "What distress is it?" said Wang; "I'm sure I'll do anything I can for you." "My parents," answered she, "loved money, and they sold me as concubine into a rich family, where the wife was very jealous, and beat and abused me morning and night. It was more than I could stand, so I have run away." Wang asked her where she was going; to which she replied that a runaway had no fixed place of abode. "My house," said Wang, "is at no great distance; what do you say to coming there?" She joyfully acquiesced; and Wang, taking up her bundle, led the way to his house. Finding no one there, she asked Wang where his family were; to which he replied that that was only the library. "And a very nice place, too," said she; "but if you are kind enough to wish to save my life, you mustn't let it be known that I am here." Wang promised he would not divulge her secret, and so she remained there for some days without anyone knowing anything about it. He then told his wife, and she, fearing the girl might belong to some influential family, advised him to send her away. This, however, he would not consent to do; when one day, going into the town, he met a Taoist priest, who looked at him in astonishment, and asked him what he had met. "I have met nothing," replied Wang. "Why," said the priest, "you are bewitched; what do you mean by not having met anything?" But Wang insisted that it was so, and the priest walked away, saying, "The fool! Some people don't seem to know when death is at hand." This startled Wang, who at first thought of the girl; but then he reflected that a pretty young thing as she was couldn't well be a witch, and began to suspect that the priest merely wanted to do a stroke of business. When he returned, the library door was shut, and he couldn't get in, which made him suspect that something was wrong; and so he climbed over the wall, where he found the door of the inner room shut too. Softly creeping up, he looked through the window and saw a hideous devil, with a green face and jagged teeth like a saw, spreading a human skin upon the bed and painting it with a paint-brush. The devil then threw aside the brush, and giving the skin a shake out, just as you would a coat, threw it over its shoulders, when lo! it was the girl. Terrified at this, Wang hurried away with his head down in search of the priest, who had gone he knew not whither; subsequently finding him in the fields, where he threw himself on his knees and begged the priest to save him. "As to driving her away," said the priest, "the creature must be in great distress to be seeking a substitute for herself; ② besides, I could hardly endure to injure a living thing." ③ However, he gave Wang a fly-brush, and bade him hang it at the door of the bedroom, agreeing to meet again at the Ch'ing-ti temple. Wang went home, but did not dare enter the library; so he hung up the brush at the bedroom door, and before long heard a sound of footsteps outside. Not daring to move, he made his wife peep out; and she saw the girl standing looking at the brush, afraid to pass it. She then ground her teeth and went away; but in a little while came back, and began cursing, saying, "You priest, you won't frighten me. Do you think I am going to give up what is already in my grasp?" Thereupon she tore the brush to pieces, and bursting open the door, walked straight up to the bed, where she ripped open Wang and tore out his heart, with which she went away. Wang's wife screamed out, and the servant came in with a light; but Wang was already dead and presented a most miserable spectacle. His wife, who was in an agony of fright, hardly dared cry for fear of making a noise; and next day she sent Wang's brother to see the priest. The latter got into a great rage, and cried out, "Was it for this that I had compassion on you, devil that you are?" proceeding at once with Wang's brother to the house, from which the girl had disappeared without anyone knowing whither she had gone. But the priest, raising his head, looked all round, and said, "Luckily she's not far off." He then asked who lived in the apartments on the south side, to which Wang's brother replied that he did; whereupon the priest declared that there she would be found. Wang's brother was horribly frightened and said he did not think so; and then the priest asked him if any stranger had been to the house. To this he answered that he had been out to the Ch'ing-ti temple and couldn't possibly say: but he went off to inquire, and in a little while came back and reported that an old woman had sought service with them as a maid-of-all-work, and had been engaged by his wife. "That is she," said the priest, as Wang's brother added she was still there; and they all set out to go to the house together. Then the priest took his wooden sword, and standing in the middle of the court-yard, shouted out, "Base-born fiend, give me back my fly-brush!" Meanwhile the new maid-of-all-work was in a great state of alarm, and tried to get away by the door; but the priest struck her and down she fell flat, the human skin dropped off, and she became a hideous devil. There she lay grunting like a pig, until the priest grasped his wooden sword and struck off her head. She then became a dense column of smoke curling up from the ground, when the priest took an uncorked gourd and threw it right into the midst of the smoke. A sucking noise was heard, and the whole column was drawn into the gourd; after which the priest corked it up closely and put it in his pouch. ④ The skin, too, which was complete even to the eyebrows, eyes, hands, and feet, he also rolled up as if it had been a scroll, and was on the point of leaving with it, when Wang's wife stopped him, and with tears entreated him to bring her husband to life. The priest said he was unable to do that; but Wang's wife flung herself at his feet, and with loud lamentations implored his assistance. For some time he remained immersed in thought, and then replied, "My power is not equal to what you ask. I myself cannot raise the dead; but I will direct you to someone who can, and if you apply to him properly you will succeed." Wang's wife asked the priest who it was; to which he replied, "There is a maniac in the town who passes his time grovelling in the dirt. Go, prostrate yourself before him, and beg him to help you. If he insults you, shew no sign of anger." Wang's brother knew the man to whom he alluded, and accordingly bade the priest adieu, and proceeded thither with his sister-in-law.

They found the destitute creature raving away by the road side, so filthy that it was all they could do to go near him. Wang's wife approached him on her knees; at which the maniac leered at her, and cried out, "Do you love me, my beauty?" Wang's wife told him what she had come for, but he only laughed and said, "You can get plenty of other husbands. Why raise the dead one to life?" But Wang's wife entreated him to help her; whereupon he observed, "It's very strange: people apply to me to raise their dead as if I was king of the infernal regions." He then gave Wang's wife a thrashing with his staff, which she bore without a murmur, and before a gradually increasing crowd of spectators. After this he produced a loathsome pill which he told her she must swallow, but here she broke down and was quite unable to do so. However, she did manage it at last, and then the maniac crying out, "How you do love me!" got up and went away without taking any more notice of her. They followed him into a temple with loud supplications, but he had disappeared, and every effort to find him was unsuccessful. Overcome with rage and shame, Wang's wife went home, where she mourned bitterly over her dead husband, grievously repenting the steps she had taken, and wishing only to die. She then bethought herself of preparing the corpse, near which none of the servants would venture, and set to work to close up the frightful wound of which he died.

While thus employed, interrupted from time to time by her sobs, she felt a rising lump in her throat, which by-and-by came out with a pop and fell straight into the dead man's wound. Looking closely at it, she saw it was a human heart; and then it began as it were to throb, emitting a warm vapour like smoke. Much excited, she at once closed the flesh over it, and held the sides of the wound together with all her might. Very soon, however, she got tired, and finding the vapour escaping from the crevices, she tore up a piece of silk and bound it round, at the same time bringing back circulation by rubbing the body and covering it up with clothes. In the night she removed the coverings, and found that breath was coming from the nose; and by next morning her husband was alive again, though disturbed in mind as if awaking from a dream and feeling a pain in his heart. Where he had been wounded, there was a cicatrix about as big as a cash, which soon after disappeared.

Notes from the Original Text:

① Impeded, of course, by her bound feet. This practice is said to have originated about 970 AD, with Yao Niang, the concubine of the pretender Li Yü, who wished to make her feet like the "new moon". The Manchu or Tartar ladies never adopted this custom, and therefore the Empresses of modern times have had feet of the natural size; neither is it in force among the

Hakkas or among the hill-tribes of China and others. The practice was forbidden in 1664 by the Manchu Emperor, K'ang Hsi; but popular feeling was so strong on the subject that four years afterwards the prohibition was withdrawn. A vigorous attempt is now being made to secure natural feet for the Chinese girl, with most chance of success.

② The disembodied spirits of the Chinese *Inferno* are permitted, under certain conditions of time and good conduct, to appropriate to themselves the vitality of some human being, who, as it were, exchanges places with the so-called "devil". The devil does not, however, reappear as the mortal whose life it has become possessed of, but is merely born again into the world; the idea being that the amount of life on earth is a constant quantity, and cannot be increased or diminished, reminding one in a way of the great modern doctrine of the conservation of energy. This curious belief has an important bearing that will be brought out in a subsequent story.

③ Here again is a Taoist priest quoting the Buddhist commandment, "Thou shalt not take life." The Buddhist laity in China, who do not hesitate to take life for the purpose of food, salve their consciences from time to time by buying birds, fishes, and letting them go, in the hope that such acts will be set down on the credit side of their record of good and evil.

④ This recalls the celebrated story of the fisherman in the *Arabian Nights*.

Notes on the Text

1. Herbert A. Giles

Herbert Allen Giles (1845—1935) was a British diplomat, sinologist, and professor of Chinese language. Giles was educated at Charterhouse School before becoming a British diplomat in China. He modified a Mandarin Chinese Romanization system earlier established by Thomas Wade, resulting in the widely known Wade-Giles Chinese Romanization System. Among his many works were translations of the masterpieces of Confucius, Lao Tzu, Chuang Tzu, and in 1892 the first widely published Chinese-English dictionary.

2. Taoist Priest

A Taoist priest, or a Taoist master, is a priest in Taoism. Some orders are monastic (Quanzhen orders), while the majority is not (Zhengyi orders). Some of the monastic orders are hermitic, and their members practice seclusion and ascetic lifestyles in the mountains, with the aim of becoming immoral beings. Non-monastic priests live among the populace and manage and serve their own temples or popular temples.

3. king of the infernal regions

King of the infernal regions (also Yama in Hinduism) is the lord of death. In the Rigveda, he is mentioned as the one who helped humankind find a place to dwell, and gave every individual the power to tread any path to which he or she wants. In Vedic tradition, Yama was considered to be the first mortal who died and espied the way to the celestial abodes. Thus, as a result, he became the ruler of the departed.

Glossary

acquiesce /ˌækwɪˈes/   v. to accept sth. without arguing, even if you do not really agree with it
e.g.: *Senior government figures must have acquiesced in the cover-up.*

alleviate /əˈliːvɪeɪt/   v. to make sth. less severe
e.g.: *A number of measures were taken to alleviate the problem.*

creep /kriːp/   v. (of people or animals) to move slowly, quietly and carefully, because you do not want to be seen or heard
e.g.: *I crept up the stairs, trying not to wake my parents.*

destitute /ˈdestɪtjuːt/   adj. without money, food and other things necessary for life
e.g.: *When he died, his family was left completely destitute.*

divulge /daɪˈvʌldʒ/   v. to give sb. information that is supposed to be a secret
e.g.: *Police refused to divulge the identity of the suspect.*

filthy /ˈfɪlθɪ/   adj. 1. very dirty and unpleasant
e.g.: *filthy rags/streets*
    2. very rude and offensive and usually connected with sex
e.g.: *filthy language/words*

grovel /ˈɡrɒvl/   v. 1. to behave in a very humble way towards sb. who is more important than you or who can give you sth. you want
e.g.: *He went groveling to her for forgiveness.*
    2. to move along the ground on your hands and knees, especially because you are looking for sth.
e.g.: *She was groveling around on the floor, looking for her contact lens.*

grunt /ɡrʌnt/   v. (of people) to make a short low sound in your throat, especially to show that you are in pain, annoyed or not interested; to say sth. using this sound
e.g.: *He grunted something about being late and rushed out.*

mourn /mɔːn/   v. to feel and show sadness because sb. has died; to feel sad because sth. no longer exists or is no longer the same
e.g.: *Today we mourn for all those who died in two world wars.*

prostrate /ˈprɒstreɪt/   v. (*usually passive*) to make sb. feel weak, shocked, and unable to do anything
e.g.: *For months he was prostrated with grief.*

rave /reɪv/   v. to talk or shout in a way that is not logical or sensible
e.g.: *He wandered the streets raving at passers-by.*

repent /rɪˈpent/   v. to feel and show that you are sorry for sth. bad or wrong that you have done
e.g.: *God welcomes the sinner who repents.*

smite /smaɪt/   *v.* to have a great effect on sb. especially an unpleasant or serious one
                         e.g.: *Suddenly my conscience smote me.*
spectacle /ˈspektək(ə)l/   *n.* an usual or surprising sight or situation that attracts a lot of attention
                         e.g.: *I remember the sad spectacle of her standing in her wedding dress.*
startle /ˈstɑːt(ə)l/   *v.* to surprise sb. in a way that slightly shocks or frightens them
                         e.g.: *I didn't mean to startle you.*
substitute /ˈsʌbstɪtjuːt/   *n.* a person or thing that you use or have instead of the one you normally use or have
                         e.g.: *The course teaches you the theory but there's no substitute for practical experience.*
thrashing /ˈθræʃɪŋ/   *n.* an act of hitting sb. very hard, especially with a stick
                         e.g.: *A sound thrashing might teach the individual to refrain from complaining.*

While Reading

I. Please fill in the blanks with the words in the parentheses with the appropriate part of speech.

1. In waiting for that important interview, I felt my own pulse _____ and my memory become a complete blank. (quickly)
2. There are so many facets to this exploration that I'm still exploring it—which is actually a part of my purpose: to _____ explore. (joy)
3. More than 170 people were hurt by flying glass, shrapnel, ball bearings and nails, some of them _____. (grief)
4. Investigators say nearly $ 100,000 was wired into the _____'s bank accounts. (suspicion)
5. In addition to its auspicious connotations in political texts, the fox was perceived as a spectral animal able to metamorphose and to _____ people. (witch)
6. The _____ of the country mourning over the death of the beloved President was beyond description. (lament)
7. His statement was seen as an _____ to the recent drug-related killings. (allude)
8. But such an _____ of my anguish is forbidden to my reason. (alleviate)
9. The doctor was quite certain that if any _____ busybody were later to insist on an _____, he would be found innocent. (inquire)
10. The conflict turned their country into a battlefield _____ ravaged by looting and civil war. (subsequence)

II. Please choose one word or phrase that best completes the sentence.

1. Check out a few of these smart ideas and determine how they _____ your site, your customers, and your industry's niche.

A. apply to   B. apply for
   C. call for   D. call in
2. Most people don't have time to linger over a cappuccino or _____ the handsome man or the beautiful woman on the next bike.
   A. look at   B. leer at
   C. peer at   D. glance at
3. Detectives _____ professional training and caution, and looked for a different explanation.
   A. threw into   B. threw on
   C. threw apart   D. threw aside
4. If you want people to _____ you, you must make your accomplishments visible.
   A. take notice of   B. make notice of
   C. take note of   D. make note of
5. When we step outside and _____ ourselves in this natural world, we open ourselves to the enlightenment that is all around, just waiting to be reflected in each one of us.
   A. involve   B. interrupt
   C. immerse   D. intervene
6. While an individual site may not _____ too much personal information, the aggregate of all the information may reveal more about them than people realize.
   A. announce   B. declare
   C. disclosure   D. divulge

III. Translation

1. Please translate the following from English into Chinese.
   1) A runaway had no fixed place of abode.
   2) to be bewitched
   3) to grind one's teeth
   4) in a little while
   5) to approach sb. on one's knees
   6) Every effort to find somebody was unsuccessful.
   7) to mourn over one's dead husband
   8) to quicken one's pace
   9) to throw aside the brush
   10) to move along with some difficulty

2. Please translate the following from Chinese into English.
   1）解愁忧
   2）世固有死将临而不悟者！
   3）二八姝丽
   4）仰首四望
   5）惶遽无色
   6）起死回生
   7）勿怒
   8）热气腾蒸
   9）恍惚若梦
   10）长跪乞救

Unit 10
The Painted Skin

3. Please translate each sentence with at least one key word or its derivative.

Key Words: alleviate, consent, endure, startle, substitute

1）尽管手术不一定能够保证治愈疾病，但却经常可以减轻病人的疼痛和不适，阻止疾病蔓延。
2）关税并不能代替政策上的刺激，但在预算平衡期，金本位国家 (gold-standard countries) 只有这条路可走。
3）双方达成共识，在谈话中避而不谈他们去那儿的原因。
4）他们集中精力减轻难民的苦难。
5）企业、市场和政府在微观层次上是可以互相替代的，在宏观层次上是互相补充的。
6）牛顿得出了一个简单却令人震惊的结论：太阳的白光事实上是光谱中所有颜色的混合体。
7）由于你的父母看待这件事的角度不同，他们很可能不赞成这个计划。
8）这种锻炼会明显改善体力，增加耐力。
9）当你被介绍给一位陌生人时，如果对方想和你握手，你或许不会觉得意外；但如果对方向你鞠躬，或亲吻你的脸颊，你可能会有些吃惊。
10）在战争使命结束以后，我们与阿富汗仍有合作关系，而且这种合作关系将会持续下去。

After Reading

I. Please make a sentence with the words and expressions you have learnt from the text.

1. to peep out:
2. to creep up:
3. to drive away:
4. to entreat sb. to do sth.:
5. to implore one's assistance:
6. to mourn over:

II. Paragraph Writing

1. Please write a paragraph of around 150 words about your personal experience of begging others for help.

2. Please write a paragraph of around 100 words with the following words and expressions you have learnt from the text. Make sure that the paragraph you have written is grammatically correct and coherent.

hideous; curse; frighten; tear; grunt; get away

Original Edition in Chinese

画 皮

　　太原王生，早行，遇一女郎，抱襆独奔，甚艰于步。急走趁之，乃二八姝丽，心相爱乐。问："何夙夜踽踽独行？"女曰："行道之人，不能解愁忧，何劳相问。"生曰："卿何愁忧？或可效力，不辞也。"女黯然曰："父母贪赂，鬻妾朱门。嫡妒甚，朝詈而夕楚辱之，所弗堪也，将远遁耳。"问："何之？"曰："在亡之人，乌有定所。"生言："敝庐不远，即烦枉顾。"女喜，从之。生代携襆物，导与同归。女顾室无人，问："君何无家口？"答云："斋耳。"女曰："此所良佳。如怜妾而活之，须秘密，勿泄。"生诺之。乃与寝合。使匿密室，过数日而人不知也。生微告妻。妻陈，疑为大家媵妾，劝遣之。生不听。
　　偶适市，遇一道士，顾生而愕。问："何所遇？"答言："无之。"道士曰："君身邪气萦绕，何言无？"生又力白。道士乃去，曰："惑哉！世固有死将临而不悟者！"生以其言异，颇疑女。转思明明丽人，何至为妖，意道士借魇禳以猎食者。无何，至斋门，门内杜，不得入。心疑所作，乃逾垝垣。则室门亦闭。蹑迹而窗窥之，见一狞鬼，面翠色，齿巉巉如锯。铺人皮于榻上，执彩笔而绘之。已而掷笔，举皮，如振衣状，披于身，遂化为女子。睹此状，大惧，兽伏而出。急追道士，不知所往。遍迹之，遇于野，长跪乞救。道士曰："请遣除之。此物亦良苦，甫能觅代者，予亦不忍伤其生。"乃以蝇拂授生，令挂寝门。临别，约会于青帝庙。
　　生归，不敢入斋，乃寝内室，悬拂焉。一更许，闻门外戢戢有声。自不敢窥也，使妻窥之。但见女子来，望拂子不敢进；立而切齿，良久乃去。少时，复来，骂曰："道士吓我。终不然，宁入口而吐之耶！"取拂碎之，坏寝门而入。径登生床，裂生腹，掬生心而去。妻号。婢入烛之，生已死，腔血狼藉。陈骇涕不敢声。
　　明日，使弟二郎奔告道士。道士怒曰："我固怜之，鬼子乃敢尔！"即从生弟来。女子已失所在。既而仰首四望，曰："幸遁未远。"问："南院谁家？"二郎曰："小生所舍也。"道士曰："现在君所。"二郎愕然，以为未有。道士问曰："曾否有不识者一人来？"答曰："仆早赴青帝庙，良不知。当归问之。"去，少顷而返，曰："果有之。晨间一妪来，欲佣为仆家操作，室人止之，尚在也。"道士曰："即是物矣。"遂与俱往。仗木剑，立庭心，呼曰："孽魅！偿我拂子来！"妪在室，惶遽无色，出门欲遁。道士逐击之。妪仆，人皮划然而脱，化为厉鬼，卧嗥如猪。道士以木剑枭其首，身变作浓烟，匝地作堆。道士出一葫芦，拔其塞，置烟中，飗飗然如口吸气，瞬息烟尽。道士塞口入囊。

— 196 —

共视人皮，眉目手足，无不备具。道士卷之，如卷画轴声，亦囊之，乃别欲去。

　　陈氏拜迎于门，哭求回生之法。道士谢不能。陈益悲，伏地不起。道士沉思曰："我术浅，诚不能起死。我指一人，或能之，往求必合有效。"问："何人？"曰："市上有疯者，时卧粪土中。试叩而哀之。倘狂辱夫人，夫人勿怒也。"二郎亦习知之。乃别道士，与嫂俱往。

　　见乞人颠歌道上，鼻涕三尺，秽不可近。陈膝行而前。乞人笑曰："佳人爱我乎？"陈告之故。又大笑曰："人尽夫也，活之何为？"陈固哀之。乃曰："异哉！人死而乞活于我。我阎摩耶？"怒以杖击陈。陈忍痛受之。市人渐集如堵。乞人咯痰唾盈把，举向陈吻曰："食之！"陈红涨于面，有难色，既思道士之嘱，遂强啖焉。觉入喉中，硬如团絮，格格而下，停结胸间。乞人大笑曰："佳人爱我哉！"遂起，行已不顾。尾之，入于庙中。迫而求之，不知所在。前后冥搜，殊无端兆，惭恨而归。

　　既悼夫亡之惨，又悔食唾之羞，俯仰哀啼，但愿即死。方欲展血敛尸，家人伫望，无敢近者。陈抱尸收肠，且理且哭。哭极声嘶，顿欲呕。觉膈中结物，突奔而出，不及回首，已落腔中。惊而视之，乃人心也，在腔中突突犹跃，热气腾蒸如烟然。大异之，急以两手合腔，极力抱挤。少懈，则气氤氲自缝中出，乃裂缯帛急束之。以手抚尸，渐温。覆以衾裯。中夜启视，有鼻息矣。天明，竟活。为言："恍惚若梦，但觉腹隐痛耳。"视破处，痂结如钱，寻愈。

　　异史氏曰："愚哉世人！明明妖也，而以为美。迷哉愚人！明明忠也，而以为妄。然爱人之色而渔之，妻亦将食人之唾而甘之矣。天道好还，但愚而迷者不寤耳。可哀也夫！"

Text B

John Minford's Version

The Painted Skin

　　A certain gentleman by the name of Wang, from the city of Taiyuan, was out walking early one morning when a young woman passed him carrying a bundle, hurrying along on her own, though with considerable difficulty. He caught up with her, and saw at once that she was a girl of about sixteen, and very beautiful.

　　'What are you doing out here all alone at this early hour?' he asked, instantly smitten.

　　'Why do you bother to ask, since you are only a passer-by and can do nothing to ease my troubles?' was her reply.

　　'Tell me, what has caused this sorrow of yours? I will do anything I can to help you.'

　　'My parents were greedy for money,' she replied sadly, 'and sold me as a concubine into a rich man's household. The master's wife was jealous of me, and she was always screaming at me and beating me, until in the end I could bear it no longer and decided to run away.'

'Where are you going?'

'I am a fugitive. I have no place to go.'

'My own humble abode is not far from here,' said Wang. 'I should be honoured if you were to accompany me there.'

She seemed only too pleased at this suggestion and followed him home, Wang carrying her bundle for her. When they arrived, she observed that the house was empty.

'Do you have no family of your own?' she asked.

'This is my private study,' he replied.

'It seems an excellent place to me,' she said. 'But I must ask you to keep my presence here a secret and not to breathe a word of it to anyone. My very life depends on it.'

He swore to this.

That night they slept together, and for several days he kept her hidden in his study without anyone knowing that she was there. Then he decided to confide in his wife, the lady Chen. She feared the consequences if the girl should turn out to have escaped from some influential family, and advised him to send her away. But he paid no heed to her advice.

A few days later, in the marketplace, Wang ran into a Taoist priest, who studied his face with grave concern. 'What strange thing have you encountered?'

'Why, nothing!' replied Wang.

'Nothing? Your whole being is wrapped in an evil aura,' insisted the Taoist. 'I tell you, you are bewitched!'

Wang protested vehemently that he was speaking the truth.

'Bewitched!' muttered the Taoist, as he went on his way. 'Poor fool! Some men blind themselves to the truth even when death is staring them in the face!'

Something in the Taoist's strange words set Wang wondering, and he began to have serious misgivings about the young woman he had taken in. But he could not bring himself to believe that such a pretty young thing could have cast an evil spell on him. Instead he persuaded himself that the Taoist was making it all up, trying to put the wind up him in the hope of being retained for a costly rite of exorcism. And so he put the matter out of his mind and returned home.

He reached his study to find the outer door barred. He was unable to enter his own home. His suspicions now genuinely aroused, he clambered into the courtyard through a hole in the wall, only to find that the inner door was also closed. Creeping stealthily up to a window, he peeped through and saw the most hideous sight, a green-faced monster, a ghoul with great jagged teeth like a saw, leaning over a human pelt, the skin of an entire human body, spread on the bed—on *his* bed. The monster had a paintbrush in its hand and was in the process of touching up the skin in lifelike colour. When the painting was done, it threw down the brush, lifted up the skin, shook it out like a cloak and wrapped itself in it—whereupon it was instantly transformed into his pretty young 'fugitive' friend.

Wang was absolutely terrified by what he had seen, and crept away on all fours. He went at once in search of the Taoist, but did not know where to find him. He looked for him everywhere and eventually found him out in the fields. Falling on his knees, he begged the priest to save him.

'I can drive her away for you,' said the Taoist. 'But I cannot bring myself to take her life. The poor creature must have suffered greatly and is clearly close to finding a substitute and thus ending her torment.'

He gave Wang a fly-whisk and told him to hang it outside his bedroom door, instructing him to come and find him again in the Temple of the Green Emperor.

Wang returned home. This time he did not dare to go into his study, but slept with his wife, hanging the fly-whisk outside their bedroom. Late that night he heard a faint sound at the door, and not having the courage to look himself, he asked his wife to go. It was the 'girl'. She had come, but had halted on seeing the fly-whisk and was standing there grinding her teeth. Eventually she went away, only to return after a little while.

'That priest thought to scare me!' she cried. 'I'll never give up! Not now, not when I am so close! Does he think I'm going to spit it out, when I'm so near to swallowing it!'

She tore down the fly-whisk and ripped it to pieces, then broke down the door and burst into the bedroom. Climbing straight up on to the bed, she tore open Wang's chest, plucked out his heart and made off with it into the night. Wang's wife began screaming, and a maid came hurrying with a lamp, to find her master lying dead on the bed, his chest a bloody pulp, and her mistress sobbing in silent horror beside him, incapable of uttering a word.

The next morning, they sent Wang's younger brother off at once to find the Taoist.

'To think that I took pity on her!' cried the priest angrily. 'Clearly that fiend will stop at nothing!'

He followed Wang's brother back to the house. By now, of course, there was no trace of the 'girl'. The Taoist gazed around him. 'Fortunately she is still close at hand.'

He went on to ask, 'Who lives in the house to the south?'

'That is my family compound,' replied Wang's brother.

'That is where she is now,' said the priest.

Wang's brother was appalled at the idea and could not bring himself to believe it.

'Has a stranger come to your house today?' asked the priest.

'How would I know?' replied the brother. 'I went out first thing to the Temple of the Green Emperor to fetch you. I shall have to go home and ask.'

Presently he returned to report that there had indeed been an old lady. 'She called first thing this morning, saying she wanted to work for us. My wife kept her on, and she is still there.'

'That's the very person we're looking for!' cried the Taoist. He strode next door immediately with the brother, and took up a stance in the middle of the courtyard, brandishing his wooden sword.

'Come out, evil one!' he cried. 'Give me back my fly-whisk!'

The old woman came hurtling out of the building, her face deathly pale, and made a frantic attempt to escape, but the Taoist pursued her and struck her down. As she fell to the ground the human pelt slipped from her, to reveal her as the vile fiend she really was, grovelling on the ground and grunting like a pig. The Taoist swung his wooden sword again and chopped off the monster's head, whereupon its body was transformed into a thick cloud of smoke hovering above the ground. The Taoist now took out a bottle-gourd, removed the stopper and placed it in the midst of the smoke. With a whooshing sound the smoke was sucked into the gourd, leaving no trace in the courtyard. He replaced the stopper and slipped the gourd back into his bag.

When they examined the pelt, it was complete in every human detail—the eyes, the hands and feet. The Taoist proceeded to roll it up like a scroll (it even made the same sound), placed it in his bag and set off. Wang's wife, who was waiting for him at the entrance, beseeched him to bring her husband back to life, and when the Taoist protested that he had already reached the limits of his powers, she became more and more hysterical and inconsolable, throwing herself on the ground and absolutely refusing to get up. The Taoist seemed to ponder the matter deeply.

'Truly, I cannot raise the dead,' he said eventually. 'But I can tell you of one who may be able to do so. Go to him, ask him, and I dare say he will be able to help you.'

Wang's wife asked him whom he was referring to.

'He is a madman who frequents the marketplace and sleeps on a dunghill. You must go down on your knees and beg him to help you. If he insults you, madam, you must on no account go against him or be angry with him.'

Wang's brother knew of this beggar. He took his leave of the Taoist, and accompanied his sister-in-law to the marketplace, where they found the man begging by the roadside, singing a crazy song. A good three inches of mucus trailed from his nose, and he was so foul it was unthinkable to go near him. But Wang's wife approached him on her knees.

'Do you love me, my pretty?' leered the mad beggar.

She told him her tale, and he laughed loudly.

'There's plenty of fine men in this world for you to marry! Why bother bringing *him* back to life?'

She pleaded with him.

'You're a strange one!' he said. 'You want me to raise the dead? Who do you take me for—the King of Hell?'

He struck her with his stick and she bore it without a murmur. By now quite a crowd had gathered around them. The beggar spat a great gob of phlegm into the palm of his hand and held it up to her mouth.

'Eat!'

She flushed deeply and could not bring herself to obey his order. Then she remembered what the Taoist had commanded and steeled herself to swallow the congealed phlegm. As it went down her throat it felt hard like a lump of cotton wadding, and even when, after several gulps, she managed to swallow it down, she could still feel it lodged in her chest. The madman guffawed.

'You really do love me then, don't you, my darling?'

And with those words, off he went. The meeting was clearly over, and he paid her no further attention. She followed him into the temple, determined to plead with him again, but though she searched every corner of the temple, she could find no trace of him. So she returned home, greatly downcast, filled with grief at her husband's appalling death, and overcome with shame and self-disgust at the treatment she had tolerated from the mad beggar. She wailed pathetically and for a time contemplated taking her own life.

When eventually she went to wash the blood from her husband's corpse and prepare it for the coffin, her women stood to one side watching, none of them having the stomach to approach their dead master's corpse. She lifted him up in her arms and started carefully replacing his internal organs, sobbing so fiercely that she began to choke and feel nauseous. Then she felt the lump of phlegm rising in her gullet and brought it up, so suddenly that she had no time to turn away, but spat it directly into the gaping wound in her husband's chest. She stared aghast: the phlegm had become a human heart and lay there throbbing, hot and steaming. In disbelief, she brought the sides of the wound together with both her hands, pressing with all her strength. If she relaxed her grip for an instant, she saw hot steam leaking from the wound. She tore a strip of silk from her dress and bound the wound tightly. In a little while, when she touched her husband's corpse, she felt the warmth returning. She drew the bedcovers fully over it. In the middle of the night when she lifted the covers, he was already breathing through his nose. By the next morning, he was fully alive.

'I was drifting,' he said. 'Everything was confused. It was like a dream. But all the time I felt this pain deep in my heart.'

The wound formed a scar the size of a coin, which disappeared with time.

Notes on the Text

1. About the text

The present text is taken from *Strange Tales from a Chinese Studio* translated by John Minford, published by Penguin Group in 2006.

2. John Minford

John Minford, an emeritus professor of Chinese at the Australian National University, is a sinologist and literary translator. He is primarily known for his translations of Chinese classics such as *Strange Tales from a Chinese Studio*, *The Story of the Stone*, and *The Art of War*. Minford's most recent work, a translation of the famous Chinese divination text, the *I Ching*, was published in 2014 by Penguin Books.

Unit 11

Lin Ru-Hai Recommends a Private Tutor to His Brother-in-Law and Old Lady Jia Extends a Compassionate Welcome to the Motherless Child (excerpt)

Reading Guide

This text is excerpted from Chapter 3 "Lin Ru-Hai Recommends a Private Tutor to His Brother-in-Law and Old Lady Jia Extends a Compassionate Welcome to the Motherless Child" of *The Story of the Stone* translated by David Hawkes, a British sinologist and translator. Over nearly 10 years, Prof. Hawkes completed the translation of the first 80 chapters of the novel, which were published in three volumes (1973, 1977 and 1980) by Penguin Books. The final 40 chapters, which appeared after Cao Xueqin's death, were translated by his son-in-law, the sinologist John Minford. Prof. Hawkes was considered the most outstanding non-Chinese Redology (the academic study of *The Story of the Stone*) expert. In a review of the translation, Frederic Wakeman, Jr., a prominent American scholar of East Asian history, described it as a "masterpiece" and the work of a "literary genius" in *"The New York Review of Books"*.[①]

This excerpt is one of the most intriguing scenes in *The Story of the Stone*, which vividly portrays the first meeting between Lin Dai-yu and Jia Bao-yu. Having to depend on her uncle for a living shortly after her mother's death, Dai-yu knows well to be perceptive about others' expressions and words there. Nonetheless, when discovering that Dai-yu doesn't have a special jade like his, Bao-yu flows into a rage and hurls his jade on the floor, leaving the others shocked and terrified. Bao-yu's willfulness and irritability contrast starkly with Dai-yu's delicacy and

---

① This review is quoted from "The New York Review of Books", and the website is http://www.nybooks.com/articles/1980/06/12/the-genius-of-the-red-chamber/.

Unit 11
Lin Ru-Hai Recommends a Private Tutor to His Brother-in-Law and Old Lady Jia Extends a Compassionate Welcome to the Motherless Child (excerpt)

sensitivity. Besides, their physical appearance is pictured in great details to boot in the text. Prof. Hawkes's translation is worth careful reading for its fine rendering of the characterization of appearance and psychology.

Before Reading

I. Preview Requirements: Please make a preparatory research on the background information, key words and phrases of this text.

1. Do research on the translator David Hawkes.
2. Do research on the historical context of the Qing Dynasty and the life of Cao Xueqin.
3. Do research on the reception of *The Story of the Stone* in the West.
4. Find and study the new words in the text such as *augment, appraisal, bestow, chide, surmise,* and *terminate*.
5. Learn the useful expressions in the text such as *seek out, catch sight of, pay ones' respect to, cling to,* and *in a nasty temper*.

II. Preview Questions: Please answer some questions about the understanding of the main content of the text.

1. What is the most impressive scene in the text?
2. What can be suggested from the detailed description of Dai-yu's and Bao-yu's appearance?
3. Why do you think Dai-yu gave different answers to Grandmother Jia's and Bao-yu's questions concerning study of books? What made her withhold the truth?
4. Why did Dai-yu and Bao-yu both feel that they had met each other before? In any sense can we assume that they were destined to meet?
5. What is the importance of the fact that Bao-yu threw his jade on the ground? How does this fact contribute to the development of the plot?
6. What do you make of the first meeting between Dai-yu and Bao-yu?
7. What is the central theme of *The Story of the Stone*?
8. Compare and contrast the writing styles of Cao Xueqin and Zhang Henshui, whose masterpieces are *A Family of Distinction* and *Fate in Tears and Laughter* respectively.
9. According to Aristotle, what is tragedy? Do you regard Dai-yu's life as a tragedy? Why?
10. How do you view the love story between Bao-yu and Dai-yu?

Text A

David Hawkes's Version

Lin Ru-Hai Recommends a Private Tutor to His Brother-in-Law and Old Lady Jia Extends a Compassionate Welcome to the Motherless Child (excerpt)

.....

Grandmother Jia asked Dai-yu what books she was studying.

'*The Four Books,*' said Dai-yu, and inquired in turn what books her cousins were currently engaged on.

'Gracious, child, they don't study books,' said her grandmother; 'they can barely read and write!'

While they were speaking, a flurry of footsteps could be heard outside and a maid came in to say that Bao-yu was back.

'I wonder,' thought Dai-yu, 'just what sort of graceless creature this Bao-yu is going to be!'

The young gentleman who entered in answer to her unspoken question had a small jewel-encrusted gold coronet on the top of his head and a golden headband low down over his brow in the form of two dragons playing with a large pearl.

He was wearing a narrow-sleeved, full-skirted robe of dark red material with a pattern of flowers and butterflies in two shades of gold. It was confined at the waist with a court girdle of coloured silks braided at regular intervals into elaborate clusters of knotwork and terminating in long tassels.

Over the upper part of his robe he wore a jacket of slate-blue Japanese silk damask with a raised pattern of eight large medallions on the front and with tasselled borders.

On his feet he had half-length dress boots of black satin with thick white soles.

As to his person, he had:

a face like the moon of Mid-Autumn,

a complexion like flowers at dawn,

a hairline straight as a knife-cut,

eyebrows that might have been painted by an artist's brush,

a shapely nose, and

eyes clear as limpid pools,

that even in anger seemed to smile,

and, as they glared, beamed tenderness the while.

Around his neck he wore a golden torque in the likeness on a dragon and a woven cord of coloured silks to which the famous jade was attached.

Dai-yu looked at him with astonishment. How strange! How very strange! It was as though she had seen him somewhere before, he was so extraordinarily familiar. Bao-yu went straight past her and saluted his grandmother, who told him to come after he had seen his mother, whereupon he turned round and walked straight out again.

Quite soon he was back once more, this time dressed in a completely different outfit.

The crown and circlet had gone. She could now see that his side hair was dressed in a number of small braids plaited with red silk, which were drawn round to join the long hair at the back in a single large queue of glistening jet black, fastened at intervals from the nape downwards with four enormous pearls and ending in a jewelled gold clasp. He had changed his robe and jacket for a rather more worn-looking rose-coloured gown, sprigged with flowers. He wore the gold torque and his jade as before, and she observed that the collection of objects round his neck had been further augmented by a padlock-shaped amulet and a lucky charm. A pair of ivy-coloured embroidered silk trousers were partially visible beneath his gown, thrust into black and white socks trimmed with brocade. In place of the formal boots he was wearing thick-soled crimson slippers.

She was even more struck than before by his fresh complexion. The cheeks might have been brushed with powder and the lips touched with rouge, so bright was their natural colour.

    His glance was soulful,
        yet from his lips the laughter often leaped;
            a world of charm upon that brow was heaped;
            a world of feeling from those dark eyes peeped.

In short, his outward appearance was very fine. But appearances can be misleading. A perceptive poet has supplied two sets of verses, to be sung to the tune of *Moon on West River*, which contain a more accurate appraisal of our hero than the foregoing descriptions.

1

Oft-times he sought out what would make him sad;
Sometimes an idiot seemed and sometimes mad.
Though outwardly a handsome sausage-skin,
He proved to have but sorry meat within.
A harum-scarum, to all duty blind,
A doltish mule, to study disinclined;
His acts outlandish and his nature queer;
Yet not a whit cared he how folk might jeer!

Prosperous, he could not play his part with grace,
Nor, poor, bear hardship with a smiling face.
So shamefully the precious hours he'd waste.
That both indoors and out he was disgraced.
For uselessness the world's prize he might bear;
His gracelessness in history has no peer.
Let gilded youths who every dainty sample
Not imitate this rascal's dire example!

'Fancy changing your clothes before you have welcomed the visitor!' Grandmother Jia chided indulgently on seeing Bao-yu back again. 'Aren't you going to pay your respects to your cousin?'

Bao-yu had already caught sight of a slender, delicate girl whom he surmised to be his Aunt Lin's daughter and quickly went over to greet her. Then, returning to his place and taking a seat, he studied her attentively. How different she seemed from the other girls he knew!

Her mist-wreathed brows at first seemed to frown, yet were not frowning;
Her passionate eyes at first seemed to smile, yet were not merry.
Habit had given a melancholy cast to her tender face;
Nature had bestowed a sickly constitution on her delicate frame.
Often the eyes swam with glistening tears;
Often the breath came in gentle gasps.
In stillness she made one think of a graceful flower reflected in the water;
In motion she called to mind tender willow shoots caressed by the wind.
She had more chambers in her heart than the martyred Bi Gan;
And suffered a tithe more pain in it than the beautiful Xi Shi.

Having completed his survey, Bao-yu gave a laugh.

'I have seen this cousin before.'

'Nonsense!' said Grandmother Jia. 'How could you possibly have done?'

'Well, perhaps not,' said Bao-yu, 'but her face seems so familiar that I have the impression of meeting her again after a long separation.'

'All the better,' said Grandmother Jia. 'That means that you should get on well together.'

Bao-yu moved over again and, drawing a chair up beside Dai-yu, recommenced his scrutiny.

Presently: 'Do you study books yet, cousin?'

'No,' said Dai-yu. 'I have only been taking lessons for a year or so. I can barely read and write.'

'What's your name?'

Dai-yu told him.

'What's your school-name?'

'I haven't got one.'

Bao-yu laughed. 'I'll give you one, cousin. I think "Frowner" would suit you perfectly.'

'Where's your reference?' said Tan-chun.

'In the *Encyclopedia of Men and Objects Ancient and Modern* it says that somewhere in the West there is a mineral called "dai" which can be used instead of eye-black for painting the eyebrows with. She has this "dai" in her name and she knits her brows together in a little frown. I think it's a splendid name for her.'

'I expect you made it up,' said Tan-chun scornfully.

'What if I did?' said Bao-yu. 'There are lots of made-up things in books—apart from the *Four Books*, of course.'

He returned to his interrogation of Dai-yu.

'Have you got a jade?'

The rest of the company were puzzled, but Dai-yu at once divined that he was asking her if she too had a jade like the one he was born with.

'No,' said Dai-yu. 'That jade of yours is a very rare object. You can't expect everybody to have one.'

This sent Bao-yu off instantly into one of his mad fits. Snatching the jade from his neck he hurled it violently on the floor as if to smash it and began abusing it passionately.

'Rare object! Rare object! What's so lucky about a stone that can't even tell which people are better than others? Beastly thing! I don't want it!'

The maids all seemed terrified and rushed forward to pick it up, while Grandmother Jia clung to Bao-yu in alarm.

'Naughty, naughty boy! Shout at someone or strike them if you like when you are in a nasty temper, but why go smashing that precious thing that your very life depends on?'

'None of the girls has got one,' said Bao-yu, his face streaming with tears and sobbing hysterically. 'Only I have got one. It always upsets me. And now this new cousin comes here who is as beautiful as an angel and she hasn't got one either, so I *know* it can't be any good.'

'Your cousin did have a jade once,' said Grandmother Jia, coaxing him like a little child, 'but because when Auntie died she couldn't bear to leave her little girl behind, they had to let her take the jade with her instead. In that way your cousin could show her mamma how much she loved her by letting the jade be buried with her; and at the same time, whenever Auntie's spirit looked at the jade, it would be just like looking at her own little girl again.

'So when your cousin said she hadn't got one, it was only because she didn't want to boast about the good, kind thing she did when she gave it to her mamma. Now you put yours on again like a good boy, and mind your mother doesn't find out how naughty you have been.'

So saying, she took the jade from the hands of one of the maids and hung it round his neck for him. And Bao-yu, after reflecting for a moment or two on what she had said, offered no further resistance.

Notes on the Text

1. The Four Books

Chinese classic texts illustrating the core value and belief systems in Confucianism, including *Great Learning*, *Doctrine of the Mean*, *Analects* and *Mencius*.

2. Bi Gan

A prominent Chinese figure during the Shang Dynasty. Notorious for his corruptness, Di Xin (about 1105 BC—1046 BC), the last emperor of the Shang Dynasty, was annoyed by Bi Gan's advice to mend his ways. He ordered Bi Gan's execution through the extraction of his heart, with the terrifying excuse of curiosity "whether the Sage's heart has seven openings". Bi Gan was honored by Confucius as "one of the three men of virtue" of the Shang Dynasty, together with Weizi and Jizi.

3. Xi Shi

One of the renowned "Four Beauties of Ancient China" (the other three were Wang Zhaojun, Diao Chan, and Yang Yuhuan). She was said to have lived during the end of the Spring and Autumn Period in Zhuyi, the capital of the ancient State of Yue.

Glossary

appraisal /əˈpreɪzl/	*n.* an act of assessing sth. or sb.
	e.g.: *Initially, the physician should do a health-risk appraisal of each patient.*
augment /ɔːgˈment/	*v.* to make sth. greater by adding to it; to increase
	e.g.: *He augmented his summer income by painting houses.*
bestow /bɪˈstəʊ/	*v.* to confer or present (an honour, right, or gift)
	e.g.: *The office was bestowed on him by the monarch of this realm.*
caress /kəˈres/	*v.* to touch or stroke gently or lovingly
	e.g.: *Birds were chirping happily as the bright rays of the sun touched and caressed her skin.*
chide /tʃaɪd/	*v.* to scold or rebuke
	chide sb. for (doing) sth. e.g.: *She chided him for not replying to her letters.*
coax /kəʊks/	*v.* persuade sb. gradually or gently to do sth.

Unit 11
Lin Ru-Hai Recommends a Private Tutor to His Brother-in-Law and Old Lady Jia Extends a Compassionate Welcome to the Motherless Child (excerpt)

	coax sb. into/out of (doing) sth. e.g.: *He coaxed her into letting him take her to the cinema.*
divine /dɪˈvaɪn/	*v.* 1. to discover sth. by guesswork or intuition
	e.g.: *She has had remarkable success in divining those names.*
	2. to have supernatural or magical insight into (future events)
	e.g: *Black cats were considered to be reincarnated beings with the ability to divine the future.*
dire /daɪə/	*adj.* extremely serious or urgent
	e.g.: *Misuse of drugs can have dire consequences.*
encrust /ɪnˈkrʌst/	*v.* to cover or decorate sth. with a hard surface layer
	e.g.: *Every surface is encrusted in sponges, corals and weed.*
interrogation /ɪnˌterəˈgeɪʃ(ə)n/	*n.* the action of interrogating or the process of being interrogated
	e.g.: *He had conducted hundreds of criminal interrogations.*
limpid /ˈlɪmpɪd/	*adj.* (of a liquid) completely clear and transparent
	e.g.: *The limpid grey eyes gazed trustfully at her.*
salute /səˈluːt/	*v.* to give sb. a salute, to greet sb.
	e.g.: *She waved cheerfully and Kyle saluted her right back.*
surmise /səˈmaɪz/	*v.* to suppose sth. without having evidence that makes it certain; to guess
	e.g.: *With no news from the explorers we can only surmise their present position.*
terminate /ˈtɜːmɪneɪt/	*v.* to come to an end or bring sth. to an end
	e.g.: *He was advised to terminate the contract.*

While Reading

I. Please fill in the blanks with the words in the parentheses with the appropriate part of speech.

1. Classical architecture was a metaphorical imitation of this _____ ordered nature. (divine)
2. Unfortunately, with the exception of blood tests for anemia, there are no assessments that accurately _____ your nutritional status. (appraisal)
3. She refused to participate in political bribery, which is the _____ prerequisite backbone of her country. (speak)
4. Stevens paused again, changing the sound of his voice to an _____ tone. (interrogation)
5. Even the most successful elections later this year cannot possibly scrub away decades of _____ corruption and inaction. (crust)
6. Audiences today are not only _____ to listen to new music, they're reluctant to listen to anything unfamiliar. (incline)

7. We all know Baron is loathed for the _____ way in which he betrayed the Cleverland Cooperation. (grace)

8. When I was still studying in college, I was pretty _____ of mainstream movies. (scorn)

9. Once the audience is _____, you start feeling the feedback, and continue to learn in the process. (attention)

10. That the portraits of Beethoven did not bear much _____ to the composer could be deemed a deliberate transgression. (like)

II. Please choose one word or phrase that best completes the sentence.

1. Through successful marketing programs, these companies have acquired loyal customer bases willing to seek them _____ and buy their brands on-line.
   A. from
   B. out
   C. away
   D. up

2. The anxious looks they _____ backwards were not directed at her.
   A. cast
   B. casted
   C. express
   D. expressed

3. The narrator explains that all these stories are _____, but they are true anyway, because they explain what Vietnam was like.
   A. made with
   B. made for
   C. made up for
   D. made up

4. My parents are sending me _____ to summer camp to get some exercise and fresh air.
   A. off
   B. for
   C. away
   D. up

5. Lisa suffers from _____ sudden rage and unbearable fatigue.
   A. fit of
   B. spell of
   C. fits of
   D. spells of

6. The Presidential Medal of Freedom is the highest honor a President can _____ a civilian.
   A. bestow with
   B. bestow on
   C. be bestowed with
   D. be bestowed on

III. Translation

1. Please translate the following from English into Chinese.

1) a graceless creature
2) flowers at dawn
3) eyes clear as limpid pools
4) queer nature
5) to have no peer
6) tender willow shoots caressed by the wind
7) gilded youths
8) a slender, delicate girl
9) to send sb. into mad fits
10) a hairline straight as a knife-cut

Unit 11
Lin Ru-Hai Recommends a Private Tutor to His Brother-in-Law and Old Lady Jia Extends a Compassionate Welcome to the Motherless Child (excerpt)

2. Please translate the following from Chinese into English.

1）罕物　　　　　　　2）二龙抢珠
3）寄名锁　　　　　　4）笼烟眉
5）黑亮如漆　　　　　6）含情目
7）唇若施脂　　　　　8）护身符
9）远别重逢　　　　　10）不生别论

3. Please translate each sentence with at least one key word or its derivative.

Key Words: bestow, coax, salute, indulge, perceive

1）一位好的教师应对学生取得的进步非常敏感。如果学生的进步被忽视，他们就会感到沮丧。
2）当女孩闷闷不乐地坐下时，治疗师指导妈妈不要哄她出去玩，而只是叙述女儿正在做什么。
3）他们过分纵容孩子，这对孩子的性格有不良影响。
4）总统对那些为国战斗者的英勇精神表示敬意。
5）"网络舆论暴力"（"Consensus Violence" in Web）产生的原因在于网络的隐匿性特征，它使得网民的行为容易放纵和过激。
6）这是因为人们给曾经对他们很重要的东西赋予了价值。
7）关键任务是让学生自己认识到成功和努力之间的关系。
8）政府承诺给他们发放暂住证，诱哄他们放弃罢工。
9）我们跟村里的每个人都相处得很好。连当地的警察骑着自行车经过时，我们都会向他敬礼。
10）你应该多花点时间去工作而少花点时间去幻想。

After Reading

I. Please make a sentence with the words and expressions you have learnt from the text.

1. to augment:
2. to chide:
3. to catch sight of:
4. to caress:
5. to terminate:

II. Paragraph Writing

1. Please write a paragraph of around 150 words to depict the character of Dai-yu and Bao-yu with the evidence in the text.

2. Please write a paragraph of around 100 words with the following words and expressions you have learnt from the text. Make sure that the paragraph you have written is grammatically correct and coherent.

> gracious; dire; barely; mist-wreathed; surmise

Original Edition in Chinese

托内兄如海荐西宾 接外孙贾母惜孤女（节选）

……

贾母因问黛玉念何书。黛玉道："刚念了《四书》。"黛玉又问姊妹们读何书，贾母道："读什么书，不过认几个字罢了！"

一语未了，只听外面一阵脚步响，丫鬟进来报道："宝玉来了。"黛玉心中想："这个宝玉不知是怎生个惫懒人物！"及至进来，原是一位青年公子，头上戴着束发嵌宝紫金冠，齐眉勒着二龙抢珠金抹额，一件二色金白蝶穿花大红箭袖，束着五彩丝攒花结长穗宫绦，外罩石青起花八团倭缎排穗褂，登着青缎粉底小朝靴；面若中秋之月，色如春晓之花，鬓若刀裁，眉如墨画，鼻如悬胆，睛若秋波，虽怒时而似笑，即瞋视而有情；项上金螭璎珞，又有一根五色丝绦，系着一块美玉。

黛玉一见便吃大一惊，心中想道："好生奇怪，倒像在那里见过的，何等眼熟！"只见这宝玉向贾母请了安，贾母便命："去见你娘来。"即转身去了。一回再来时，已换了冠带，头上周围一转的短发，即结成小辫，红丝结束，共攒至顶中胎发，总编一根大辫，黑亮如漆，从顶至梢，一串四颗大珠，用金八宝坠脚；身上穿着银红撒花半旧大袄；仍旧带着项圈、宝玉、寄名锁、护身符等物；下面半露松绿撒花绫裤，锦边弹墨袜，厚底大红鞋。越显得面如傅粉，唇若施脂；转盼多情，语言若笑。天然一段风韵，全在眉梢；平生万种情思，悉堆眼角。看其外貌，最是极好，却难知其底细，后人有作《西江月》二词批宝玉极确，其词曰：

无故寻愁觅恨，有时似傻如狂；纵然生得好皮囊，腹内原来草莽。潦倒不通庶务，愚顽怕读文章；行为偏僻性乖张，那管世人诽谤！

富贵不知乐业，贫穷难耐凄凉；可怜辜负好韶光，于国于家无望。天下无能第一，古今不肖无双；寄言纨绔与膏粱：莫效此儿形状！

却说贾母笑道："外客未见就脱了衣裳！还不去见你姊妹。"宝玉早已看见了一个姊妹，便料定是林姑妈之女，忙来作揖，相见毕归坐，细看形容，与众各别：

Unit 11
Lin Ru-Hai Recommends a Private Tutor to His Brother-in-Law and Old Lady Jia Extends a Compassionate Welcome to the Motherless Child (excerpt)

两弯似蹙非蹙笼烟眉，一双似喜非喜含情目。态生两靥之愁，娇袭一身之病。泪光点点，娇喘微微。闲静时如娇花照水，行动如弱柳扶风。心较比干多一窍，病如西子胜三分。

宝玉看罢，笑道："这个姊妹我曾见过的。"贾母笑道："可又是胡说，你何曾见过他？"宝玉笑道："虽然未曾见过他，然看着面善，心里像倒是旧相认识，恍若远别重逢的一般。"贾母笑道："好，好！若如此更相和睦了。"

宝玉便走向黛玉身边坐下，又细细打量一番，因问："妹妹可曾读书？"黛玉道："不曾读书，只上了一年学，些须认得几个字。"宝玉又道："妹妹尊名？"黛玉便说了名，宝玉又道："表字？"黛玉道："无字。"宝玉笑道："我送妹妹一字，莫若'颦颦'二字极妙。"探春便道："何处出典？"宝玉道："《古今人物通考》上说：'西方有石名黛，可代画眉之墨。'况这妹妹眉尖若蹙，用取这两个字岂不甚美？"探春笑道："只恐又是杜撰。"宝玉笑道："除《四书》，杜撰的太多，偏只我是杜撰不成？"又问黛玉："可有玉没有？"众人都不解。黛玉便忖度着："因他有玉，故问我有无。"因答道："我没有。那玉亦是件罕物，岂能人人皆有？"

宝玉听了，登时发作起狂病来，摘下那玉，就狠命摔去，骂道："什么罕物！人的高下不识，还说灵不灵呢！我也不要这劳什子！"吓的地下众人一拥争去拾玉。贾母急的搂了宝玉道："孽障！你生气要打骂人容易，何苦摔那命根子！"宝玉满面泪痕泣道："家里姐姐妹妹都没有，单我有，我说没趣，如今来了这个神仙似的妹妹也没有，可知这不是个好东西。"贾母忙哄他道："这妹妹原有玉来的，因你姑妈去世时，舍不得你妹妹，无法可处，遂将他的玉带了去，一则全殉葬之礼，尽你妹妹之孝心；二则你姑妈之灵亦可权作见了你妹妹之意。因此他只说没有玉，也是不便自己夸张之意。你如今怎比得他，还不好生慎重带上，仔细你娘知道了。"说着便向丫鬟手中接来，亲与他带上。宝玉听如此说，想一想，也就不生别论了。

Text B

Yang Hsien-yi & Gladys Yang's Version

Lin Ju-hai Recommends a Tutor to His Brother-in-Law The Lady Dowager Sends for Her Motherless Grand-Daughter(excerpt)

......

Then her grandmother asked Tai-yu what books she had studied.

"I've just finished the *Four Books*," said Tai-yu."But I'm very ignorant." Then she inquired what the other girls were reading.

"They only know a very few characters, not enough to read any books."

The words were hardly out of her mouth when they heard footsteps in the courtyard and a maid came in to announce, "Pao-yu is here."

Tai-yu was wondering what sort of graceless scamp or little dunce Pao-yu was and feeling reluctant to meet such a stupid creature when, even as the maid announced him, in he walked.

He had on a golden coronet studded with jewels and a golden chaplet in the form of two dragons fighting for a pearl. His red archer's jacket, embroidered with golden butterflies and flowers, was tied with a coloured tasselled palace sash. Over this he wore a turquoise fringed coat of Japanese satin with a raised pattern of flowers in eight bunches. His court boots were of black satin with white soles.

His face was at radiant as the mid-autumn moon, his complexion fresh as spring flowers at dawn. The hair above his temples was as sharply outlined as if cut with a knife. His eyebrows were as black as if painted with ink, his cheeks as red as peach-blossom, his eyes bright as autumn ripples. Even when angry he seemed to smile, and there was warmth in his glance even when he frowned.

Round his neck he had a golden torque in the likeness of a dragon, and a silk cord of five colours, on which hung a beautiful piece of jade.

His appearance took Tai-yu by surprise. "How very strange!" she thought. "It's as if I'd seen him somewhere before. He looks so familiar."

Pao-yu paid his respects to the Lady Dowager and upon her instructions went to see his mother.

He returned before long, having changed his clothes. His short hair in small plaits tied with red silk was drawn up on the crown of his head and braided into one thick queue as black and glossy as lacquer, sporting four large pearls attached to golden pendants in the form of the eight precious things. His coat of a flower pattern on a bright red ground was not new, and he still wore the torque, the precious jade, a lock-shaped amulet containing his Buddhistic name, and a lucky charm. Below could be glimpsed light green flowered satin trousers, black-dotted stockings with brocade borders, and thick-soled scarlet shoes.

His face looked as fair as if powdered, his lips red as rouge. His glance was full of affection, his speech interspersed with smiles. But his natural charm appeared most in his brows, for his eyes sparkled with a world of feeling. However, winning as his appearance was, it was difficult to tell what lay beneath.

Someone subsequently gave an admirable picture of Pao-yu in these two verses written to the melody of *The Moon over the West River*:

> Absurdly he courts care and melancholy
> And raves like any madman in his folly;

For though endowed with handsome looks is he,
His heart is lawless and refractory.

Too dense by far to understand his duty,
Too stubborn to apply himself to study,
Foolhardy in his eccentricity,
He's deaf to all reproach and obloquy.

Left cold by riches and nobility,
Unfit to bear the stings of poverty,
He wastes his time and his ability.
Failing his country and his family.

First in this world for uselessness is he,
Second to none in his deficiency.
Young fops and lordlings all, be warned by me:
Don't imitate this youth's perversity!

    With a smile at Pao-yu, the Lady Dowager scolded, "Fancy changing your clothes before greeting our visitor. Hurry up now and pay your respects to your cousin."

    Of course, Pao-yu had seen this new cousin earlier on and guessed that she was the daughter of his Aunt Lin. He made haste to bow and, having greeted her, took a seat. Looking at Tai-yu closely, he found her different from other girls.

    Her dusky arched eyebrows were knitted and yet not frowning, her speaking eyes held both merriment and sorrow; her very frailty had charm. Her eyes sparkled with tears, her breath was soft and faint. In repose she was like a lovely flower mirrored in the water; in motion, a pliant willow swaying in the wind. She looked more sensitive than Pi Kan, more delicate than Hsi Shih.

    "I've met this cousin before," he declared at the end of his scrutiny.

    "You're talking nonsense again," said his grandmother, laughing. "How could you possibly have met her?"

    "Well, even if I haven't, her face looks familiar. I feel we're old friends meeting again after a long separation."

    "So much the better." The Lady Dowager laughed. "That means you're bound to be good friends."

    Pao-yu went over to sit beside Tai-yu and once more gazed fixedly at her.

    "Have you done much reading, cousin?" he asked.

    "No," said Tai-yu. "I've only studied for a couple of years and learned a few characters."

    "What's your name?"

    She told him.

"And your courtesy name?"

"I have none."

"I'll give you one then," he proposed with a chuckle. "What could be better than Pin-pin[①]?"

"Where's that from?" put in Tan-chun.

"*The Compendium of Men and Objects Old and New* says that in the west is a stone called *tai* which can be used instead of graphite for painting eyebrows. As Cousin Lin's eyebrows look half knit, what could be more apt than these two characters?"

"You're making that up, I'm afraid," teased Tan-chun.

"Most works, apart from *the* [*The*] *Four Books*, are made up; am I the only one who makes things up?" he retorted with a grin. Then, to the mystification of them all, he asked Tai-yu if she had any jade.

Imagining that he had his own jade in mind, she answered, "No, I haven't. I suppose it's too rare for everybody to have."

This instantly threw Pao-yu into one of his frenzies. Tearing off the jade he flung it on the ground.

"What's rare about it?" he stormed. "It can't even tell good people from bad. What spiritual understanding has it got? I don't want this nuisance either."

In consternation all the maids rushed forward to pick up the jade while the Lady Dowager in desperation took Pao-yu in her arms.

"You wicked monster!" she scolded. "Storm at people if you're in a passion. But why should you throw away that precious thing your life depends on?"

His face stained with tears, Pao-yu sobbed, "None of the girls here has one, only me. What's the fun of that? Even this newly arrived cousin who's lovely as a fairy hasn't got one either. That shows it's no good."

"She did have one once," said the old lady to soothe him. "But when your aunt was dying and was unwilling to leave her, the best she could do was to take the jade with her instead. That was like burying the living with the dead and showed your cousin's filial piety. It meant, too, that now your aunt's spirit can still see your cousin. That's why she said she had none, not wanting to boast about it. How can you compare with her? Now put it carefully on again lest your mother hears about this."

She took the jade from one of the maids and put it on him herself. And Pao-yu, convinced by her tale, let the matter drop.

Notes on the Text

About the text

The present text is taken from *A Dream of Red Mansions* translated by Yang Hsien-yi and Gladys Yang, published by Foreign Languages Press in 2010.

---

① knitted brows.

Unit 12

At the Foot of Mount Li the Traces of an Ancient Emperor; By the Side of Lake Ming the Song of a Beautiful Girl (excerpt)

Reading Guide

This text is an excerpt from the 2nd episode "At the Foot of Mount Li the Traces of an Ancient Emperor; By the Side of Lake Ming the Song of a Beautiful Girl" of *The Travels of Lao Ts'an* translated and edited by Harold Shadick. The first full-length English version of *The Travels of Lao Ts'an* was translated by Lin Yijin and Ko Te-shun named as *Tramp Doctor's Travelogue*, published by Commercial Press in 1939. In 1947, the version translated by Yang Hsien-yi and Gladys Yang was published by Nanjing Independent Publishing Company. Thereafter, many other full-length versions were published, among which the version by Harold Shadick, published in 1952 by Cornell University Press, gained its influence in the Western world. Shadick was born in the United States, later moved to Canada, and graduated from the University of Toronto. Having acted as the director of the Department of Western Languages in Yenching University in the 1930s, he had a perfect mastery of both Chinese and Western culture, and therefore his version is faithful to the original, especially the notes in the book well facilitate readers' understanding. Besides, the illustrations, an embodiment of the novel's cultural connotations, are well received by the readers. This version is so popular with Western readers that it has been reprinted several times.

This excerpt is a well-known and representative episode from *The Travels of Lao Ts'an*. The Western readers had their first contact with modern Chinese novels between 1920s and 1930s, starting with *The Travel of Lao Ts'an*. As early as 1929, "The Sing Girl", the second episode translated by Arthur Waley was published on magazine *Asia*, which displays the great talent of Liu E to Western readers. This excerpt depicts the fantastic performance of the Accompanist, the Dark Maid, and the Fair Maid. Particularly its vivid depiction of the exquisite singing by the Fair

Maid is a great reflection of achievement of the traditional Chinese art. Singing, being intangible, appeals to people's ears and is difficult to describe in words. However, by applying various techniques like appealing to people's sense of sight, sense of taste and sense of touch, the writer successfully presents readers with the exquisite singing of the Fair Maid.

Before Reading

I. Preview Requirements: Please make a preparatory research on the background information, key words and phrases of this text.
1. Do research on the translator Harold Shadick.
2. Do research on *Quyi*, especially the storytelling with drum accompaniment in the northeastern region of China.
3. Do research on Confucius and Confucianism.
4. Do research on the rhetorical device such as simile and synaesthesia.
5. Find and study the new words in the text such as *intricate, oblong, prevail, sober, rumble* and *wedge*.
6. Learn the useful expressions in the text such as *except for, be wedged into, in accompaniment to, gossip away, in any case,* and *in a circular motion.*

II. Preview Questions: Please answer some questions about the understanding of the main content of the text.
1. What is the writing style of the text? Exposition, description, narration or argumentation?
2. What is the story about? Can you describe the most impressive scene in the text?
3. When did Lao Ts'an arrive at the Ming Lake House? When did the show begin? Were the seats taken?
4. What are the musical instruments that were used in the performance? Do you feel surprised when you find how popular the art was with the local people and how exquisite the art could be in the author's description even though it involved very simple musical instruments?
5. What did the people do in the audience? Were they just folk people? Did they have different social status?
6. How did the local people like the accompanist's performance? Did people listen attentively when he started to play? What drew people's attention to the accompanist's playing?
7. Can you find out the words and expressions the author uses to describe the Dark Maid's singing? What did the audience say about the Dark Maid's performance compared with that of the Fair Maid?
8. Why does the author go to lengths to describe the performance of the accompanist and the Dark Maid if the Fair Maid is the best singer? Why doesn't the author directly describe the singing of the Fair Maid?

9. Can you find out the words and expressions the author uses to describe the Fair Maid's performance? How are the descriptions different from those of the Dark Maid? What senses does the author appeal to when he describes the Fair Maid's singing?
10. How did the audience comment on the Fair Maid's performance?

Text A

Harold Shadick's Version

At the Foot of Mount Li the Traces of an Ancient Emperor; By the Side of Lake Ming the Song of a Beautiful Girl (excerpt)

......

The next day he got up at six o'clock and first went to see the Shun Well inside the South Gate. Then he went out of the South Gate to the foot of Lishan to see the place where, according to the tradition, the great Shun ploughed the fields in ancient times. When he returned to his inn, it was already about nine o'clock, so he made a hasty breakfast and then went to the Ming Lake House, where he arrived before ten o'clock. It turned out to be a large theater. In front of the stage were more than a hundred tables, and to his surprise when he entered the gate he found all the seats taken, except for seven or eight empty tables in the middle section. These tables had red paper slips pasted on them which said, "Reserved by the Governor, " "Reserved by the Director of Education, " and so on.

Lao Ts'an looked for a long time but could not find a place. Finally he slipped two hundred cash to an attendant, who arranged a short bench for him in a gap between the tables. On the stage he saw an oblong table on which was placed a flat drum. On the drum were two pieces of iron and he knew that these must be the so-called pear-blossom castanets. Beside them was a three-stringed banjo. Two chairs stood behind the table, but no one was on the stage. When you saw this huge stage, quite bare except for these few things, you couldn't help wanting to laugh. Ten or twenty men were walking up and down among the audience with baskets on their heads, selling sesame-seed cakes and *yu-t'iao* [fritters] to those who had come to the theater without having breakfast.

By eleven o'clock sedan chairs began to crowd at the door. Numerous officials in informal dress came in one after another, followed by their servants. Before twelve o'clock the empty tables in the front were all full. People still kept coming to see if there were seats, and short benches had to be wedged into the narrow spaces that were left. As this crowd of people arrived there were mutual greetings, many genuflections, and a few low bows. Loud and animated conversation, free and easy talk, and laughter prevailed. Apart from those at the ten or so tables in front, the rest of the audience was made up of tradespeople, except for a few who looked like the scholars of the place. They all gossiped away, *ch'i-ch'i, ts'a-ts'a*, but since there were so many people, you couldn't hear clearly what they were saying. In any case, it was nobody's business.

At half-past twelve a man wearing a long blue cloth gown appeared through the curtained door at the back of the stage. He had a longish face, covered with lumps, like the skin of a Foochow orange dried by the wind. But ugly as he was, you felt that he was quiet and sober. He came out on the stage and said nothing but sat down on the chair to the left, behind the oblong table. Slowly he took up the three-stringed banjo, in a leisurely way tuned up the strings, and then played one or two little melodies, to which, however, the audience did not listen with much attention. After this he played a longer piece, but I don't know the name of the tune. I only remember that as it went on he began to pluck the strings in a circular motion, with all his fingers one after another, until the sounds now high, now low, now simple, now intricate, entered the ears and stirred the hearts of the listeners so with their variety that there might have been several tens of strings and several hundreds of fingers playing on them. And now continuous shouts of approval were heard, not interfering, however, with the sound of the banjo. When he had finished this piece, he rested, and a man from the wings brought him a cup of tea.

After a pause of several minutes a girl came out from behind the curtains. She was about sixteen or seventeen years old with a long duck's egg face, hair down into a knot, and silver earrings in her ears. She wore a blue cotton jacket and a pair of blue cotton trousers with black piping. Although her clothes were of coarse material, they were spotlessly clean. She came to the back of the table and sat down on the chair to the right. The banjo player then took up his instrument and began to pluck the strings, *chen-chen, ts'ung-ts'ung*. The girl stood up, took the pear-blossom castanets between the fingers of her left hand and began to clap them, *ting-ting, tang-tang*, in time with the banjo. With her right hand she took up the drumstick and then, after listening carefully to the rhythm of the banjo, struck the drum a sharp blow and began to sing. Every word was clear-cut and crisp; every note smooth-flowing like a young oriole flying out of a valley or a young swallow returning to the nest. Every phrase had seven words and every part several tens of phrases, now slow, now fast, sometimes high, sometimes low. There were endless changes of tune and style so that the listener felt that no song, tune, melody, or air ever invented could equal this one piece, that it was the peak of perfection in song.

There were two men sitting at Lao Ts'an's side, one of whom asked the other in a low voice, "I suppose this must be the Fair Maid?" The other man said, "No, this is the Dark Maid, the Fair Maid's younger sister. All her songs were taught by the Fair Maid. If you compare her with the Fair Maid, it's impossible to estimate the distance that separates them! You can talk about her skill, but the Fair Maid's can't be put into words. The Dark Maid's skill can be learned by others, but the Fair Maid's can't possibly be learned. For several years now everybody has tried to sing like them. Even the singsong girls have tried! And the most anyone has done is to sing two or

Unit 12
At the Foot of Mount Li the Traces of an Ancient Emperor, By the Side of Lake Ming the Song of a Beautiful Girl (excerpt)

three phrases as well as the Dark Maid. As to the Fair Maid's merits, why, there's never been anybody who could do a tenth as well as she."

While they were talking, the Dark Maid had already finished singing and went out at the back. And now all the people in the theater began to talk and laugh. Sellers of melon seeds, peanuts, red fruit, and walnuts shouted their wares in a a loud voice. The whole place was filled with the sound of human voices. Just when the uproar was at its height, another girl appeared at the back of the stage. She was about eighteen or nineteen years old, and her costume differed in no detail from that of the first. She had a melon-seed face and a clear white complexion. Her features were not particularly beautiful; she was attractive without being seductive, pure but not cold. She came out with her head slightly bent, stood behind the table, took up the pear-blossom castanets and clapped them together several times, *ting-tang*. It was most amazing! They were just two bits of iron, and yet in her hand they seemed to contain all the five notes and the twelve tones. Then she took up the drumstick, lightly struck the drum twice, lifted her head, and cast one glance at the audience. When those two eyes, like autumn water, like winter stars, like pearls, like two beads of black in quicksilver, glanced left and right, even the men sitting in the most distant corners felt: Little Jade Wang is looking at me! As to those sitting nearer, nothing need be said. It was just one glance, but the whole theater was hushed, quieter than when the Emperor comes forth. Even a needle dropped on the ground could have been heard.

Little Jade Wang then opened her vermilion lips, displaying her sparkling white teeth, and sang several phrases. At first the sound was not very loud, but you felt an inexpressible magic enter your ears, and it was as though the stomach and bowels had been passed over by a smoothing iron, leaving no part unrelaxed. You seemed to absorb ambrosia through the thirty-six thousand pores of the skin until every single pore tingled with delight. After the first few phrases her song rose higher and louder till suddenly she drew her voice up to a sharp high-pitched note like a thread of steel wire thrown into the vault of the sky. You could not help secretly applauding. Still more amazing, she continued to move her voice up and down and in and out at that great height. After several turns her voice again began to rise, making three or four successive folds in the melody, each one higher than the last. It was like climbing T'aishan from the western face of the Aolai Peak. First you see the thousand-fathom cleft wall of Aolai Peak and think that it reaches the sky. But when you have wound your way up to the top, you see Fan Peak far above you. And when you have got to the top of Fan Peak, again you see the South Gate of Heaven far above Fan Peak. The higher you climb, the more alarming it seems—the more alarming, the more wonderful.

After Little Jade Wang had sung her three or four highest flourishes, suddenly her voice dropped, and then at a powerful spirited gallop, in a short time, with a thousand twists and turns she described innumerable circles like a flying serpent writhing and turning among the thirty-six peaks of the Yellow Mountains. After this the more she sang, the lower her voice became; the lower she sang, the more delicate it was, until at last the sound could be heard no more.

Every person in the theater held his breath and sat intently, not daring to move. After two or three minutes it was as though a small sound came forth from under the ground. And then the voice again rose like a Japanese rocket which shoots into the sky, bursting and scattering with innumerable strands of multicolored fire. The voice soared aloft until endless sounds seemed to be coming and going. The banjo player too plucked his strings with a circular movement of all his fingers, now loud, now soft, in perfect accompaniment to her voice. It was like the wanton singing of sweet birds on a spring morning in the garden. The ears were kept so busy that you couldn't decide which note to listen to. Just as it was becoming most intricate, one clear note sounded, and then voice and instrument both fell silent. The applause from the audience was like the rumbling of thunder.

After a while the uproar abated slightly and from the front row one could hear a young man of about thirty say with a Hunan accent, "When I was a student and came across that passage where the ancient writer describes the merits of good singing in the words 'The sound circles the beams and stops not for three days,' I could not understand what was meant. If you think of it in the abstract, how can sound go round and round the beams? And how can it go on for three days? It was not until I heard Little Jade Wang sing that I realized how appropriate the words of the ancient writer are. Every time I hear her sing, her song echoes in my ears for many days. No matter what I'm doing my attention wanders. Rather I feel that the 'three days' of 'stops not for three days' is too short. The 'three months' of the saying about Confucius, 'For three months he knew not the taste of meat', would describe it much more adequately. " Those around him all said, "Mr. Meng Hsiang expresses it so aptly that he arouses my envy."

Notes on the Text

1. Shun Well

The Shun Well is named after the legend of Shun. According to the ancient book *Mencius*, Shun had a tough childhood after his mother died at a young age. He was persecuted by his stepmother and his little brother. They deceived Shun into digging the well and then threw stones into the well to kill him. Fortunately, Shun escaped from the hole in the wall of the well which led to the outside and accidentally discovered a spring. There is a chain now hanging over the mouth of the well. The legend is that the chain was used to lock the dragon which was destroying the river channel at the time when Yu the Great tamed the flood and could only be released when the iron tree blossomed.

2. Mount Li

Mount Li is the name of Mount Qianfo in ancient times. Mount Qianfo gained its name during the reign of Sui Kai, when Buddhism prevailed and thousands of Buddha statues were carved in the mountain. Located in the south of Jinan City, it is among the three tourist attractions together with Baotu Spring and Daming Lake.

Unit 12
At the Foot of Mount Li the Traces of an Ancient Emperor; By the Side of Lake Ming the Song of a Beautiful Girl (excerpt)

3. **Three-stringed banjo**

   It first came into use in the Qin Dynasty. It has three strings and three parts, namely, a head, a neck and a body. The instrument makes a husky and loud sound. It is an indispensable instrument of traditional *Quyi*, such as the Northern Drum Music and Suzhou Pingtan.

4. **Genuflection**

   Originated as a Manchu custom, it became a popular etiquette of greeting among men in the Qing Dynasty. When greeting others with the etiquette, one should be in a posture with the left knee bent forward, right hand drooping and upper body leaning forward.

5. **Aolai Peak**

   Aolai Peak is one of the most famous peaks in the west of Mount Tai with an altitude of 987 meters. Though it can't be compared with Mount Tai in altitude, it has an air of never succumbing to Mount Tai with its sharp and towering cliff.

6. **Fan Peak**

   Fan Peak is located in the west of Xixi of Mount Tai. It has towering and steep cliffs shaped like a fan, hence the name of Fan Peak. It offers a panoramic view of Aolai Peak, which lies in its west.

7. **Confucius**

   Confucius (551 BC—479 BC) was a Chinese teacher, editor, politician, and philosopher of the Spring and Autumn Period in Chinese history. The philosophy of Confucius, also known as Confucianism, emphasizes the importance of benevolence, a virtuous life, filial piety, ancestor worship, and inner moral harmony. His followers competed successfully with many other schools during The Contention of a Hundred Schools of Thought only to be suppressed by the Legalists during the Qin Dynasty. Following the victory of Han over Chu after the collapse of Qin, Confucius's thoughts received an official sanction and were further developed into a system known in the West as Neo-Confucianism, and later New Confucianism (Modern Neo-Confucianism).

Glossary

accompaniment /əˈkʌmpənɪmənt/ *n.* 1. sth. that happens at the same time as another thing
e.g.: *High blood pressure is a common accompaniment to this disease.*

2. music that is played to support singing or another instrument
e.g.: *The pianist improvised an accompaniment to the song.*

animated /ˈænɪmeɪtɪd/ *adj.* full of interest and energy
e.g.: *The performance was followed by an animated discussion.*

cleft /kleft/ — *n.* a natural opening or crack, for example in the ground or in rock, or in a person's chin
e.g.: *The climber fell down a cleft in the rocks.*

complexion /kəmˈplekʃ(ə)n/ — *n.* the natural colour and condition of the skin on a person's face
e.g.: *Rain water was once considered to be good for the complexion.*

lump /lʌmp/ — *n.* a swelling under the skin, sometimes a sign of serious illness
e.g.: *Check your breasts for lumps every month.*

intricate /ˈɪntrɪkət/ — *adj.* having a lot of different parts and small details that fit together
e.g.: *He knows his way around the intricate maze of European law.*

oblong /ˈɒblɒŋ/ — *adj.* an oblong shape has four straight sides, two of which are longer than the other two, and four angles of 90°
e.g.: *There is an oblong table in the middle of the room.*

paste /peɪst/ — *v.* to stick sth. to sth. else using glue or paste
e.g.: *He pasted the pictures into his scrapbook.*

prevail /prɪˈveɪl/ — *v.* to exist or be very common at a particular time or in a particular place
e.g.: *Those beliefs still prevail among certain social groups.*

rumble /ˈrʌmbl/ — *v.* to make a long deep sound or series of sounds
e.g.: *The machine rumbled as it started up.*

sesame /ˈsesəmi/ — *n.* a tropical plant grown for its seeds and their oil that are used in cooking
e.g.: *Old Cheng picked a sesame seed from between his teeth.*

sober /ˈsəʊbə/ — *adj.* serious and sensible
e.g.: *On sober reflection, I don't think I really need a car after all.*

successive /səkˈsesɪv/ — *adj.* following immediately one after the other
e.g.: *This was their fourth successive win.*

uproar /ˈʌprɔː(r)/ — *n.* a situation in which people shout and make a lot of noise because they are angry or upset about sth.
e.g.: *Her comments provoked an uproar from the*

Unit 12
At the Foot of Mount Li the Traces of an Ancient Emperor; By the Side of Lake Ming the Song of a Beautiful Girl (excerpt)

vault /vɔːlt/	*audience.* *n.* a roof or ceiling in the form of an arch or a series of arches e.g.: *The vault of this cathedral is very high.*
vermilion /vəˈmɪljən/	*adj.* of a vivid red to reddish-orange color e.g.: *Nine doornails are on the vermillion gate.*
wedge /wedʒ/	*v.* to put or squeeze sth. tightly into a narrow space, so that it cannot move easily e.g.: *The boat was now wedged between the rocks.*
writhe /raɪð/	*v.* to twist or move your body without stopping, often because you are in great pain e.g.: *She was writhing around on the floor in agony.*

While Reading

I. Please fill in the blanks with the words in the parentheses with the appropriate part of speech.
1. Smoking is becoming increasingly _____ among younger women. (prevail)
2. His fingers were rubbing back and forth on the photo, as if he was trying to _____ his baby back to life. (animation)
3. Tom was _____ of his brother's success in business. (envy)
4. The _____ to the show is a wall lined with books that conceals a secret door. (enter)
5. After 57 years of _____ operation, the theatre closed, was sold to a private company, and scheduled for demolition. (continue)
6. At this point there were murmurings of _____ from the experts. (approve)
7. The price depends on the _____ of the work. (intricate)
8. Technological innovations have brought _____ benefits. (number)
9. It is necessary to distinguish the policies of two _____ governments. (success)
10. It is unrealistic to believe _____ is an attainable goal. (perfect)

II. Please choose one word or phrase that best completes the sentence.
1. _____ her illnesses, she had had a particularly happy childhood.
   A. Except for   B. Apart from
   C. Other than   D. Without exception
2. Food is _____ carbohydrates, proteins and fats.
   A. made from   B. made up of
   C. made out of   D. made up for
3. It may rain tomorrow, but I miss my parents so much that I'm going home _____.
   A. in no way   B. at any rate
   C. at any cost   D. in any case

4. He did not particularly want to _____ a competitive sport.
   A. take out   B. take in
   C. take up   D. take on
5. He learned to walk safely _____ the stairs.
   A. up and down   B. left and right
   C. in and out   D. back and forth
6. Don't be intolerant of people whose opinions _____ yours.
   A. conform to   B. agree with
   C. differ from   D. differentiate from

III. Translation

1. Please translate the following from English into Chinese.

1) to plough the fields   2) to walk up and down
3) one after anther   4) a sedan chair
5) to be wedged into   6) a melon-seed face
7) to pluck the strings   8) shouts of approval
9) a long duck's egg face   10) now slow, now fast
11) in accompaniment to   12) to arouse my envy
13) in a circular motion

2. Please translate the following from Chinese into English.

1）高谈阔论   2）说笑自如
3）抑扬顿挫   4）入耳动心
5）转腔换调   6）歌曲腔调
7）秀而不媚   8）清而不寒
9）五脏六腑   10）千回百折
11）屏气凝神   12）余音绕梁，三日不绝。
13）新莺出谷   14）乳燕归巢
15）朱唇皓齿

3. Please translate each sentence with at least one key word or its derivative.

Key Words: equal, scatter, arouse, wander, prevail

1）他们的迫害只会激起人民对他们的反抗。
2）政治抱负和个人野心开始压倒经济利益。
3）树倒猢狲散。
4）他克制着自己，不让思想在工作时开小差。
5）政府承诺要为妇女争取平等的权利。
6）詹姆斯缄口不提任何可能使人们对他的动机产生怀疑的话题。
7）野蛮的习俗在这一山区仍然流行。

8）我没法从远处疏疏落落的众多面孔中把他辨认出来。

9）妈妈生怕我们迷路，不准我们走远。

10）她讨厌书，其程度之深只有她对人的厌恶可以相比。

After Reading

I. Please make a sentence with the words and expressions you have learnt from the text.

1. to tingle:
2. to writhe:
3. to glance left and right:
4. to be in accompaniment to:
5. to separate ... from ... :

II. Paragraph Writing

1. Please write a paragraph of around 150 words about the popularity of the performance among the local people, and the audience's comments on the performance of the Dark Maid and the Fair Maid.

2. Please write a paragraph of around 100 words about the Fair Maid's performance with the following words and expressions you have learnt from the text. Make sure that the paragraph you have written is grammatically correct and coherent.

> cast one glance; pass over; tingle with delight; vault of the sky; hold one's breath; rumbling of thunder

Original Edition in Chinese

历山山下古帝遗踪　明湖湖边美人绝调（节选）

……

次日六点钟起，先到南门内看了舜井。又出南门，到历山脚下，看看相传大舜昔日耕田的地方。及至回店，已有九点钟的光景，赶忙吃了饭，走到明湖居，才不过十点钟时候。那明湖居本是个大戏园子，戏台前有一百多张桌子。那知进了园门，园子里面已经坐的满满的了，只有中间七八张桌子还无人坐。桌子却都贴着"抚院定""学院定"等类红纸条儿。老残看了半天，无处落脚，只好袖子里送了看坐儿的二百个钱，才弄了一张短板凳，在人缝里坐下。看那戏台上，只摆了一张半桌，桌子上放了一面板鼓，鼓上放了两个铁片儿，心里知道这就是所谓梨花简了；旁边放了一个三弦子，半桌后面放了两张椅子，并无一个人在台上。偌大的个戏台，空空洞洞，别无他物，看了不觉有些好笑。园子里面，顶着篮子卖烧饼油条的有一二十个，都是为那不吃饭来的人买了充饥的。

到了十一点钟，只见门口轿子渐渐拥挤，许多官员都着了便衣，带着家人，陆续进来。不到十二点钟，前面几张空桌俱已满了，不断还有人来，看坐儿的也只是搬张短凳，在夹缝中安插。这一群人来了，彼此招呼，有打千儿的，有作揖的，大半打千儿的多。高谈阔论，说笑自如。这十几张桌子外，看来都是做生意的人，又有些像是本地读书人的样子，大家都喊喊喳喳的在那里说闲话。因为人太多了，所以说的什么话都听不清楚，也不去管他。

到了十二点半钟，看那台上，从后台帘子里面，出来一个男人，穿了一件蓝布长衫，长长的脸儿，一脸疙瘩，仿佛风干福橘皮似的，甚为丑陋。但觉得那人气味倒还沉静，出得台来，并无一语，就往半桌后面左手一张椅子上坐下，慢慢的将三弦子取来，随便和了和弦，弹了一两个小调，人也不甚留神去听。后来弹了一支大调，也不知道叫什么牌子。只是到后来，全用轮指，那抑扬顿挫，入耳动心，恍若有几十根弦、几百个指头在那里弹似的。这时台下叫好的声音不绝于耳，却也压不下那弦子去。这曲弹罢，就歇了手，旁边有人送上茶来。

停了数分钟时，帘子里面出来一个姑娘，约有十六七岁，长长鸭蛋脸儿，梳了一个抓髻，戴了一副银耳环，穿了一件蓝布外褂儿，一条蓝布裤子，都是黑布镶滚的。虽是粗布衣裳，倒十分洁净。来到半桌后面右手椅子上坐下。那弹弦子的便取了弦子，铮铮鈜鈜弹起。这姑娘便立起身来，左手取了梨花简，夹在指头缝里，便丁丁当当的敲，与那弦子声音相应；右手持了鼓捶子，凝神听那弦子的节奏。忽羯鼓一声，歌喉遽发，字字清脆，声声宛转，如新莺出谷，乳燕归巢。每句七字，每段数十句，或缓或急，忽高忽低；其中转腔换调之处，百变不穷，觉一切歌曲腔调俱出其下，以为观止矣。

旁坐有两人，其一人低声问那人道："此想必是白妞了罢？"其一人道；"不是。这人叫黑妞，是白妞的妹子。他的调门儿都是白妞教的，若比白妞，还不晓得差多远呢！他的好处人说得出，白妞的好处人说不出；他的好处人学得到，白妞的好处人学不到。你想，这几年来，好顽耍的谁不学他们的调儿呢？就是窑子里的姑娘，也人人都学，只是顶多有一两句到黑妞的地步。若白妞的好处，从没有一个人能及他十分里的一分的。"说着的时候，黑妞早唱完，后面去了。这时满园子里的人，谈心的谈心，说笑的说笑。卖瓜子、落花生、山里红、核桃仁的，高声喊叫着卖，满园子里听来都是人声。

正在热闹哄哄的时节，只见那后台里，又出来了一位姑娘，年纪约十八九岁，装束与前一个毫无分别，瓜子脸儿，白净面皮，相貌不过中人以上之姿，只觉得秀而不媚，清而不寒。半低着头出来，立在半桌后面，把梨花简丁当了几声，煞是奇怪：只是两片顽铁，到他手里，便有了五音十二律似的。又将鼓捶子轻轻的点了两下，方抬起头来，向台下一

Unit 12
At the Foot of Mount Li the Traces of an Ancient Emperor; By the Side of Lake Ming the Song of a Beautiful Girl (excerpt)

盼。那双眼睛，如秋水，如寒星，如宝珠，如白水银里头养着两丸黑水银，左右一顾一看，连那坐在远远墙角子里的人，都觉得王小玉看见我了；那坐得近的，更不必说。就这一眼，满园子里便鸦雀无声，比皇帝出来还要静悄得多呢，连一根针吊（掉）在地下都听得见响！

王小玉便启朱唇，发皓齿，唱了几句书儿。声音初不甚大，只觉入耳有说不出来的妙境：五脏六腑里，像熨斗熨过，无一处不伏贴；三万六千个毛孔，像吃了人参果，无一个毛孔不畅快。唱了十数句之后，渐渐的越唱越高，忽然拔了一个尖儿，像一线钢丝抛入天际，不禁暗暗叫绝。那知他于那极高的地方，尚能回环转折。几啭之后，又高一层，接连有三四叠，节节高起。恍如由傲来峰西面攀登泰山的景象：初看傲来峰削壁千仞，以为上与天通；及至翻到傲来峰顶，才见扇子崖更在傲来峰上；及至翻到扇子崖，又见南天门更在扇子崖上：愈翻愈险，愈险愈奇。

那王小玉唱到极高的三四叠后，陡然一落，又极力骋其千回百折的精神，如一条飞蛇在黄山三十六峰半中腰里盘旋穿插，顷刻之间，周匝数遍。从此以后，愈唱愈低，愈低愈细，那声音渐渐的就听不见了。满园子的人都屏气凝神，不敢少动。约有两三分钟之久，仿佛有一点声音从地底下发出。这一出之后，忽又扬起，像放那东洋烟火，一个弹子上天，随化作千百道五色火光，纵横散乱。这一声飞起，即有无限声音俱来并发。那弹弦子的亦全用轮指，忽大忽小，同他那声音相和相合，有如花坞春晓，好鸟乱鸣。耳朵忙不过来，不晓得听那一声的为是。正在撩乱之际，忽听霍然一声，人弦俱寂。

这时台下叫好之声，轰然雷动。停了一会，闹声稍定，只听那台下正座上，有一个少年人，不到三十岁光景，是湖南口音，说道："当年读书，见古人形容歌声的好处，有那'余音绕梁，三日不绝'的话，我总不懂。空中设想，余音怎样会得绕梁呢？又怎会三日不绝呢？及至听了小玉先生说书，才知古人措辞之妙。每次听他说书之后，总有好几天耳朵里无非都是他的书，无论做什么事，总不入神，反觉得'三日不绝'，这'三日'二字下得太少，还是孔子'三月不知肉味'，'三月'二字形容得透彻些！"旁边人都说道："梦湘先生论得透辟极了！'于我心有戚戚焉'！"

Text B

Yang Hsien-yi & Gladys Yang's Version

......

The next morning he got up at six o'clock and went first to the South Gate to see Shun's Well; then he went outside the gate to the foot of the mountain to see the place where in ancient times Shun was supposed to have ploughed. When he returned to the hotel it was already nine o'clock, and after a quick breakfast he went to the theatre, arriving there at about ten o'clock. This Lake Pavilion was a large theatre with over a hundred tables before the stage, but when he went in there was already a full house, with only seven or eight tables left, all marked "Reserved" for the inspector, the examiner, the governor and other high officials. Lao Can looked round for a long time but could not find a place, so he took two hundred cash from his sleeve and gave them to an attendant, who then fetched him a small stool so that he could sit down among the others. He saw a table on the stage on which there was a drum, and on the drum were two pieces of iron which he knew must be the castanets; by the side was a three-stringed guitar, and behind the table there were two chairs. There was no one on the stage, and he felt rather amused to see such a large stage entirely empty. Some twenty or thirty vendors, carrying baskets on their heads, were selling refreshments in the theatre for those who had come without their lunch.

At about eleven o'clock more sedan-chairs and carriages came to the door, all belonging to officials who were wearing ordinary dress and had brought their servants. By twelve o'clock all the reserved tables in front were full, but people continued to come in, and the attendants brought small stools for them and squeezed them in among the others. The newcomers greeted each other, some of them kneeling on one knee and some giving a more casual greeting, but most of them knelt on one knee. They all talked at the top of their voices, laughing and chattering. The other tables were occupied by people who looked like merchants or local scholars, all gossiping noisily. Because there were so many people it was impossible to catch what they were saying, and he did not try.

When it was about half past twelve a man came out from behind the screen wearing a blue cloth gown; he had a long face as full of pimples as a dried orange peel, and was excessively ugly, but he seemed quite self-possessed. He came out without uttering a word, slowly took up the guitar and casually tuned it, after which he played a few tunes to which the audience paid very little attention. Then he played a long piece, the name of which Lao Can did not know; but towards the end all the fingers were called into play and the melody, high and low, quick and slow, moved people's hearts as if there were dozens of strings and hundreds of fingers playing in harmony. At that time there were incessant "Bravos" from the auditorium, but the tune could still be distinctly heard. After this piece was finished he stopped, and an attendant brought him some tea.

After a few minutes a girl appeared from behind the screen, who seemed sixteen or seventeen years old. She had an oval face and her hair was gathered in a knot on her neck; she was wearing silver ear-rings and a blue cloth tunic and trousers, both with a yellow border; but although her clothes were only made of coarse cloth they were spotlessly clean. She sat on the chair on the right-hand side behind the table, and when the accompanist took up the guitar again and started playing, the girl stood up with the castanets in her left hand, holding them between her fingers and clashing them to the tune played by the guitar, while in her right hand she took the drumstick and listened carefully to the rhythm; then with one beat of the drum she burst out singing. Every word was clear and every note was mellow, like young orioles emerging from a valley or young swallows returning to their nest. There were seven words to every line, and some dozen lines to every stanza. Some lines were slow and some quick, some low and some high, while as for the variations in the melody, they were innumerable. All other songs and tunes that Lao Can had heard seemed inferior to this, and he felt that she had attained the peak of perfection.

Unit 12
At the Foot of Mount Li the Traces of an Ancient Emperor; By the Side of Lake Ming the Song of a Beautiful Girl (excerpt)

There were two people sitting beside him, and one whispered to the other, "I suppose this is White Sister?" But the other said, "No, this is Black Sister, her younger sister. She learnt all her tunes from White Sister, but she is much inferior to her. People can analyse her good points whereas they can't analyse White Sister's good points, and people can learn her goods whereas they can't learn White Sister's good points. All these years pleasure-loving people have learnt her tunes, and even the singsong girls have imitated her but at the most they can only sing one or two lines as well as Black Sister, while nobody can sing even one-tenth as well as White Sister."

As they were speaking Black Sister finished her song and went to the back. Then all the people in the theatre chattered and laughed and all the pedlars selling melon-seeds, monkey-nuts, fruit-jellies and walnuts, cried their wares, until the whole theatre was a babel of human voices. In the middle of this tumult a girl came out from behind the stage who was eighteen or nineteen years old. She was dressed in every respect like the other, and had a long, melon-seed shaped face, white skin and average good looks, appearing delicate but not seductive and distinguished but not disdainful. She came out with lowered head, seated herself behind the table, and clashed her castanets; and strange to relate, although these were only two pieces of ordinary iron, yet between her fingers they seemed instruments of great range. Then beating the drum softly twice she raised her head to look at the spectators, and her eyes appeared like autumn pools, like frosty stars, like pearls or black crystals kept in quick-silver. When she glanced right and left even the people far away felt that Little Jade was looking at them, to say nothing of those seated near her, and thereupon the whole theatre became so still that even if the emperor himself had appeared there could not have been greater quiet. One could have heard a pin drop.

Little Jade then parted her lips and sang a few lines: the sound was low but indescribably sweet. All the organs of the body seemed smoothed as if by an iron, each into its proper place, while the whole body felt as if after drinking nectar, and there was not a pore that was not relaxed. After she had sung a few dozen lines she gradually sang higher and higher, until suddenly she soared to a very high pitch as if a steel rope had been flung into the sky, and Lao Can was secretly amazed. But even at that high pitch her voice could still circle and revolve, and after several trills it rose to an even higher note and ascended the scale for three or four notes more. It was like climbing Taishan Mountain from the Aolai Cliff on the west side: first you see the precipice reaching up to heaven, but when you attain the summit you realise that another peak is still ahead, and when you reach this you realise that there is yet another peak above. Thus with every turn the sense of insecurity increases, and as the sense of insecurity increases so also does one's amazement.

When Little Jade reached the highest pitch her voice suddenly dropped and, winding skillfully with all its art, seemed like a flying snake weaving its way down through the many ridges of the mountain and circling round and round in a very short space. Her voice dropped lower and lower until it gradually became inaudible, and all the people in the theatre held their breath in suspense and dared not make the least movement. In two or three minutes there seemed to be a small voice coming slowly out from beneath the ground to flare up again like foreign firecrackers or like a rocket soaring up and multiplying into a thousand trails of coloured light before scattering down again. After this crescendo of sound many songs seemed to start all together. The accompanist also used all his fingers and played high and low in harmony with the voice, like many birds singing at dawn amid spring flowers, so that people's ears could not contain all the sounds and did not know to which melody to listen. In this medley they suddenly heard a final sound, and both voice and strings became mute, while "Bravos" sounded from before the stage like thunder.

After a little while when the tumult had begun to die down, a young man less than thirty years old in the front seat nearest the stage started to speak with a Hunan accent, saying, "When I studied in the past and read descriptions of good singers, it was said that the echoes of their songs would linger about the roof for three days but I would not believe it, thinking it was the writer's fancy—for how could echoes linger in the roof, and how could they hover there for three days? But since I heard Miss Wang sing, I realise how well the ancient scholars expressed it; for every time I have heard her I can hear her voice in my ears for several days, so that I cannot give my whole attention to anything I do. Indeed I feel that even three days is rather inadequate, and would rather use Confucius' words: 'For three months I cannot taste the flavour of meat.' Three months would be more correct. "

All the people beside him said, "His comment is quite correct, and expresses our own feelings."

Notes on the Text

About the text

The present text is taken from *The Travels of Lao Can* translated by Yang Hsien-yi and Gladys Yang, published by Chinese Literature in 1983.

Key to the Exercises

Unit One

I. Please fill in the blanks with the words in the parentheses with the appropriate part of speech.

1. sorrowful
2. Rebellious
3. righteousness
4. zealot
5. extinction
6. descendant
7. admirable
8. thirst
9. utterance
10. surveyor

II. Please choose one word or phrase that best completes the sentence.

1. A   2. D   3. C   4. C   5. B   6. B

III. Translation

1. Please translate the following from English into Chinese.

1）流火
2）卒岁
3）春日迟迟
4）万寿无疆
5）忧心烈烈／忧心忡忡
6）杨柳依依
7）雨雪霏霏
8）百世
9）济济多士
10）自求多福
11）允文允武

2. Please translate the following from Chinese into English.

1) to take one's way to the fields
2) With the spring days the warmth begins.
3) to begin one's spinning
4) young prince
5) The cicada gives out its note.
6) The leaves fall.
7) the spirits for the spring
8) to recommence one's sowing
9) No one knows my sadness.
10) an old country
11) with his horse looking so grand

3. Please translate each sentence with at least one key word or its derivative.

1) He outlined his plans and then proceeded to explain them in more detail.

2) He tried desperately to convey how urgent the situation was.

3) They are concerned for the fate of the forest and the Indians who dwell on it.

4) We are looking for people who would be willing to assist in the group's work.

5) The police insist that Michael did not follow the correct procedure in applying for a visa.

6) Here are some good sources of information to assist you in making the best selection.

7) Normally, such an outward display of affection is reserved for his mother.

8) Should you reach the summit, you would have only one desire—to descend and live with those who dwell in the deepest valley.

9) The pipes convey hot water from the boiler to the radiators.

10) He has displayed remarkable courage in his efforts to reform the party.

Unit Two

I. Please fill in the blanks with the words in the parentheses with the appropriate part of speech.

1. bash
2. straighten
3. lofty
4. vacancy
5. encouragement
6. companionship
7. security
8. Fortunately
9. inspiration
10. Creative

II. Please choose one word or phrase that best completes the sentence.

1. A   2. B   3. C   4. D   5. D   6. A

III. Translation

1. Please translate the following from English into Chinese.

1）折花   2）青梅
3）低头   4）展眉
5）一壶酒   6）独酌
7）举杯   8）浣女
9）空山   10）渔舟

2. Please translate the following from Chinese into English.

1) both of us young and happy-hearted   2) not to turn to one's thousand calls

3) Raising my cup, I asked the bright moon.   4) to bring me my shadow and make us three

5) Leaves are dropping down like the spray of a waterfall.

6) I watch the long river always rolling on.

7) moonlight in its groves of pine   8) stones of crystal in its brooks

9) Take home an armful, for my sake.   10) as a symbol of our love

3. Please translate each sentence with at least one key word or its derivative.

1) The guide led the way and we trotted along behind him.

2) In Britain, jazz is losing its elitist tag and gaining a much broader audience.

3) Share prices continued to tumble today on the Tokyo stock market.

4) We don't want to go out with a whimper. We know we have to be cautious, but we cannot be over-cautious.

5) A dark red stain was spreading across his shirt.

6) The girl broke into a trot and disappeared around the corner.

7) The country no longer wanted to be tagged as a Third World nation.

8) Both of the wrestlers tried to tumble their rivals with all their strength.

9) I clamped my teeth to keep from uttering a single whimper.

10) You can stain the wood with this special liquid to give it a pleasing color.

Unit Three

I. Please fill in the blanks with the words in the parentheses with the appropriate part of speech.

1. Beauty, beautify   2. sorrow
3. perfectionists   4. afloat
5. thickens   6. prelude
7. startling   8. sentimental
9. height   10. heroic

II. Please choose one word or phrase that best completes the sentence.

1. D   2. A   3. A   4. C   5. C   6. D

III. Translation

1. Please translate the following from English into Chinese.

1）这次第，怎一个愁字了得！   2）物是人非事事休

3）少年不识愁滋味   4）为赋新词强说愁

5）人有悲欢离合   6）月有阴晴圆缺

7）明月几时有   8）把酒问青天

9）此事古难全   10）起舞弄清影

2. Please translate the following from Chinese into English.

1) I would not have it told.
2) my acquaintances of old
3) I'd like to go upstair.
4) Life is but like a dream.
5) Rocks tower in the air.
6) Waves beat on the shore.
7) Beyond the clouds seven or eight stars twinkle.
8) Before the hills two or three raindrops sprinkle.
9) So let us wish that man live as long as he can!
10) Though miles apart, we'll share the beauty she displays.

3. Please translate each sentence with at least one key word or its derivative.

1) It is difficult for him to part with his extravagant habits.
2) In Britain, at least among the middle-class downshifters of my acquaintance, they have different reasons for seeking to simplify their lives.
3) Old age hasn't dimmed her memory.
4) In coming years, researchers may also be able to shed light on the impact of language on subtler areas of perception.
5) Family was a huge part of my grandpa's life; he was always happiest when he had his entire family around him.
6) Until recently business tended to take a dim view of the idea that the climate was changing.
7) "As a young person grows up," Socrates told us, "he has an ample opportunity to acquaint himself with the way of life in his community."
8) The streets look gay with bright flags and colored lights.
9) I disliked the dim light, and on the second day fixed, at my own expense, a more powerful electric bulb.
10) Proper pronunciation is extremely important, so repeat the name of your new acquaintance to be sure you're pronouncing it correctly.

Unit Four

I. Please fill in the blanks with the words in the parentheses with the appropriate part of speech.

1. temperate
2. leisurely
3. narration
4. competitive
5. departure
6. discerning
7. glorious
8. reclusive
9. meditate
10. dominating

Key to the Exercises

II. Please choose one word or phrase that best completes the sentence.
1. C 2. C 3. A 4. D 5. B 6. B

III. Translation

1. Please translate the following from English into Chinese.

1）枯藤 2）客梦回
3）晚霞 4）意马收
5）名利场 6）无与伦比
7）柳绵 8）白衣
9）科举 10）玉管

2. Please translate the following from Chinese into English.

1) a small bridge, the murmuring water 2) passion-ridden tear in vain
3) The lamplight is dim. 4) pink with flowers that fly
5) a thatched shop 6) a cosy and peaceful nest
7) the secular world 8) things of worldly kind
9) the end of the earth 10) the eastern hedge
11) red sleeves 12) to split the rock and pierce the cloud

3. Please translate each sentence with at least one key word or its derivative.

1) Did you plod through the day at the office?
2) We tried to repress feelings of disappointment, and take the responsibility of accomplishing the task that was given to us.
3) The sergeant was whining about how hard he had been forced to work recently.
4) The sparrows chirp outside the window every morning.
5) With a "bang" of his stamp on my visa, I was free to roam much of Europe.
6) After two decades of plodding developments in personal computing, a host of new platforms has popped up.
7) Dialogue and agreement should supplant violence and repression.
8) Do not give in to your child's whining or crying, as it only reinforces the behavior.
9) You could hear the chirping of the locator devices the firefighters wear and see only the lights flashing red and yellow through the haze.
10) You might also have roaming service from your telephone service provider.

Unit Five

I. Please fill in the blanks with the words in the parentheses with the appropriate part of speech.

1. ruinous
2. respectful
3. manipulation, manipulate
4. remission
5. idler
6. generosity
7. trustworthiness
8. customary
9. banishment
10. refugees, refugees

II. Please choose one word or phrase that best completes the sentence.

1. A   2. C   3. A   4. D   5. B   6. B

III. Translation

1. Please translate the following from English into Chinese.

1）执杯相谢
2）不成家业
3）祭祀
4）盘缠
5）辞别
6）做个人情
7）安排筵席
8）发迹
9）时来运转
10）日远日疏，日亲日近。
11）寸步不离
12）耽误

2. Please translate the following from Chinese into English.

1) to pluck up one's courage
2) to work out a tactic
3) a personal aide
4) playing the flute, strumming a guitar, singing and dancing
5) to be taken with
6) to await one's opportunity
7) to find refuge with
8) propitious winds and timely rains
9) to proclaim an amnesty throughout the empire
10) to squander a fortune
11) to take out a writ against somebody
12) to mount one's horse

3. Please translate each sentence with at least one key word or its derivative.

1) Naturally, hardly anyone could afford to squander so much time every day.
2) He would always be haunted by that scene in Well Park.
3) That escaped convict would be pardoned after serving five years of his sentence.
4) She could harbor a grudge against anyone who betrayed her trust.
5) But at least Edison did not squander vast quantities of public money on installing cinema screens in schools around the country.

6) It remained very difficult to procure food, fuel, and other daily necessities at the end of the Second World War.

7) The Wanglang Nature Reserve in western Sichuan is the haunt of giant pandas.

8) I have all the evidence necessary to convict this young criminal now.

9) We have now worked with forty-one countries around the world on improving the transparency, competitiveness and efficiency of government procurement.

10) As for people who love us but whom we do not love, we may be indifferent, or at least would not harbor such a deep overall concern.

Unit Six

I. Please fill in the blanks with the words in the parentheses with the appropriate part of speech.

1. unjustifiable/unjustified
2. assignment
3. acknowledgement
4. disclosed, disclosures
5. detection, detective
6. wintry
7. invulnerability
8. coincidental, coincidence
9. engaging
10. reckoning, reckoning

II. Please choose one word or phrase that best completes the sentence.

1. C   2. A   3. B   4. A   5. D   6. A

III. Translation

1. Please translate the following from English into Chinese.

1）神机妙算
2）贺喜
3）诡谲小计
4）泄密
5）碌碌庸才
6）恕我直言
7）军中无戏言
8）受重罚
9）自有妙用
10）通天文
11）识地利
12）命系于天

2. Please translate the following from Chinese into English.

1) to make no move
2) to be taken up with military concerns
3) to miss one's advice
4) to do sb. harm/ to pull a trick on sb.
5) to make defense
6) Tremendous fogs spread across the heavens.
7) to make a sally
8) The color left one's face.
9) to use sth. against the enemy
10) to spoil everything
11) to fix one's punishment
12) to examine the maps of deployment

3. **Please translate each sentence with at least one key word or its derivative.**

1) The storm got worse and worse. Finally, I was obliged to abandon the car and continue on foot.

2) Grandparents are often tempted to spoil their grandchildren whenever they come to visit.

3) During that year of agony and the following year of my grieving, everything stopped for me in my life.

4) If the operation cannot be restored within a short time, the CRC line-operating unit shall organize the dispersion and transfer of passengers.

5) Bitterly I thought in my mind that the storm came on purpose to spoil my happiness; all its malice was against me.

6) If I submitted to their demands, they would not press the allegations.

7) The police ordered the dispersal of the crowds gathering around that building.

8) He fell awkwardly and lied down in agony clutching his right knee.

9) We called up three economists to ask how to eliminate the deficit and they obliged with very straightforward answers.

10) In desperation, Mrs. Smith submitted to an operation on her right knee to relieve the pain.

Unit Seven

I. *Please fill in the blanks with the words in the parentheses with the appropriate part of speech.*

1. compassionate, compassion
2. Commandments
3. momentary
4. trustful
5. countless
6. falsehood
7. uninhabited
8. unbelieving
9. attendant
10. unworthy

II. *Please choose one word or phrase that best completes the sentence.*

1. B   2. A   3. C   4. A   5. B   6. D

III. *Translation*

1. Please translate the following from English into Chinese.

1）杏眼
2）斯文气象
3）斋僧
4）招女婿
5）香米饭
6）农忙时节
7）炒面筋
8）做善事
9）胡说八道
10）还愿

Key to the Exercises

2. Please translate the following from Chinese into English.

1) with a face like the moon and features like flowers

2) The good man will have Heaven's reward. 3) to repay one's kindness

4) to change one's mind 5) to relieve one's hunger

6) an uninhabited region 7) to shake with horror

8) fiery eyes and diamond pupils

3. Please translate each sentence with at least one key word or its derivative.

1) You put a little by each week, and you'll be surprised how it mounts up.

2) He committed the equally serious offence of interrupting the conversation.

3) When he saw his brother's pleading expression, his heart softened.

4) When I was a mere lad, and had never ridden a horse before, my father made me mount one and gallop by his side, with no qualms about me.

5) She was caught cheating at exams, but her parents pleaded that she should be given one more chance.

6) Don't take any notice of the boy. If you scold him, he will only start acting up.

7) If all else fails, I'll go over to the offensive/ take the offensive.

8) I'm not going to defer these decisions just because they are not immediately politically popular.

9) Whenever I do not behave myself, I will get a scolding from my parents.

10) I refused to discuss the matter out of deference to my employer.

Unit Eight

I. Please fill in the blanks with the words in the parentheses with the appropriate part of speech.

1. desperation 2. grieve
3. ineffable 4. mockery
5. seclusion 6. weary
7. pretense 8. pursuit
9. graceful 10. affectionately

II. Please choose one word or phrase that best completes the sentence.

1. A 2. B 3. C 4. D 5. B 6. A

III. Translation

1. Please translate the following from English into Chinese.

1）自言自语 2）发咒禁当

3）无眠一夜
5）撩人
7）前生
9）杳无人迹
11）霎时间

4）女儿心性未分明
6）书生
8）一*丝丝*
10）白日青天
12）缓留连

2. Please translate the following from Chinese into English.

1) a crow in charge of a phoenix
2) one's life's true love
3) three meals a day
4) to pursue one's dream through endless twistings
5) in dreams "no fluttering side by side of splendid phoenix wings"
6) between hearts the one minute thread from root to tip of the magic horn
7) The ground is carpeted with fallen petals.
8) a small secluded court
9) to live or die at will
10) So be it.
11) to bind the heart
12) to fill one's vision

3. Please translate each sentence with at least one key word or its derivative.

1) She couldn't withstand the lure of money and was dragged into the mire.
2) He grabbed her arm and dragged her into the room.
3) Who among us has never been moved to snap a sunset on the horizon, a flowing river, a blossom in spring?
4) The inventions make possible things the capitalists cannot envision.
5) A lot of people moaned about the parking problems.
6) A number of big-budget movies managed to lure moviegoers into theaters in the US during the Christmas holidays despite a sluggish economy.
7) If you don't like your life, see yourself changing it. Sure enough, what you envision will come about.
8) If even one mistake can drag your life down, you can imagine what kind of damage bad habits can do.
9) When I walked into the room, I saw my roommate sit on the floor, moaning.
10) He broke off the twig with a snap.

Unit Nine

I. Please fill in the blanks with the words in the parentheses with the appropriate part of speech.

1. compelling
2. melancholy
3. marriage
4. mistaken

5. imploration
6. stupefyingly
7. avenger
8. inscriptions
9. hasty
10. undignified

II. Please choose one word or phrase that best completes the sentence.
1. B   2. A   3. C   4. A   5. D   6. B

III. Translation
1. Please translate the following from English into Chinese.

1）月老
2）错花星
3）报喜
4）聘礼
5）母女分离
6）摘翠
7）守节
8）寻个权宜之法
9）上轿
10）前途保重

2. Please translate the following from Chinese into English.

1) I beg you take care of yourself.
2) to dress sb. up as a bride
3) It is now the third watch of night.
4) the token of the solemn vow
5) I am blameless in this matter.
6) the fair complexion
7) close kinsmen
8) the embroidered gown
9) That is out of the question.
10) We are bound to meet again.

3. Please translate each sentence with at least one key word or its derivative.

1) We implore all of you to remain calm and assure that you are in a safe place.
2) The Chairman shall preside at all meetings of the Board of Directors and shall cast the deciding vote in the case of a tie.
3) Perhaps casual chatting with colleagues in the pantry over a cup of tea for a good fifteen minutes will soothe the mid-day crisis symptoms.
4) A few hundred million euros a year would suffice for poor western areas.
5) I didn't get a lot of that because of your accent, but the general tone was soothing, and somehow I feel better.
6) He did attend the lecture this morning but somehow he did not seem to attend to it.
7) There can be a pension, not enormous but sufficient, for her sister for the remainder of her life.
8) The President always has six bodyguards in close attendance.
9) The time has come for institutional reform of organizations that preside over the world economy.
10) Then it struggled to break loose and flied higher and higher regardless of the girl's

imploration in tears.

Unit Ten

I. Please fill in the blanks with the words in the parentheses with the appropriate part of speech.

1. quicken
2. joyfully
3. grievously
4. suspect
5. bewitch
6. lamentation
7. allusion
8. alleviation
9. inquisitive, inquiry/ inquisition
10. subsequently

II. Please choose one word or phrase that best completes the sentence.
1. A   2. B   3. D   4. A   5. C   6. D

III. Translation

1. Please translate the following from English into Chinese.

1）在亡之人，乌有定所。
2）邪气萦绕
3）切齿
4）少顷
5）膝行而前
6）不知所踪
7）悼夫
8）急走
9）掷笔
10）甚艰于步

2. Please translate the following from Chinese into English.

1) to alleviate one's distress

2) Some people don't seem to know when death is at hand.

3) a pretty girl of about sixteen   4) to raise one's head and look all around

5) in a great state of alarm   6) to bring sb. to life/ to raise the dead

7) to show no sign of anger   8) to emit a warm vapor

9) to be disturbed in mind as if awaking from a dream

10) to throw himself/herself on his/her knees and beg somebody to save him/her

3. Please translate each sentence with at least one key word or its derivative.

1) Although surgery is not always a cure, it is often the best way to alleviate pain and discomfort and stop the spread of disease.

2) Tariffs were a poor substitute for policy stimulus, but in an era of balanced budgets they were all that gold-standard countries had.

3) By common consent, their talk avoided the reason for their being there at all.

4) Their energies were focused on the alleviation of the refugees' misery.
5) Firms, markets and governments are substitutive for each other at the micro level, and are complementary for each other at the macro level.
6) Newton came to a simple but startling conclusion: the white light of the sun was in fact a mixture of all the colors of the spectrum.
7) As your parents see the matter in a different angle, they will probably not consent to the plan.
8) The exercise will obviously improve strength and endurance.
9) You would not be surprised if a stranger tried to shake hands with you when you were introduced, but you might be a little startled if they bowed or kissed you on both cheeks.
10) Beyond the end of our combat mission, we will still have a partnership with Afghanistan, which will endure.

Unit Eleven

I. Please fill in the blanks with the words in the parentheses with the appropriate part of speech.

1. divinely
2. appraise
3. unspoken
4. interrogative
5. encrusted
6. disinclined
7. graceless
8. scornful
9. attentive
10. likeness

II. Please choose one word or phrase that best completes the sentence.

1. B   2. A   3. D   4. A   5. C   6. B

III. Translation

1. Please translate the following from English into Chinese.

1）怠懒人物
2）春晓之花
3）睛若秋波
4）性格乖张
5）无双
6）弱柳扶风
7）纨绔
8）一个袅袅婷婷的女孩
9）狂病发作
10）鬓若刀裁

2. Please translate the following from Chinese into English.

1) rare objects
2) two dragons playing with a large pearl
3) a padlock-shaped amulet
4) mist-wreathed brows
5) glistening jet black
6) passionate eyes

7) the lips touched with rouge   8) a lucky charm

9) to meet sb. again after a long separation   10) to offer no further resistance

3. Please translate each sentence with at least one key word or its derivative.

1) A good teacher should be very perceptive to his students' progress. If their progress is ignored, the students will feel discouraged.

2) When the girl sat glumly, the mother was instructed not to coax her into playing, but simply describe what she was doing.

3) They indulge their child too much; it's bad for his character.

4) The president saluted the courage of those who had fought for their country.

5) The concealed character of Web brings about "Consensus Violence" in Web, which makes Web users self-indulgent and too drastic.

6) That's because they bestow value upon things that once mattered to them.

7) A key task is to get pupils to perceive for themselves the relationship between success and effort.

8) The government coaxed them to give up their strike by promising them temporary residence permits.

9) We were on good terms with everyone in the village, and we even gave a salute to the local policeman as he passed on his bicycle.

10) You should bestow more time to work and less to daydreaming.

Unit Twelve

I. Please fill in the blanks with the words in the parentheses with the appropriate part of speech.

1. prevalent   2. animate
3. envious   4. entrance
5. continuous   6. approval
7. intricacy   8. innumerable
9. successive   10. perfection

II. Please choose one word or phrase that best completes the sentence.

1. A   2. B   3. D   4. C   5. A   6. C

III. Translation

1. Please translate the following from English into Chinese.

1）耕地   2）走来走去
3）一个接一个   4）轿子

5）安插 6）瓜子脸
7）拨动琴弦 8）叫好声
9）长鸭蛋脸 10）或急或缓
11）相和相合 12）于我心有戚戚焉
13）循环

2. Please translate the following from Chinese into English.

1) a loud and animated conversation
2) Free and easy talk and laughter prevail
3) now high, now low, now simple, now intricate
4) to enter the ears and stir the heart
5) change of tune and style
6) song, tune, melody, or air
7) attractive without being seductive
8) pure but not cold
9) the stomach and bowels
10) a thousand twists and turns
11) to hold one's breath and sit intently
12) The sound circles the beams and stops not for three days.
13) young oriole flying out of a valley
14) a young swallow returning to the nest
15) vermilion lips and sparkling white teeth

3. Please translate each sentence with at least one key word or its derivative.

1) Their persecution only serves to arouse the opposition of the people.
2) Political and personal ambitions are starting to prevail over economic interests.
3) When the tree falls, the monkeys scatter.
4) He was constraining his mind not to wander from the task.
5) The government is committed to achieving equal rights for women.
6) James scrupulously avoided any topic likely to arouse suspicion as to his motives.
7) Barbaric customs still prevail in the mountainous area.
8) I couldn't distinguish him among the scatter of distant faces.
9) Because our mother is afraid we'll get lost, we aren't allowed to wander far.
10) Her distaste for books was equaled only by her dislike of people.